A Sealed and Secret Kinship

PUBLIC ISSUES IN ANTHROPOLOGICAL PERSPECTIVES

General Editors: William O. Beeman and David Kertzer, Department of Anthropology, Brown University

Volume 1

Braving the Street: The Anthropology of Homelessness
Irene Glasser and Rae Bridgman

Volume 2

War on the Home Front: An Examination of Wife Abuse
Shawn D. Haley and Ellie Braun-Haley

Volume 3

A Sealed and Secret Kinship: The Culture of Policies and Practices in American Adoption
Judith S. Modell

A Sealed and Secret Kinship

The Culture of Policies and Practices in American Adoption

Judith S. Modell

Berghahn Books
New York • Oxford

First published in 2002 by
Berghahn Books
www.berghahnbooks.com

© 2002 Judith S. Modell

Library of Congress Cataloging-in-Publication Data

Modell, Judith Schachter, 1941-
    A sealed and secret kinship : the culture of policies and practices in American adoption / Judith S. Modell.
        p. cm. -- (Public issues in anthropological perspectives ; v. 3)
    Includes bibliographical references and index.
    ISBN 1-57181-077-3 (cl. : alk. paper) -- ISBN 1-57181-324-1 (pb. : alk. paper)
        1. Adoption--Government policy--United States. 2. Open adoption--United States. 3. Adoptees--United States--Identification. 4. Adoptive parents--United States--Family relationship. I. Title. II. Public issues in anthropological perspective ; v. 3.

    HV875.55 .M643 2001
    362.73'4'0973--dc21   2001049957

British Library Cataloguing in Publication Data

A catalogue record for this book is available from the British Library.

Printed in the United States on acid-free paper

9/09

Contents

Acknowledgments   vi

Chapter 1   Opening the Subject of Adoption   1

Chapter 2   Banishing Secrecy, Banishing
                Confidentiality, and Opening Adoption   24

Chapter 3   From "Drifting" to "Permanency"—
                Adoption Policy and Practice   75

Chapter 4   Taking (Care of) the Children—
                Adoptive Parents in the
                Twenty-first Century   124

Chapter 5   Opening the Confines of Kinship—
                Twenty-first Century American
                Child Placement   176

Bibliography   201

Index   210

Acknowledgments

When David Kertzer phoned and asked me to contribute a book to the new Berghahn series, Key Public Issues in Anthropological Perspective, he started me on a path that turned out to be more complicated and longer than either of us anticipated. David, his co-editor William Beeman, and publisher Marion Berghahn, have all three been as helpful, supportive, and understanding as any author could have desired. I know them personally, and have enjoyed working with them professionally in a way that recognizes the personal dimensions of such contacts—over time. They are the first to be thanked.

Many others fill the ranks of those to whom I am grateful. As always, the people whose lives are intertwined with adoption, foster care, and child placement went beyond the call of cooperation to tell me their stories, their problems, and their views on this deeply important public issue. Personal accounts, like theirs, keep anthropology on its toes and, I hope, kept me honest as an anthropologist who brings disciplinary views of kinship and family to the issue. The accounts I heard, too, intersect with my own experiences of being a biological and an adoptive parent: thanks again to my daughter Jennifer and my son Matthew. It is impossible to name all the parents, children, social workers, and others I talked to during the course of this project, and some did not want to be identified. A few names represent the many who helped: Max Baer, Wayne Carp, LeAnn Fields, Gordon Finley, Renee Garfinkel, Harriet Gross, David Herring, Judy Horgan, Marianne Novy, Carol Sanger, Glenda

Shay, Vicki Sirockman, Jania Sommers, Jean Vincent. I've had the good fortune of a group of anthropological colleagues, who talk and present papers with me at annual meetings; these include: Gail Landsman, Linda Layne, Helena Ragone, Linda Stone, Janelle Taylor, Danielle Wozniak, and unfailingly insistent that I include class analysis, Rayna Rapp.

Colleagues at Carnegie Mellon are important in another way, granting me time off, listening to my ideas, understanding my preoccupation with "getting my book done": especially but not only Charlee Mae Brodsky, Barbara Lazarus, Richard Maddox, Steven Schlossman. Jane Bernstein has read through several versions of my work on adoption, giving me her fine responses to writing. Dan Resnick, a historian of policy, read the early version of Chapter One, and pointed me in the right directions for thinking about policy; so, too, did Albrecht Funk, all along the way. And then there are the students, who listen, who ask, and who occasionally sigh when the word "adoption" passes my lips. They have been in my classes. Three students have worked closely with me over several years, hunting for everything from obscure library sources to the missing commas in a final manuscript. Naomi Langer was the first one on board, and she was terrific at such hunting; sitting over the dining room table, we battered out what were still inchoate ideas and confused movements into the area of policy. Then came a PhD candidate in History, Rebecca Marie Kluchin; not only did she read my chapters closely and carefully, but she brought her strong feminist perspective to all our conversations. When she began her own inquiries into abortion and sterilization in the United States, she opened my eyes to further aspects of the story I have been telling in my own writings. Last but by no means least, Melissa McMahon, whose calm sense of order took me through the last stages of manuscript preparation. I, of course, am ultimately responsible for the interpretations and viewpoints expressed in the following pages.

Family and friends are important in diffuse and enduring ways: Jennifer Modell-McLoughlin and her family, Matthew Modell and his family, Oscar Schachter, Muriel Sackler, Ellen Leventhal, Mary Dwan, Paul Sides, Susanne Slavick, Caroline Acker, Carol Zisowitz. Albrecht Funk occasionally despaired at how many times I rewrote a chapter or section or paragraph, a chore that did not go on in silence, but through it all he gave me the most wonderful, tolerant, and loving sustenance. I thank them all.

Chapter 1

Opening the Subject of Adoption

Spotlight on adoption

Not so long ago veiled in secrecy and closed records, American adoption is now dramatically *out*. Out of locked file cabinets, out of the immediate family, out of the domain of social work, adoption struts boldly across the stage of American culture. Adoption is out in another way as well. Today the subject draws engaged attention not only from participants, experts, and journalists but also from scholars in an array of disciplines.[1]

Spread across daily newspapers, stories of "reunions," of two mothers "sharing one child," and of "infants from abroad" show how thoroughly adoption tantalizes the American public these days. The stories also indicate the depth of change in adoption—the groundswell that profoundly alters the look of an age-old custom of "transferring" children. As recently as spring 2000, the state of Oregon unlocked previously sealed records, granting adult adoptees access to an original birth certificate. The leader of the movement for reform, an adoptee who had found her birthmother, posed for a *New York Times* photographer, confident that she had brought justice to the adoptees in her state. Yet in Oregon, at the very same moment, a group of birthparents complained about the injustice: they had lost their rights to privacy, betrayed by a state that had promised them permanent confidentiality.[2]

What does all this mean? New words appear on the horizon of adoptive kinship, like search and access, rights and privileges, autonomy and, too, betrayal. But the dominant word is *open*. A concept of openness epitomizes changes in American adoption that have been creeping upon participants and observers for over three decades. The connotations are clear, the denotation murky. Connotations of sunshine rather than shadow, of honesty rather than deceit, of exposure rather than secrecy mark the contemporary use of the word. Exactly what "openness" signifies for practices and policies, however, is fiercely contested. "Open" refers to access to records—but which records? "Open" also refers to contact between participants in an adoption—but what kind of contact and for how long? "Open" suggests the visibility of adoptive families, as fewer of those families look like the conventional nuclear family—but how far can individuals stretch the understanding of "family" and remain within the domain of American kinship?

These are anthropological questions. For decades anthropologists who wrote about adoption called it *fictive*, implying a *true* kinship based on relationships of birth not contract, on nature not law. *Fictive* evoked the creativity of cultural beings, and found its most common application in theories of marriage, an arrangement individuals (presumably) design. Until recently, moreover, adoption appeared in the annals of anthropology mainly to describe the customs of others, strangers not those at home. The "others" who practiced adoption occasionally included groups within the United States, like Native-Americans and African-Americans, whose customs of moving children from household to household contrasted with those of the majority, white and middle class, who gave the picture of adoption its most familiar face. And even when the subject was treated in far away places or among cultural minorities within North America's borders, it quickly blended into subjects considered more weighty and more significant. Much early anthropological work on adoption located the transaction in a larger system—of inheritance and property rights, say, or of population and land management, or of marriage, descent, and alliance. And while those are important—variously important, depending on time and place—they slight the importance of adoption itself.[3]

In the 1960s, the well-known British anthropologist Jack Goody wrote a classic analysis of adoption customs throughout the world.[4] Yet few took up his implicit call, to put adoption forward as a revealing and an encompassing subject; when an American anthropologist did take up the call, she (or he) avoided familiar forms of "child exchange" at home. We left that discussion to social workers, psychologists, physicians, adoptees, adoptive parents, and participants in adoption.

Why? Just as the cultural anthropologist David Schneider criticized anthropologists for not looking beyond their own views of kinship to find other visions, one might comment that American anthropologists accepted a view of adoption that erased it as an academic topic.[5] Adoption in the United States, after all, is a benign, pleasurable, apparently uneventful event—except to those who are involved. Even when scholars recognized its personal significance, they tended to disregard the importance of American adoption as a social and a cultural phenomenon.

The disregard arose partly because adoption *was* perceived as personal, a way of taking care of a child or forming a family. As a transition from one life-phase to another, adoption did not spark much interest. Partly, too, the disregard came about because anthropologists (and other social scientists) respected the secrecy American adoption had acquired over the years. Even when a child knew she had been adopted, the rest of the world did not; even when a couple had to adopt, the rest of the world was supposed to forget that beginning of the family. Cultural discourse is revealing: a clue to interpretations lies in the "had been," in the past nature of adoption. Another clue lies in the "had to adopt," in the presumption of constraint not of choice in the decision. Both elements "closed" the event. Secrecy surrounds American adoption still, enforced by law and by custom. Once an adoption is finalized in the United States, the arrangement leaves no visible public traces. The child's birth certificate carries the names of his or her adopting parents. The birthparent is anonymous.

This description refers to "stranger" adoptions, the prototype in the United States for the reallocation of parental rights to a child. Stranger adoptions are the subject of my book. This form of adoption, in which the child is not already linked to one or both adoptive parents, exposes the contradictions, confusions, uncertainties, and controversies that surround the transfer of a child, legally and permanently, from a genealogical to a non-genealogical parent.

Anthropologists occasionally use the word "exchange" to describe adoption in non-Western societies of the world. The implication is that one person gives her child to another, establishing a relationship and an ongoing reciprocity. By contrast, any suggestion of "exchange" is anathema in an American culture of adoption, whether referring to gift or commercial transactions. Exchange implies a face to face contact that vanished from American adoption throughout most of the twentieth century. Furthermore, "exchange" suggests market principles, an intrusion of money, worth, returns, and credits, which are piously kept out of child placement scenarios in the United States—the more piously the more such principles and calculations actually determine the movement of a child from parent to parent.

Reluctance to apply the term exchange at home stems from a strenuous effort to keep "market" out of discussions of child placement practices. The reluctance also reinforces the convention that adoption is private, not a matter of external and objective calculations, but of individual emotions, needs, and desires. In the United States, at the start of the twenty-first century, adoption remains ideally and intensely a personal event, a moment in an individual's life.

The secrecy of American adoption came to seem natural to all but the most involved observers. The conviction that a stranger can fit seamlessly into a new family shapes popular interpretations of the event. Cultural anthropologists accepted the rule of custom and ignored the transaction. Once legalized, the transfer of parenthood was no longer visible—or interesting. After all, ideally and boringly, the American adoptive family was "just like" the family created out of sexual intercourse, pregnancy, and birth.

As-if-begotten

"Adoption is the legal proceeding whereby an adult person takes another adult or minor person into the relation of child and thereby acquires the rights and incurs the responsibilities of parent with respect to said adult or minor."[6] In legal language, this constitutes adoption in the United States: an adult becomes as-if parent to a child not hers or his by birth.

The central premise of American adoption is written into law in the phrase "as if begotten." From the first laws of the mid-nineteenth century through modifications in the twentieth century, the premise holds, supported by every twist and turn in state statutes.[7] Even when individuals complain about the diverse (and often confusing) provisions of adoption law, few dare to reject the biological model that sustains the judicially created family. Behind the appeal of adoption in the United States lies the principle (enshrined in law) that a court constituted parent-child tie cannot be distinguished from a biologically constituted parent-child tie.

American adoption customs recognize a genealogical model in three primary ways. First, by law adoption transforms the identity and the kinship status of the child. Second, adoption practices replicate the "signs" of a biological relationship by matching child to adoptive parents. Third, according to American conventions the adoptive family is indistinguishable from any other family. In every state of the union, the adopted child receives a new birth certificate: the names of the birthparents are erased and the names of the adopting parents written in instead. By state law, adoption records are permanently sealed and the history of the adoption remains a secret forever.[8] Legally an adopted child is *just like* a child born to the adoptive parents.

The numerous revisions of legal statutes, while respecting core concepts of kinship, at the same time indicate the problems perceived in permanently re-making a parent-child tie. All states provide a mechanism for transforming the adoptee's identity through an altered birth certificate, but there the smooth replication of a "birth family" ends. Laws regarding the transmission of property, arcane and detailed, test the meaning of "as if begotten" or at least show that the meaning does not go uncontested.[9]

In some states, for instance, an adopted child has no claim to the property of an adoptive parent in a non-testamentary death. In other states, an adopted child retains a claim on the property of his or her biological parent. Rules regarding the transmission of property expose the primacy of blood and of the biological tie in American conceptualizations of kinship.

Inheritance laws indicate where as-if-begotten starts and ends. In instances where there is no will and the adopted child is excluded from the family property, adoptive kinship clearly has a limited continuity. In those instances, kinship exists between parent and child but does not extend to a descent group. Adoption, then, is a one-generational phenomenon. In states where the adopted child may legally inherit from a biological parent, a notion of "natural right" exposes the limits of adoption. In the United States, adoption links parent and child; legally as well as customarily, the arrangement may bind no one else.

Despite these caveats and limitations, as-if-begotten dominates the law of adoption in every state. In North American culture, where the proverb "blood is thicker than water" measures kinship, it is not surprising that "blood" symbolizes strong and true ties. The symbolism guides participants and lawmakers through the morass of "non-blood" relationships. The symbolism tells observers and participants alike that parental love is grounded in a facsimile of the connection perceived to arise from conception, pregnancy, and birth.[10]

As-if-begotten informs everyday language about adoption in the United States. If not in the archaic sounding legal phrase, still the idea appears in what people say about adoption, whether they are directly involved or not. It is not rare for an adoptive parent to hear (and perhaps agree with) the comment: "Aren't you lucky that the baby looks just like you?" Why "lucky?" Primarily because in the eye of the beholder, looking alike—resemblances—*essentialize* the tie, make it (seem) inherent, inevitable, and enduring. Resemblances between parent and adopted child give the impression of an absolute bond, and an impression counts for a lot in substantiating fictive kinship. In recent decades, the resemblance of an adopted child to her adopting parents gives the impression that her "genetic make up" is close to that of her adoptive family—and such closeness, too, is considered all to the good.

On a more mundane level, having a child who looks like you or an adoptive father whom people say you are the "spitting image of" normalizes the adoptive relationship, putting it into the same picture gallery as the biological family. From the point of view of professionals who arrange and finalize adoptions, the family that looks like all others promises to be secure and enduring.[11]

Why are those presumptions among the most indisputable in American adoption practice? One might argue, as some adoptive parents do, that it is easier to bond with a familiar-looking child. Or one might argue, as some adoptees do, that it *feels like* belonging when there are visible resemblances to family members. Or one might argue, as some professionals do, that attachments are more likely to persist among relatives who "share traits." Behind those arguments lies the cultural conviction that blood holds people together and that, consequently, the more evidently an adoptive family replicates a blood family, the more enduring it is likely to be. And there may be fewer social and psychological pressures on a family that looks exactly the way it is supposed to look.

Social workers take the matter of resemblance seriously, and decisions about an adoption support the adage of blood's thickness. Throughout the twentieth century, the practice of matching dominated placement decisions: the baby to be placed in an adoptive home should "match" the parents in that home. Match in race and in religion, of course, but also in physique, intelligence, and temperament. Blue-eyed babies to blue-eyed parents is the tip of an iceberg that may in a new century prompt genetic screening for all participants in an adoption. It is oddly paradoxical that birth and adoptive parents are *social strangers* at the same time as they ideally share *intimate* traits—but paradox is the history of American adoption.

Matching displays the ways in which the American population is divided up. Decade by decade, matching is a barometer of what are culturally considered the most significant traits in a person. Yet, as I indicated, matching is clothed in another language: the language of bonding, belonging, and enduring solidarity. In the United States, matching bridges the gap adoption opens up between "genealogical connection" and "parental love." Matching reveals a fundamental anxiety about the reallocation of parental rights to a child.

Practices of matching, proverbs about blood and water, and even the legal dictum of as-if-begotten are undergoing a gradual slippage. Adoption may slip through the pens of scholars but it inspires intense interpretive exercises on the part of those who arrange, who participate in, and who muse over the personal implications of "fictive" kinship. As the twenty-first century begins, debates over the meaning of kinship are even more energetic, absorbing and attending to changes in adoption practice. These debates continue to exploit the symbol of blood, with its multivocal references, including everything from genetics to love. Under the cover of an old symbolism, new ideologies of kinship, family, parenthood, and identity are slowly taking form.

The sounds of change

Over the past three decades, cracks have appeared in the wall of secrecy and silence surrounding American adoption. Stories about adoption dominate television and newspapers. Here a scene of happy reunion between long-lost relatives, there a birthparent claiming she never agreed to the adoption; here a birth mother handing "our" baby to an adoptive mother, there a photo of an agency's available "child of the week." Other stories appear as well: Russian children reported to have been slapped and pinched by adopting American parents; a picnic for African-American children "freed" from foster care and in need of a permanent home; a child in a wheelchair flanked by hale and hearty adoptive parents. At the start of a new century, American adoption is *noisy* on a lot of fronts.

Adoptees first broke the silence of American adoption.[12] Birthparents followed soon after, on the heels of relinquished children. No more closed records and permanent secrets, announce adoptees, we want to know who we really are. No more denying the fact of birth, say birthparents, we want to know our biological offspring. Both arguments draw on the resonances of birth, blood, and genetics in an American cultural context. Outspoken adoptees and birthparents protest against the provisions of American law using the very symbolism the law sanctifies. For such activists, an amended birth certificate, closed records, and the anonymity of birth and adoptive families violate the cultural meanings of as-if-begotten. Each obscures the importance of blood ties. To those who advocate reform of American adoption, the provisions in laws make no cultural sense.

Breaking silence, the adopted person claims an adoptive family is *not* just like a biological family, being taken in is not the same as being born into a family, having parents by law is different from having them "naturally." From this point of view, adoption is unique, incomparable, and special. Everyone else, adoptees say, has a birth story—the midnight rush to the hospital, for instance—and everyone else knows someone whose features are a mirror to one's own. Everyone else has a long line of ancestors and can confidently insert their names on a family tree.[13] No pieces are missing when you remain where you were born, the argument continues, whereas the adopted person always has a "gap" and the gap is sanctioned by law.

Taking up the terms of dominant kinship discourse, birthparents claim they cannot forget a child they have conceived, begotten, and sometimes named. They cannot, they argue, forget a child who carries their genetic substance. Operating in a culture that values and romanticizes birth, birthparents ask why they should be told to erase that experience and paste it over with "pretend" documents. The argument is ostensibly gender-free, although most birthparent activists are women and an imagery of "motherhood" controls the texts presented by advocates of reform.

Leaning on "motherhood" is, of course, not surprising. In a North American context, "mother" represents the ideal parent, and by the laws of heaven, science, and the state she maintains that position.[14] Mothers are the chief players in scenes of parenting, and mothers are the first to take credit or be given credit for the well-being of a child. From statutes to surrender papers, a mother holds the reigns of a child's fate; in relinquishing and in adopting, by custom and by convention *she* has the final word. At the same time, use of an imagery of motherhood creates yet another paradox in discussions of adoption and, I show, in policies regulating child placement in the United States. "Mother" affirms the bonds of birth and evokes an emotional rather than a calculating actor on the stage of life. Activist birthparents use that imagery to argue for reform.

The shared symbols of kinship, of birth, and of motherhood unite birthparents and adoptees in their pleas for reform. Rallying behind familiar symbols, the number of those who actually criticize the institution of American adoption is less important than the effectiveness of the banners they carry. That the May 2000 decision in Oregon to grant adoptees access to their original birth certificates made front-page headlines across the nation shows how "loud" a legislative change in adoption can be. Neither in Oregon nor in the nation as a whole does any one know exactly how many adoptees object to the terms of their relationships; no one knows how many birthparents would like (or dislike) having their identities known. Mystery surrounds the steps that are taken after records are opened and identities exposed. Even the number of adoptees and of birthparents in the United States is unknown; one of the most dramatic aspects of the secret and sealed nature of American adoption is the lack of statistics on the phenomenon.[15] Good guesses are made, and more careful guesses are made when something is at stake—as is the case today, with vociferous protests against the sealed records everyone once accepted.

Adoptive parents are not silent. The third member of the triad, in the last three decades adoptive parents have been adding to the "noise" surrounding American adoption.[16] Adoptive parents offer their own variations on the theme of as-if-begotten, as much influenced by the symbolism of "blood" in American kinship as are adoptees and birthparents.

Adoptive parents enter contemporary discussions with the history of adoption law shadowing them, a history that to a large extent seems to be of their own making. The usual explanations of state laws of adoption are that parents interested in adopting grew impatient with the slow, formal process of gaining legislative approval and demanded quicker judicial proceedings. Granted statutory rights to a child, the story continues, adoptive parents demanded protection of those rights. Demands resulted in the laws of confidentiality and anonymity passed in the first half of the twentieth century.

A rewritten birth certificate designates the adoptive as the *only* parents of the child. The maneuver alters parental status and identity as thoroughly as it redesigns the child's identity. And though a transformation of the child's identity is not unusual in adoption, the complete replacement of a biological by a social parent is unusual. By law in the United States, a birth-parent vanishes from the adoptee's records and by custom she disappears from the social networks of the adoptive family. Adoptive parents read manuals that encourage them to claim absolute entitlement to the child.[17] As-if-begotten inscribed on a certificate and reiterated in manuals is presumed to insure an adoptive parent's permanent commitment to the child.

Why then do adoptive parents challenge American adoption policy and practice? Historical accounts of their impact on adoption law aside, adoptive parents do not have a position of unadulterated strength. In a cultural milieu that assumes children *make* a family, being childless by choice elicits condemnation; being childless by "fate" elicits pity and concern. Of those in the second category, an increasing number now enter the complex arena of American adoption. There they must *petition* for a child, becoming clients of an agency or, in independent adoptions, of an adoption facilitator. Potential adoptive parents are dependent on others in order to "have" a child and, too, they depend upon a supply of available children. As clients or consumers, adoptive parents assess the rules of the game and the terms of the "market." Confronting odds that are increasingly *not* in their favor—a shortage of infants, restrictive agency rules—adoptive parents modify the traditional mechanisms of transferring a child in the United States. They take over the routes to adopting, avoiding agencies, going abroad, finding brokers, and using the Internet. Through new practices, adoptive parents challenge the terms of fictive kinship as thoroughly as do their companions in the triad, adoptees and birthparents.

The adoption triad is an intense and intimate one. Questions about birth and bonds by those who are adopted and by those who relinquish inevitably affect the legal parents in the constellation. In addition, in the twenty-first century, issues of genetics are in the air, not surprisingly appropriated by participants in an arrangement that prompts self-consciousness about nature and nurture, inherent traits and learned characteristics.

Combine this new vocabulary with a perceived shortage of children among whom potential parents can find a baby "just like one's own," and the as-if-begotten premise of American adoption begins to falter.

Growing adoptive parent demand for adoptable children shakes up the meanings of birth, blood, biology, and genetics (blurred as these are in everyday speech). International adoptions, adoptions of older children, adoption of a sibling group— an instantly large family—do not eliminate traditional views of kinship, parenthood, and identity so much as they subject these views to an extraordinary burst of interpretive creativity. The premise of as-if-begotten, deeply engrained, is incrementally shifting its meaning. No longer bound to the facsimile of birth represented by a rewritten birth certificate, as-if-begotten translates into something more like "in one's own image." And if this captures a part of the meaning of blood in American culture, still the interpretation has stretched far beyond the language in even the most loosely constructed state law of adoption.

Clearly adoptees, birthparents, and adoptive parents do not all share the same interpretations of blood, birth, as-if-begotten, and identity. Nor do people who occupy the same place in the triad share motives for engaging in adoptive kinship or perspectives on the practices that reallocate parental rights in the United States. At the same time, it is equally clear that in the last several decades few within the triad are silent and hidden about their places. Individuals involved in adoption in the United States negotiate meanings of blood, biology, and genetics in the course of creating, experiencing, and reflecting on the "nature" of family ties.

Meanings are not clearly oppositional or dichotomous. A close look reveals that there are few either-or's in the history of American adoption. But there are many if's, and's, and but's— many inconsistencies and uncertainties. The story of adoption in the United States features individuals who embark upon a culturally *non-ordinary* kinship. Inevitably, such individuals get caught between the dominant model for parent-child relationships and a changing pool of available, adoptable children—*inevitably*, inasmuch as the transfer of children occurs predominantly in the public domain where models rule. The decision by an individual to give a child permanently or by another to take a child as her or his own rarely goes on in a private familial domain as it does in cultures where state paraphernalia is less significant for reallocating rights to a child. And even that situation—described, for instance, by anthropologists in two fine volumes on adoption in Pacific Island societies—diminishes with the global spread of modern instruments for arranging kinship.[18]

Towards the policy domain

In the United States, child welfare and family issues have long occupied the attention of policy makers. The federal guidelines and model acts they institute become cultural documents which in turn frame popular interpretations of family, kinship, parenthood, and identity. Federal guidelines and model acts filter down through their impact on state statutes, on budgetary allotments, and on the stories reported in newspapers, on television, and on the Internet. Anyone can know what is happening in the domain of child placement, foster care, and adoption these days.

One recently heralded piece of knowledge is how frequently the biological bonds between parent and child fail to hold. The assumption that "birth" ensures a secure place for a child collapses in the face of America's growing population of at-risk children. Members of Congress, of state legislatures, and of local child-welfare agencies can no longer refer to the "natural" parent or to conceptualizations of maternal bonds to find a reliable source of responsibility, care, and love.

The crisis of collapsing parental bonds brings adoption to the forefront of attention. Furthermore, the crisis brings a traditional view of adoption forward, closely linked to the as-if-begotten seals the parent-child relation. The conviction is evident regardless of whether the speaker supports closed records, argues for doing away with confidentiality, or tries for a compromise position.

Passionate and antagonistic as the debate currently is, opposing groups remain in the same ballpark, playing the same game across the same bases. No one explicitly argues that adoption should be eliminated and no one offers an entirely new model for kinship— even when many critize the anachronistic criteria for a fit parent, like heterosexuality or marriage or residential stability.

Behind the safety of traditional symbols, American adoption practices are shifting, decision by decision, case by case. And the elastic ideology of as-if-begotten is tugged and pulled to cover diverse situations: a child shared by birth and adoptive parents, white parents adopting a black child, a special needs placement of three siblings into one family, and so on. At the moment, the elastic is pulling taut, and one might well predict a sudden tear in the institution of American adoption in the twenty-first century. Will a radical change in adoption mean a revolution in interpretations of kinship?

Month by month the debate over American adoption enlarges, drawing in a wide array of spokespersons. What began with upstart search groups now can be called a social movement, including adoptive parents, social workers, lawyers, and members of Congress. And sometimes the diversity of voices blends into a swelling comment on how and with whom America's children can have permanent homes. Sometimes the diversity erupts into sharp attack.

The debate is fraught with feeling. Behind the altruism of "the best interests of the child" principle lie infinite special interests. In contemporary American society, the subject of adoption has (apparently) broken through old boundaries; talk of adoption veers into discussion of the ethics of judging a fit parent, the social consequences of same-race placement policies, and the definition of a family. Arguments officially offering one agenda harbor another: for instance, a pro-adoption stance may amount to a strike against abortion. Advocacy of special needs adoption may hide a bitter condemnation of the American foster care system. And as with all policy debates that focus on domestic issues, these points of debate expose the most profound concerns of modern American society. Will a next generation be cared for? What kind of a setting gives a child security and a route to productive adulthood? Who should make the choices about a child's life?

Behind these questions lie others: can core cultural symbols of blood, birth, and ancestry withstand the debate over adoption? Can these symbols withstand the challenges posed by colloquial opinion and by discrete events? Will American kinship as we have known it endure or are changes in adoption a signal of profound—still subterranean—shifts in conceptualizations of kinship?

The questions do not lend themselves to quick or easy answers. But in tackling them, a cultural-anthropological perspective is vital. Trained to observe *at a distance*, we are now just beginning to develop ways of gaining distance on our own cultures, situations, and, even, modes of parenthood. The realization that what we assume to be "obvious" is as constructed as meanings and behaviors elsewhere brings new methods for analyzing discourses, life-stories, and the implications of actions which are comfortably familiar. David Schneider threw a shock into those of us who study kinship with his 1984 announcement that not every one thinks of birth as core to the construction of kinship. But the anthropologist at home can add to that insight: inasmuch as "birth" *is* core to American views of kinship, we must use other techniques to assess the significance of diverse experiences of that premise. Adoption is a perfect case.

Analysis of adoption in the United States requires a recognition of the importance of rhetoric and of the competition to be heard that is an aspect of all social action. Central to recent anthropological theory, the focus on voice implies a difference in access both to the capacity to "speak" and to the likelihood of gaining a hearing. Because of its position on the threshold of the private yet under the eye of the public, adoption is especially vulnerable to changing formulations of family, of parenthood, and of kinship. The matter of who regulates the "discourse" is crucial to understanding the phenomenon and its evolution in American society. At the same time, to the extent that adoption is "about" family and the self, those who compete for voice compete with the same set of core symbols, adjusting and re-adjusting their meanings with the ups and downs of practice. Moreover, as anthropologists insist, control of discourse is deeply embedded in the material conditions as well as the categorical discriminations of any society. Ours is no exception.

I also had the experience of looking elsewhere before (and while) applying anthropological theory to kinship at home. In the late 1980s, I began a project on child placement in Hawaii, specifically to investigate the impact of an American legal system on the reported casual, easy-going, and open practice of "exchanging" children within the Hawaiian population. The practices and the language of those who consider themselves Hawaiian show little of the secrecy and silence that American laws of adoption impose in the fiftieth state. My experience with an open, casual, and explicitly generous transfer of children illuminated the arguments against secrecy and confidentiality raging on the mainland. And though the benefits of openness, ease, and generosity cannot be carried wholesale from *there* to *here*, the lessons of a personalized, affectionate, and sociable—as well as a legal—reallocation of parental rights can be.

American anthropologists have come home, often bringing the lessons of a distant culture—but not invariably. Studies of American culture, especially in the fields of kinship and family, are no longer always preceded by a study of the strange, exotic, or foreign. That phase of our disciplinary development is fading or, rather, in a post-modern world the designation of the "strange" can be applied anywhere.

For me the lesson is personal as well as professional. I adopted a child at a time when secrecy was the norm, when information about the birthparent came in a well-honed "background sketch," and when those customs seemed perfectly reasonable. I knew the age, health, education, and hobbies of my son's birthmother. I knew what she reported about his birth father. When my son was sixteen I gave him all the information I had, and he was pleased. He stored those papers away with other collections he keeps of school papers, photographs, and precious documents.

His adoption is, and remains, in the full meaning of the words, *sealed and secret*. The birthparent is anonymous to us and we are anonymous to her. Our identities are not known to one another. And while we are content with the arrangement, neither my son nor I any longer consider secrecy and closed records the only way to think about adoption.

Secrets and sealed records

This is my second book on adoption in the United States. I began research on adoption with some reluctance. Inspired by Robert Levy's brilliant account in *Tahitians*, I also was deeply aware of the inspiration in my own experiences.[19] Influenced by a culture in which adoption is considered private, by sensitivity to my children's feelings, and by unease about how personal an anthropology should be, I began cautiously—with an inquiry into kinship structured by the work of my forebears in anthropology, especially David Schneider.

The resulting book, *Kinship with Strangers*, explores American cultural interpretations of kinship through the lens of adoption.[20] In it, I listen to, interpret, and analyze the multivocal narratives people tell about the experience of adoption in contemporary American society. I cast the narratives of participants against the "official" voices of experts and lawmakers. I also consider the narratives I heard in the context of arguments for reform of adoption customs and, primarily, for opening the transaction. Interest in the move from secrecy to openness did not end in the last chapter of that book, and prompts much of the discussion in this.

A Sealed and Secret Kinship reflects the increasing openness of talk about adoption in general—not just among scholars, but also among parents, children, kin and non-kin to adoptive families. The burst of adoption into the news, as dinner party conversation, and within congressional debates over other issues, signals the change in the American milieu more strikingly than the revision of laws and of scholarship. This book investigates a change whose impact diffuses through a population. In the process of writing, I have had to reconsider the doctrines I accepted as an adoptive parent and as an early scholar of the phenomenon at home.

Things had begun to change well before I finished the first book, but the attention given to those changes has intensified enormously in the past ten years. Expressing a point of view on adoption is no longer the privilege of those in an adoptive family, professionals who arrange adoption, or lawmakers who control its form. Everyone can talk about the phenomenon. That adoption is "good to talk" is a sign that the subject incorporates numerous other concerns: about the fate of the American family, about the relationship between diversity in a population and diversity at home, about obligations to the greater social good and the importance of nurturing the development of "self." Adoption touches on matters of life and death, not only because it has become part of the abortion debate but also because of its bearing on concepts of the self, the social order, and the mainsprings of a culture.

In the following pages, I draw from "talk" that occurs in different arenas. Some talk is directed toward the public, some only happens at home or in the office of a social worker; some talk has a deliberate goal, and some meanders over the core concepts of a central cultural problem, that of relatedness and identity. Regardless of where and how they occur, conversations about adoption are not just a clue to but a *cause of* changes in ideologies of kinship, family, and identity in the United States. *A Sealed and Secret Kinship* is about the vast, often unintended, consequences of a competitive, heated, controversial, and very public debate over the "true" definition of family.

The book also addresses changes in the political climate and in welfare policy. In recent years, adoption has entered the public domain not only from the point of view of family, but also from the point of view of "rescue." Once connected with subjects like marriage, infertility, and family size, adoption now appears in the news in the guise of providing a safe place for endangered children.[21] Adoption is presented as an efficient, cost-saving, and ideologically pleasing way of caring for children who are in harm's way. Entering the public domain in this manner, adoption veers between an old picture of benign social policy—making a family—and a new picture of children who cannot safely live with a birthparent. The shift is enlarged by the attention of policymakers and by the pronounced involvement of the federal government in presumably local child placement practices.

As long as American society maintains a restricted and often punitive welfare system, adoption becomes an alternative to offering services to drug-addicted or otherwise dysfunctional parents. From another perspective—for other policy-makers— adoption is the generous and good solution for an unplanned pregnancy, especially compared with the "evil" of abortion. Furthermore, as I describe below, adoption has become the "good" to the "bad" of foster care, a distinction that reflects the checkered history in the United States of placing children. Seeming to solve so many social problems, adoption is a more prominent aspect of family and welfare policy than ever before.

Are these developments completely disconnected from the parents and children who belong to adoptive families? From the significant others and extended kin of those individuals? From the social workers and judges who arrange the movement of a child from one family to another? The answer is neither a yes nor a no, and my book describes the negotiations among all these players as American adoption moves into the twenty-first century.

I start with the earliest outspoken individuals: adoptees who declare dissatisfaction with the terms of adoption. Following their "children" come the birthparents who choose to declare a once hidden and stigmatized identity. Borrowing the phrase "out of the closet," birthparents vociferously object to the norms that forced secrecy on them, the customs that made a central fact of their existence invisible to the world. Chapter Two, "Banishing Secrecy, Banning Confidentiality, and Opening Adoption" tells the story of an eruption in adoption circles that seemed sudden but whose energy had been smoldering for decades. Adoptees and birthparents who are critical of American adoption do not operate in a vacuum; those who speak out, join groups, march in Washington, and publish memoirs share a context with other critics of child placement practice, including social workers, lawmakers, professors, and physicians. The proclamations and arguments produced by adoptee and birthparent reform groups intersect with debates over family values and family policy in the United States.

In Chapter Three, "From 'Drifting' to 'Permanency'," I focus on the policy component in the culture of adoption in North America. The constitutional system of the United States gives American adoption a special character. Unable to pass laws of adoption, the federal government instead issues guidelines, position papers, and general memoranda on the "state of the children" in modern American society. Until there is a crisis, a national discourse shields a fragmented legal structure.

Federal government documents reach a nation-wide population through legislators who recognize that talking about children, and the safe keeping of children, appeals to almost every member of a constituency. Federal government texts also reach a wide audience through their diffusion in newspapers, on television, and over the Internet. Last but not least, I show how the ideologies in such mandates reach the public through their material side: control over budget lines, regulations about subsidies to families, and ever-changing provisions regarding parenthood in federal tax laws.

In a society, like our own, which lacks common rituals, uniform rules for enacting kinship, and unambiguous scripts for "personhood," government texts constitute a master narrative when individuals formulate their own versions of these core elements of life. In the realm of adoption, laws, judicial opinions, and the model acts of a Congress are never far from individual interpretations of kinship, family, parenthood, and identity.

Chapter Four, "Taking (Care of) the Children," features the adoptive parents, the recruits for new adoption policies and practices in the United States. Until recently, the picture of an adoptive parent has been relatively benign and appealing: adults who cannot have a child of their own and generously take in a "stranger"—no more true to life than the picture of a young and vulnerable birthparent or of a perpetually adopted *child*. Nowadays, adoptive parents comprise a diversified group with diverse motives for and routes to adopting a child. The chapter also shows the extent to which adoptive parents have been homogenized by strict rules of qualification and by high standards for the person who is not a parent "biologically" or, as is still sometimes said, "naturally."

Audience for arguments made by adopted individuals and by birthparents, adoptive parents confront anew the implications of "fictive" kinship. Yet adoptive parents are caught in a bind: considered the strongest corner of the triad—politically and economically advantaged in an American context—, their experience is one of having to petition for a child; in public, they are alternately pitied or patted on the head. In many ways, speaking out is hardest for an adoptive parent, who risks losing everything she or he wants by antagonizing social workers, adoptees, and potential birthparents. Chapter Four describes the increasing complications when, added to the fact of applying for a child, adoptive parents become the "resources" for at-risk children in the United States. President Clinton's 1996 Executive Memorandum calling for doubled adoption rates by 2002 links adoptive parenthood to changes in American child-placement policy, and changes adoptive parenthood immeasurably by that fact.

The diversity and divisions among those who adopt are becoming more evident as we approach 2002. Although the lobbying groups of adoptive parents are quite different from the adoptee and birthparent support groups I describe in Chapter Two, still the "noise" adoptive and potential adoptive parents make is denting American practice as effectively as anything else on the adoption horizon.

Following the introductory first chapter, the book is organized into three major chapters, each divided into smaller sections. I do this to capture the diversity of "moves" in American adoption, carried out by a diverse population of actors. No longer just the social workers, or just the children, or just the parents, participants in American adoption at the beginning of the twenty-first century include those who legislate, those who write about, those who film, and those who analyze the phenomenon of transferring a child from one parent to another—a transaction no longer as familiar or familial as it once seemed.

Adoption in the United States is not what it used to be. Despite cautious practices and the persuasiveness of core symbols of kinship, family, parenthood, and identity, American customs of reallocating rights to children are relentlessly changing. The pages below describe what looks like a chaos of contradictory interpretations, from the halls of Congress to the corridors of adoption agencies. Out of these contradictions, I suggest, emerge whole new ways of conceptualizing the relationship between persons who are presumed to be bound to each other as "parent" and "child." Adoption is no longer simply a way of making a family or caring for a child; nor is adoption simply an aspect of family policy or a mechanism of social control of domestic arrangements. At the start of a new century, adoption is a challenge to ideas, symbols, and ideologies Americans have long held to be self-evident.

Notes

1. Pertman 2000; Carp 1998; Bartholet 1999; Webber 1998; Hollinger 1998; Modell 1994; Sanger forthcoming.
2. Verhovek, Sam Howe. *The New York Times* 4/5/00: 14.
3. Wolf and Huang 1980; Waltner 1990; E. Goody 1982; J. Goody 1969.
4. J. Goody 1969.
5. I refer here to Schneider's 1984 *A Critique of the Study of Kinship*.
6. Carrieri 1991: 317.
7. The first state to pass a law was Massachusetts in 1851, followed rapidly by every state of the union. Exactly why a law came to pass is not clear; see the discussions in, for instance, Grossberg 1985; Mason 1994; Modell 1994.
8. As Wayne Carp (1998) points out, records occur in three forms: court records, documents in a state bureau of vital statistics, and agency files. State laws of confidentiality close all three sources of information, but with differing opportunities for gaining access under "good cause." See Chapter Two.
9. Hollinger (1998) provides an excellent summary of American adoption law.
10. The "genealogical connection," David Schneider writes, is at the core of American kinship; 1984.
11. That likeness is in the eye of the beholder holds true, of course, for biologically linked parents and children as well as for adoptive parents and children. Resemblance, in other words, is a socially constructed lens through which "family members" are viewed.
12. I borrow the phrase from Jean Paton's 1954 book, *The Adopted Break Silence*.
13. Many adoptees told me the story of being instructed in elementary school to draw a family tree and being baffled by what to include on its branches and its roots.

14. See Sanger 1996.
15. There are no national bureaus or offices that collect statistics; to attempt any count of adoption would involve going from courthouse to courthouse through the nation. See Pertman 2000: 7.
16. "Triad" is part of the new language of adoption in the United States, humanizing the older "triangle."
17. "The sense of entitlement of the parents to child, of child to parents, and siblings to each other is a task unique to adoption"; Smith and Miroff 1987: 25.
18. Brady (ed.) 1976; Carroll (ed.) 1970.
19. Levy 1973.
20. Modell 1994.
21. Adoption became a "social problem" later than child abuse; Hocking 2000. Recently, the two have become yoked.

Chapter 2

Banishing Secrecy, Banning Confidentiality, and Opening Adoption

Ending a sealed and secret kinship

In the fall of 1976, in a small Pennsylvania town, a group of people got together to talk about the experience of being adopted. They had responded to a newspaper ad placed by Karen, an adoptee in her forties. This was the beginning of an adoptee support group that grew in size, ambition, and presence over the next twenty-five years. I call the group Adoptee Support Group, or ASG, a pseudonym I assured members I would use. That same year, another woman placed an ad in a Boston newspaper. Lee Campbell invited parents who had once relinquished a child to come and meet in her living room. That meeting initiated the national birthparent group, Concerned United Birthparents, or CUB. CUB was destined to become a large and public force in adoption circles in the United States.

The two groups shared concerns about conventional American adoption practices and customs. Taking non-relative adoptions as the model, the birthparents and adoptees asked why these adoptions were such a deep, dark secret. Why shouldn't an adopted person know the story of her birth, the name of her birth-mother, or her genetic heritage? Why, the birthmothers who met that fall asked, could they not know the fate of a child they had given birth to? Why shouldn't they know whether a child they had relinquished was well-placed, happy, sad, alive or dead? In American society in 1976, adoptees and birthparents were not permitted to know one another. Adopted, the individual was as if born into the adoptive family, the identity of a birth family sealed in closed records. Having relinquished a child, a birthparent was supposed to keep that parental role hidden. "Secrecy" pervaded the adoption, and had for nearly three decades.[1]

Why, then, do support groups come into being in the mid-1970s? CUB and ASG were not the first *adoption* groups, but they mark a new, activist trend in such gatherings. Partly, adoptees and birthparents, like others, were swept up by the previous decade's activism; partly, the rise of consciousness groups across the nation made them widely appealing for a variety of causes. The claims voiced by feminists and by civil rights proponents brought the "personal" into the "political," granting an opening for the same gesture to be made in the realms of parenthood and kinship. Identity politics and psychotherapy, interest in the then arcane "DNA" and the popularized "roots" coalesced for those who responded to ads like Karen's and Lee's. Finally, adoption itself had changed, at least for the adoptees in the triad. The exact number of adoptees in the American population is not known. The visibility of adoptees is evident, and that presence reassured participants in both groups who dared to reject the old premises of the arrangement. [2]

Like Lee, the birthparents who attended early meetings of CUB had relinquished at a time when "giving up" a child was shrouded in silence and in shame—the 1940s and the 1950s. They had had no news of relinquished children, most of whom would be well on the way to adulthood themselves. In a decade in which "our bodies, ourselves" was a central cultural theme, the norm that demanded a denial of "birth" toppled and, for a number of birthparents, fell. The news of CUB spread, by word of mouth and through classified ads, much the way adoptee support groups made their presence known.

Members of these groups rally around the concept of "secrecy." Different as the individuals who join local support groups are, they all share a perception that parts of their own lives are hidden from them, wrapped in closed documents or hidden behind the doors slammed by cultural condemnation. For members of support groups, the concept of secrecy summarizes the terms and the customs of American adoption, in which participants are blocked forever from knowing one another and, in the logic established at meetings, from *knowing themselves*. Closed records and confidential files, then, are only part of the story. The other part is the *suffocation* of personal identity American adoption practices entail.

Focus on personal identity resonated in a culture embarking on the trek to self-help in virtually every domain of life. A focus on personal identity, too, turned support groups away from an attack on state laws of adoption and towards a modification of the confidentiality imposed by particular statutes. The agenda of early support groups like CUB and ASG was less a revolution in American adoption than a break in the anonymity that structures American adoptive kinship. Moreover, focusing on the suppression of self and on *secreted* information captured an audience beyond those directly involved in adoption: denying a person access to facts about her or himself contradicts an American precept. As support groups pointed to the shame, secrecy, and stigma attached to adoption in the United States, they exposed one of its prominent distinctions: unlike such transactions in other places, American adoption is not construed as generous or as *social*.[3]

A focus on secrecy paradoxically leaves some elements of American adoption themselves a secret. Turning the critique of adoption into an issue of personal identity takes the spotlight away from the economic and political dimensions of the transfer of children in the United States. Sealed records and closed files are crucial to modern American adoption; so, too, are the racial and class biases that enter into the social designation of a parent. Equally significant are the cultural interpretations of gender that intersect with other criteria for "good" parenthood. Behind these considerations lies a checkered story of aid to mothers, the damping down of welfare and social services, and a moralistic view of individuals who badly time life-course events like pregnancy. While CUB and ASG emphasized the personal in the political, the effect was to bring adoption onto a new stage, a stage it had not occupied before, and a stage that drew a remarkably large audience. Thanks to such groups, child placement is a *subject* as it never was before.

Choosing "secrecy" as the point of crusade turned out to be an effective strategy. To insert secrets (even lies) into the domain of family, of intimacy, and of love provoked a reaction. In the wake of federal freedom of information acts, depriving an individual of "vital facts" about her or himself was easily construed as a denial of "rights." Culturally, "birth" is a vital fact. Adoption practices and procedures were clouded in obscurity, out of the glow of the "sunshine."[4] That generations of children, and their parents, lived behind a veil of secrecy seemed "un-American."

At the same time, throughout adoption circles, individuals favor secrecy and confidentiality. As William Pierce, president of the National Council for Adoption (NCFA) reminds his audiences, birthparents request privacy, adoptive parents have a right to non-intrusion, and, above all, children deserve to be protected from the conflicting interests of adults. Opponents of opening adoption draw on central cultural themes, including the shape of the family and the best interests of a child. The terms of debate over secrecy and sealed records are not crystal clear. Meanwhile, birthparent and adoptee support groups draw more members and more national news attention as legislators debate, social workers argue, and participants in adoption redefine the meanings of family.

Support groups serve multiple goals. Stories exchanged at meetings of ASG and of CUB carry individuals through the changing terrain of American adoption custom. At the same time, the accumulation of individual narratives contributes to a potentially vast change in the institution.

The 1970s: breaking the silence

The five adoptees who met in Karen's living room, fearful they were breaking the law, actually had a good deal of social and cultural support. By the mid-1970s, adoption had lost its patina of shame, at least for the adoptive family, and the visibility of adoptees in the United States had increased with the adoption of children from abroad and from new categories of "adoptable". In addition, adoptees are the children in the transaction, the vulnerable, and the tender; much as an adult adoptee might object to the perpetual "adopted child" convention, the role of child helps the cause of reform. If adoption is in the best interests of the child, according to American cultural and legal principles, then the "child's" demands deserve a hearing.

By the 1970s, too, adoptees had written and published books that detailed the dangers in an American system of closed records from the adoptee perspective. In 1975, Betty Jean Lifton published *Twice Born: Memoirs of an Adopted Daughter*, a small book that had a large impact on individuals involved in adoptive kinship. "I said, 'Who am I?'" the book begins. "Looking into the mirror my eyes searched for clues. There were none. Nor were there likely to be. For I am adopted."[5] And so, too, begins the quest for her birthparents described in the rest of the book. I went into the labyrinth, Lifton writes, borrowing from a Greek myth; the path she followed uncovered the facts that would complete her identity. The adoptee, the book informs its readers, is "fragmented" as long as she or he lacks a link with biological kin.

Others had gone into the labyrinth before Lifton, but their books were not so popular, either coming too early or written in a style that did not so quickly capture the reader. In 1954, under the pseudonym of Ruthena Hill Kittson a social worker, Jean Paton, published *The Adopted Break Silence*. The book made little dent. Paton published a second, more successful book, *Orphan Voyage*, in 1968 and, more significantly, established the first adoption registry, Orphan Voyage, where members of the triad looking for lost kin could register their names and hope for a match.[6] In 1975, Karen made a call to Orphan Voyage when she decided that she, too, needed to find a birth family. "At last, someone that could help!"[7]

By then, others could help as well. More adoptees were breaking silence, either to one another or in books that publishers realized appealed to readers who were not directly involved in adoption. And while Betty Jean Lifton concentrated on the psychological and cultural dimensions of being adopted, others took a more militant tone, arguing against the constraints of the institution and the *victimization* of its participants. Among these outspoken adoptees was Florence Fisher, who founded an adoptee group that attained national prominence quite quickly. In 1973 Fisher published her memoir, *The Search for Anna Fisher,* and made her advocacy of searching the core of a new adoptee organization, the Adoptees Liberty Movement Association or ALMA. Militant and never mincing words, ALMA was also too much for some adoptees, like those who gathered in Karen's house, ready to talk to one another but not yet ready to parade, make speeches, or appear before a state legislature. Nor were the early members of ASG as sure as Fisher and her group that locating a birth family was the right and necessary thing to do. At the same time, the fact that ALMA existed, and that *Twice-Born* was so convincing, gave adoptees in groups like ASG reinforcement and a vocabulary for their own stories.

By the mid-1970s, current wisdom held that every adopted child should be told about her or his adoption. At ASG meetings, narratives revealed flaws in the prescription for "telling" and an imperfect application. Members recall embarrassed looks, shortened conversations, and awkward moments when parents turned the other way. Stories of suspicion and sensitivity to whispers abound. Memories of mysteries, of hints never followed and of facts not known—weight at birth, the ride to the hospital—gained energy in a milieu in which professionals insisted on the dangers of keeping secrets within the family (though few adoption manuals insist that adoption be publicized outside the family). Moreover, the form and the content of an adoption story cannot be tightly scripted, even in manuals for adoptive parents; each case is different. Adoptees in support groups compare their experiences of learning about adoption to the common wisdom that "telling" is good, and revise their memories in the light of a wider array of possibilities for conveying information.

Karen told her story of learning she was adopted. She grew up, she remembered, with only the slightest sense that she was different from the rest of her family. Then, one spring day, she sat in her dentist's office—her dentist was her uncle. And she continued: "He was drilling my teeth, and I could not talk, and he said, 'what do you know about your real mother?'" The shock touched us all, regardless of how many times we heard Karen's story of "sudden" knowledge. Drama apart, and the metaphor of being drilled perhaps accidental, the impact of such a shift in self-image framed the stories exchanged at ASG meetings.

Details and anecdotes like Karen's built up the case against secrecy within the family. Little by little, these personal accounts accumulated, in ASG and elsewhere, to constitute the basis for a reform movement. The boundaries were permeable, and the movement swift from arguing against secrets within a family to protesting the state's maintenance of secrets about a person. Stories like Karen's illustrate the dangers of hiding facts from a child and point to the likelihood that any secret will burst into the open one fine spring day. Twenty-five years after Karen first gathered a group to protest the perpetual sealing of birth certificates, she received an award for her work from the local adoption community. No longer portrayed, as she was initially, as an individual looking for the facts of her own life, Karen is now considered an advocate of adoptee rights.

Birthparents do not win the sympathy or the favorable attention adoptees in the United States do. The four women who in 1976 answered Lee's advertisement had little support in a social and cultural setting that sternly mandated silence for a relinquishing parent. The openness prescribed for adoptive parents was not prescribed for the parents who had "given up" children. Instead, birthparents were advised to keep the decision secret, to forget the event, and to move on with their lives. Invisible for decades, birthparents do not have the place in American culture that the adopted individual, representing a benign alteration of status, has. In fact, the greatest support for the birthparents who met in Lee's living room were the adoptees who had been meeting in other towns, throughout the country. Adoptee critiques of the secrecy perpetuated by American adoption law offered birthparents support for their own evolving interpretations of the "surrender" of a child.[8]

Lee was different from Karen, in her leadership style and in her ambitions for a birthparent group. While her decision to form a group, like Karen's, surfaced out of a personal experience, Lee took the programs and the purposes of CUB further than Karen would take ASG. Lee recognized the importance of establishing a birthparent status, making the invisible parent visible, and she also recognized the strength of a rhetoric borrowed from social movements of the 1960s and 1970s.

In telling her own story, and in encouraging the exchange of stories that formed the core of the first and all subsequent meetings, Lee inscribed the birthparent experience in a language of identity and status. She drew on the women's movement, and its rhetoric of self-assertion and social equality. She also drew on the gay rights movement, especially its key metaphor: coming out of the closet. Implicitly, she referred to the civil rights movement, fitting the arguments against discrimination and oppression to the birthparent case as well. Like a musical piece, with themes whose resonances touched a variety of cultural chords, Lee's presentation effectively opened the door of the closet for numerous birthparents in the United States and, eventually, the world. Concerned United Birthparents, or CUB, was by the 1980s an influential player on the adoption playing field.

The floodgates had opened, and CUB expanded into a large and complex organization. Statements of purpose followed. Burgeoning membership brought diverse views and goals that had to be reconciled. Absorption into an increasingly public debate over secrecy and sealed records forced the organization to articulate, and rearticulate, its central principles. Possibly, too, the continued frown that "out" birthparents receive in many parts of American society forced a self-consciousness about purposes that adoptee groups, with a better press, did not need. At any rate, under Lee's leadership and then after she left, CUB stepped a distance from its early support group character. While stories continue to form the basis of local meetings, suits and lobbying constitute the group's presence in a wider domain.

Although the adoptee support groups give support and, to some extent, a vocabulary to birthparent groups, the two develop along quite different lines. A comparison of the language birthparents use to plead their case with the framing of the adoptee case reveals how divergent the two are. It appears, now, that adoptees predominate on the American scene, but the details of the predominance and its relationship to birthparent arguments reveals how deep into American culture the reform movement penetrates.

Let me start with the adoptees.

The right to know

In 1979, Lifton published another book on the experience of being adopted. *Lost and Found: The Adoption Experience* is a collection of personal testimonies, indicating how many adoptees in the United States want to know about their birth families. While condemning the sealed records of American adoption, through its wide cast of characters *Lost and Found* presents a diversity of interpretations of confidentiality, anonymity, and secrecy. By the last decade of the twentieth century, adoptees in the United States had a wealth of resources for constructing their assessments of "being adopted." The number of people speaking out against secrecy had expanded, and an adopted person could set her own biography, and its gaps, against the experiences and the opinions of individuals from all walks of life. The comfort of cultural resources and of published personal testimonies was unmistakable at the meetings of ASG I attended from 1984 through 1993.

I discovered ASG the way adoptees did, through an ad in the classified section of my local newspaper. One morning in 1984, I read a notice to "all interested persons" to come to a meeting to protest a bill that was before the state legislature. (I had just moved to the area.) The bill, if passed, would *close* hitherto available original birth certificates. The ad was my first hint of ASG's existence, and I went to the open meeting. The bill passed in January 1985, and adoptee birth certificates remain officially closed to this day.

The meetings were attended by adoptees, an occasional adoptive parent, and, until a birthparent group formed in the area, several birthparents. Age, background, and reasons for attending all varied over the years that I went; invariably, however, adoptee stories dominated the afternoon discussions. Sometimes there were only one or two people present besides me, Karen, and two other coordinators. There were Sundays when, mysteriously to me, twenty people would show up. If a news item broke about a "disrupted" adoption or, after they became more common, a happy reunion, the Sunday meetings predictably filled up. In all the years of my attendance, only a few members were non-white. Most of those who came regularly were women.

Meetings followed the model of consciousness-raising groups, opening with the exchange of stories. Common themes emerged, concerning the moment of learning about adoption, the silences adoptive parents imposed, the embarrassment of being asked to draw a family tree at school. Over the years, adoptees more freely admitted a desire to find birth relatives; adoptive parents who attended also showed an increasing willingness to meet the birthparents—generally of now adult adopted children. Karen's own story filtered in and out of almost every meeting I attended and provided a blueprint for searching. Her comment, "it was the best thing I ever did," had to influence a number of those in attendance. When the *ASG Newsletter* began keeping a count of successful searches, the die was cast.

Still, the decision to search was, as Karen put it, "scary." For members of the group, the exchange of stories at Sunday meetings made the case for breaking the law. The case rested on interpretations of the pain and anxiety caused by secrecy. Secrets, Lifton wrote in *Twice-Born*, the book everyone seemed to know, "that's what adoption is all about: secrets."[9] In the stories I heard, secrets lay like grenades, ready to explode. "So I went from 2 to that age of 12 assuming that I was a natural child to those particular parents. And at 12 my knowledge of being not a natural child to the foster parents [she was not legally adopted] came at a dinner table whereby I spilled my milk and the foster, my foster mother said something to the effect of, 'I'm very glad that you don't belong to us because I wouldn't want such a sloppy, awful child being mine.'"[10]

Even when adoptive parents told the adoptee, for those who came to ASG this did not end the secrecy in their lives. "I've known since as little as I can remember that I was an adopted kid," a man who searched for his birthmother told me. "My parents never talked about us being adopted. We were just their kids." The subject, from his (retrospective) point of view, was *taboo*. "I felt like as a child that there were a whole lot of things that I couldn't talk about. So anyway, I think this is something that's, as I say, it still does in some way affect my difficulty in knowing when I can tell people that I'm adopted."[11] Lifton's argument exactly: that "telling" does not erase the secrets and lies, which are there until the adoptee learns about his or her biological ancestry. The sense of something being wrong—that silences are damaging—pervaded the narratives at ASG. "Because I think that subconsciously you know that there is something different about you even though I used to ask if I was adopted and everybody, my mother would say, 'Oh no.'" This woman found out in young adulthood that she had in fact been adopted (personal communication).

At meetings, memories of "being different" and "suspecting something" transformed into the "right to know." Karen's own story set a goal; feelings of "vague discontent" when she was in her mid-30s brought her to ask for more information about her adoption and about her birth family. But her story was not the only inspiration for members of ASG. Most knew the argument in Lifton's books, either directly or through the popularizations of her ideas. That *not knowing* interrupts the development of a strong identity was coin-of-the-realm at adoptee support group meetings. Lifton's arguments influence adoptees and, through them the whole adoption reform movement.

Lifton links the secrecy in adoption to the difficulties individual adoptees experience in achieving an integrated identity. Specifically, she condemns keeping secrets about the birth family. "By being forced out of the natural flow of generational continuity, as others know it, it is as if one has been forced out of nature itself," she writes. "Seen in these terms, Adoptees become impotent creatures who have been denied free will."[12] With the concept of "nature," Lifton turns the matter into something inevitable, essential, and universal. In this argument, a connection with biological ancestry provides the necessary foundation for an integrated identity regardless of time, place, and culture. At the same time, Lifton's view of identity evokes distinctly American cultural values: independence, choice, and free will.

Her emphasis on individual development took the discussion of closed records out of the realm of the social (where it belongs) and placed it squarely in the realm of the self. Her emphasis quickly received backing in clinical literature and in the widely appealing symbolism of *roots*.

In 1979, three therapists in California published a book that gave the arguments in *Twice-Born* the patina of expertise. Based on their clinical practice, Sorosky, Baran, and Pannor argue that adoptees, birthparents, and adoptive parents suffer a loss of self and of self-confidence because they lack "natural ties." *The Adoption Triangle* concludes: "Taking a child from one set of parents and placing him/her with another set, who pretend that the child is born to them, disrupts a basic natural process. The need to be connected with one's biological and historical past is an integral part of one's identity formation."[13] The conclusion is the gist of the argument. Through its presentation of diverse cases, the body of the book provides any reader with an easy road map to that conclusion. *The Adoption Triangle* sat on the front table, next to *Twice-Born*, when Karen remembered to bring them both to ASG meetings.

And in 1977 there was Alex Haley's *Roots: The Saga of an American Family.* Less the book than the amazingly successful TV series made searching for family backgrounds, for biological ancestors, and for the "roots" of oneself appealing well beyond the adoption triad. For adoptees, wondering about the wisdom of requesting an unamended birth certificate or agency records, Haley's passionate account offered a sense of security and diminished the sense of marginality in their actions.

A decade later, at the end of the 1980s, publicity about DNA and genetic engineering influenced adoption discourse. The appeal of framing a call for information about "birth" in a language of science was irresistible. Always persuasive rhetoric in American culture, references to science and to "medical knowledge" justified the need-to-know adoptees had all along linked to biology.

During the Sunday afternoon meetings of ASG, however, notions of genetics and, blurred with that, of biology came clothed in stories of isolation, of emptiness, and of the "vacuum" that no conversations and no relatives ever filled. Anecdotes describing the panic at having to draw a family tree or find a family member with the same features filled adoptee stories, both altering and accentuating a culture's preoccupation with the famous helix. "I know with me, too, 'who do I look like' [was important]," an adoptee recalled her childhood concerns. " I always looked in, I remember ... just looking up in the clouds. And it's just kind of a blank. I see a body, except that the face was completely blank and trying to get the clouds to make a figure, almost ordering the clouds, go there and make a figure, show me what the face looks like." [14] And so Pam expressed her isolation and her experience of disconnectedness through the vivid memory of "missing" someone who looks like you. The trope, of lacking familiar faces in a family, formed the premise for requesting facts about a birth family, a real relative, and, ultimately, access to one's "genetic" heritage.

Other adoptees reject the "looks like me" argument. They find the phrase vague, mystical, or simply irrelevant to their concerns. In addition, many adoptees recognize the persuasiveness of alternative arguments, especially those that touch upon health and health history. A request for medical records seems down to earth, reasonable, and specific. Throughout the United States, courts hear such requests with sympathy. At ASG meetings adoptees put the medical in colloquial terms: "I had these terrible back pains and I wanted to know if someone else in my family had them" or "I wondered whether I was going to get fat in my old age." Occasionally, the plea for medical histories was a response to an illness or an emergency. As one adopted woman told me: "And the surgeon sat on my bed and wanted to know, 'OK, what did your mother have, what did your father have, what did your sister have?' I am sitting there with this blank look on my face saying, 'I can't tell you anything because I am adopted.'" [15] These requests do not address the case against sealed records in American adoption. Rather, they represent a demand by an individual for the (specific) information that will help in a crisis or ease one's own passage through life.

"Records" does not refer to a single entity in American adoption. [16] When adoptees request medical information, they define "records" in a particular way: the data kept by an agency, perhaps, or by the physician who treated a birthparent. But they are not necessarily asking for the original birth certificate or the court documents finalizing the adoption; they are not necessarily, that is, requesting a break down in confidentiality and the possibility of identifying a birthparent. In some ways, then, a request for medical information weakens the argument against secrecy, by limiting the kinds of records that should be available.

Medical concerns constitute a "good cause" claim to records in a majority of American courts. An adoptee can also plead "psychological need" and receive a sympathetic hearing in a court or an agency. Medical good cause and psychological good cause are quite different in the eyes of adoptees: "medical" implies a claim that is both urgent and rational, while "psychological need" implies for some a claim based on weakness and immaturity. Adoptees at ASG meetings were reluctant to phrase their requests for information in terms that might lead an official to define them as unstable, unhappy, or just plain crazy. Most of the adoptees I met refused such a plea, drawing a fine line between "psychological need" and the *right* to have information in order to complete one's identity. Karen enjoined this separation over the years I knew her, using her enmity for Bill Pierce of the National Council for Adoption to maintain her position against psychological good cause.

Karen began to tangle with Bill Pierce in the mid-1980s. The dispute, and the tension, between them has not ceased to this day. An issue of the *ASG Newsletter* in 1986 carried one of her first sallies. Editor and main reporter, Karen put Pierce's argument in her own words: "According to Mr. Pierce, if an adoptee needs to search he has a mental problem, he is ungrateful and he is told he would not search if he loved his [adoptive] parents. He cannot be trusted with his own mother's name." She printed her own response: "I am not sick, Mr. Pierce. I am only experiencing heartache from genetic amputation."[17]

Behind her compact sentence lies a distinction between "sickness" and soothing a "heartache." The adoptee who wants her or his records, according to Karen, is not sick but sensible.

With Pierce as her abiding scapegoat, Karen opposes any implication that frailty or mental instability prompts the adopted person to request information about her or himself. In 1999, the case still lay open. Mr. Pierce, she told readers, accused her of having a "mental health problem" because she wanted to know about her birth family.[18] And though Karen polarizes the issue by reporting her personal encounters with Pierce, her passionate defense of adoptee requests for information reflects the force of Pierce's defense of sealed records.

Questions about *why* an adoptee requests information from a sealed file remain. The media encourages such questions by speculating that those who make requests are dissatisfied and ungrateful individuals. Members of ASG respond to the negative adjectives by insisting on the maturity the request represents and by rejecting the suggestion that access to facts is a solution to "mental health (or any) problems." "I could get a psychiatrist to say that I am loony-tunes and we need the records and I could get doctors to say that there's a health problem and we need to get the records," a woman in ASG told me.[19] She scorned what she considered a humiliating route to gaining the information adoptees define as rightfully theirs.

Discussions in the press and at support group meetings carry forward the debate. Are requests for records a sign of weakness or an appropriate response to unjust deprivation? The debate is framed in cultural terms, with the contest set between an individual's *need* and an individual's *right*. Furthermore, the debate exposes the cultural assumption that there is a connection between an integrated identity and possession of the facts of one's past. These are the terms Lifton and other activists use in their arguments. Lifton, however, portrays not only the deprivation but also the desperation of the person who lacks crucial facts about her or his own life.

In the spring of 1986, in a widely reported case, an adopted boy burned down the house of his adoptive parents, killing them both. The defense lawyer argued that the boy was innocent, suffering from an "adopted child syndrome." The argument did not spare the boy but it did bring a phrase out of arcane literature into popular speculations on adoption and being adopted. A few days after the trial, in an op-ed piece in *The New York Times* Betty Jean Lifton made a stronger case for the defense. "The syndrome includes conflict with authority, preoccupation with excessive fantasy, setting fires, pathological lying, stealing, running away from home, learning difficulties, lack of impulse control." The brutal evidence of a syndrome in the boy's case, she said, "should encourage legislators and adoption specialists to consider the effects of society's secrecy about adoptees' pasts and to reexamine the need for sealed adoption records."[20]

Reference to an adopted child syndrome, while bringing the issue of sealed records to the attention of the American public, does not suit most advocates of reform in adoption laws. William Feigelman, a longtime expert on adoption, responded to Lifton's op-ed piece: "Although I fully agree adoption records should be unsealed, I am reluctant to accept her premises, including an 'adopted child syndrome.'"[21] For advocates of unsealing adoption records and doing away with secrecy, records are a resource and not a cure.

Moreover, the argument that rests on an adopted child syndrome suggests that the institution itself causes difficulties for individuals. While ASG and other adoption reform groups criticize state laws of confidentiality and anonymity, they do not condemn the institution of adoption. From this point of view, the right to know and the privilege of seeing documents about oneself accords the adopted person the resources every adult American citizen has. No one else lacks information about their birth, their background, and their "biological ancestry," argue these groups.

Yet the argument made by reform groups often comes down to considering records the foundation for individual identity. That is, the arguments are based on an assessment of the self that does not stray far from psychological interpretations like that in Lifton's 1970s *Twice-Born* and *Lost and Found*. Currently, as states review the laws of confidentiality on their books, they do so in response to the adoptee claim to a "right to know." The claim draws from American cultural constructions of the person as a psychological and a social being. Effective as the claim is, and increasingly so, it sidesteps the normative and the political functions of adoption. This becomes clear from a comparison with birthparent arguments for reform in American adoption law and custom.

Adoptees claim the right to know vital facts about themselves and their origins. Birthparents claim the right to a status, to come out in the world as the parents they know themselves to be. Using the oxymoronic phrase, a "childless mother," CUB literature points to the hypocrisy in American culture: modeling parent-child bonds on "birth" and denying parenthood to the *birthparent*. The argument differs from the one adoptees make. While adoptees demand documents—records and data—, birthparents ultimately demand a revision of cultural values and norms. At the same time, the arguments are yoked together by an emphasis on identity and by a critique of state intervention in private lives.

I. Birthparent Experiences of Relinquishment

My signature on a piece of paper

While adoptees talk about official documents, sealed away somewhere, birthparents talk of the "surrender" that shut off a whole part of their lives. In both narratives, *papers* alter forever the course of a life. In both narratives, the notion of papers stands for the whole panoply of legal regulation and of customary belief that keeps a person from knowing and from asserting her "true" identity. As adoptee and birthparent narratives put it: by sequestering and sealing documents, the state appropriates what rightly belongs to the person. But here the similarity ends. In the adoptee narrative, the documents are drawn by someone else; in the birthparent narrative, the papers are one's own, created in the moment of signing a certificate of relinquishment. This is the *surrender* that in the view of birthparents who join support groups has no legal redress in American society. "Surrender" forms a powerful trope for birthparent experiences, unifying the disparate experiences of any individual who has given up a child.

The women who met in Lee Campbell's living room that Sunday in 1976 had already reassessed the experience of relinquishment. They would not have come had they not begun the task of reconsidering the meaning of "signing away" a child. Lee had tapped an existing constituency: individuals who were no longer able to "forget" and to "freeze" a part of their lives. From their stories that afternoon came not only the origins of a national organization but also the key words for an effective alternative interpretation of adoption in the United States. The fate of that interpretation when it entered the public domain was another question.

To *surrender* a child. A moment's thought reveals the potential in the concept for carrying an elaborate interpretation of the norms and the laws guiding relinquishment in virtually all states of the union. To "surrender" is *giving up* and *giving in*, a contrast to the *giving* that defines adoption practice in other societies of the world. As CUB evolved, "surrender" condensed and communicated complicated experiences. The term resonated for every birthparent in CUB, but shared resonance was not enough to prevent conflicts and disputes in the growing organization. Reflections on the role of class and of gender eventually split the group. While members agree that surrender represents the vulnerability and lack of resources all birthparents know, some voices call this a feminist issue and some call it an issue of economic and social discrimination. The gap widened and disagreements about feminism, poverty, and social inequities appeared in the pages of the *CUB Communicator.* The political and rhetorical unity of CUB's early years dissolved. Inasmuch as surrender implies weakness, lack of leverage, and submission to forces stronger than one's own, the term evokes hierarchies of social position and access to "goods." Within CUB, there was not to be perfect agreement on the significance of social factors and of political developments to American adoption practices.

At first, however, surrender unified the purposes and the participants in CUB. The narratives and letters published in the group's newsletter, the *CUB Communicator,* drew attention to the agony of signing away a child, to the injustice of demands that the experience be erased, and to the moral condemnation of a person who took care of a child in that way. *The word surrender demonstrates the punitive cast of American adoption.* As used, surrender exposes the contradictions in a culture in which the state sanctions an act that its citizens condemn. The word sur-render, too, unifies all birthparents, including those who had deliberated the decision to relinquish and those who "lost" their rights to a child through the pressures or the policing imposed by others.[22] With surrender as the overarching symbol, everyone who signed the papers had *given up*.

Exploiting the colloquial connotations of surrender, CUB offers an alternative perspective on statutory provisions for relin-quishing a child. The emphasis on *giving up* erases the generos-ity in "giving" and throws into light the absence of choice and of decision-making CUB claims is at the heart of relinquishment under American law. Birthparent insistence on the coercion in a relinquishment, regardless of the particular circumstances, indi-cates how glaringly that gesture violates the norms of parent-hood in American culture. Moreover, the ferocity of opposition to birthparent arguments reveals the importance of that figure as scapegoat for the ills of American adoption policy. Like adoption support groups, birthparent groups took their first step in the direction of identity and social status as a parent; the second step was an attack on law and on the rigidity of statutes.

When Lee met with the four women in her living room, she told the story of her own "coming out" as a birthparent. Her story continues to be a template in CUB, influencing the many stories that have been told in the ensuing quarter century. Lee is not shy about retrieving her memories, describing them for read-ers of the *CUB Communicator* and using them as a basis for the growing scholarship on birthparent experiences.[23] I heard the story during one afternoon I spent with Lee, and later recognized the blend of elements that continue to be part of CUB rhetoric. A person needs to be self-confident, Lee told me, in order to recon-sider the experience of relinquishment. "And I did not consciously deal with the impact of the surrender until more than a decade had passed—until a time when my life was secure enough that I could allow the suffering to surface."[24] She also recognized and relished the connotations of "battle" in the term surrender.

The imagery of battle expanded in the pages of the *Com-municator* and in brochures for new members of CUB. Notably, Lee borrowed the initials MIA from the Vietnam War struggles;

MIA, she wrote, stands for Missing In Adoption. What was missing, was not the adopted child but memories and a connection to the past: birthparents were cut off, imprisoned, and sentenced to a lifetime behind the walls of strict laws of confidentiality. Members of CUB took to the imagery, reconceptualizing relinquishment as a battle against forces stronger than themselves. A number of birthparents I interviewed hoped they had at least fought back, and that the surrender had followed a battle.

"So it was in fact like a little two-year old ...," a woman mused out loud to me about the surrender of twenty years earlier. She paused before bursting out in anger at the social worker who, she said, treated her like a child who did not know her own mind. Years after the relinquishment, this birthmother learned a different story: "I was so grateful because I thought I gave in really easy and I felt so guilty about giving in. If I had really given them a fight I may not have felt so bad and I never thought I did. But here years later when my mother and I could finally talk about some things, she says, 'Oh no, you gave us a real fight.' So I was stronger than I thought I was."[25]

The majority of birthparents I met did not experience such a moment of triumph. I encountered CUB at the end of the 1970s, when I began a project on adoption and interpretations of kinship in American culture. A local group existed where I then lived, and they welcomed me with a warmth that at first surprised me. Subsequently, I realized that the group was pleased to have an adoptive parent there; in addition, most members looked forward to research and publicity about the birthparent position in American adoption. As Lee intended, the local group embraced the cause of "educating" the public about the hidden member of the triad. But the group also respected the original consciousness-raising goals, and an exchange of personal stories characterized every meeting I attended. The majority of members, during the eight years I participated, were women, Caucasian, and, as far as I could judge, middle class. Like the ASG group, this CUB group did not keep attendance records or statistics on its members.

In their stories, participants brought out into the open the "secrets" they remembered being told to keep. The central moment, for virtually everyone who came, was the moment of surrender and the permanent resignation of rights to a child. Over the years, the meanings of "surrender" stretched from the personal to the political, as the local group developed an analysis of the inequities and the hypocrisy in American cultural views of the parent who delegates parenting to another person.

Their stories are of coercion, of passivity, and of being tricked into signing the papers. "I was all doped up and this woman came in and she shoved a paper in front of me. I never knew what I signed," a birthparent told me in a conversation, recalling the relinquishment of twelve years earlier. "I had just given birth and I lay there exhausted, and there was the hospital social worker in the doorway," said another, older woman, prefacing her conclusion that she could not then refuse to sign. I heard reports of priests slipping a surrender paper into a counseling session and of girls whose parents insisted surrender was the "best" thing to do. At CUB meetings, a transformation occurred, so that to have surrendered underlined the power of the state and not the weakness of a person. The narratives constructed a state that, through its agents and its moral sanctions, suppressed the exercise of individual will, reformulated the content of an individual decision, and made the action of "giving up" a child the only option. Under Lee's influence, CUB's master narrative delineated the inequities in the institution of American adoption.

The strategy of using "surrender" as the central trope for a birthparent's experiences lifted the onus off the person and placed it squarely on external forces. [26] The ground was prepared for battles in a larger arena.

Identity politics and the bear

In her statements and publications, Lee shifted the blame from self to society and simultaneously insisted that a birthparent consider her (or his) own agency in the occurrence of an adoption. She created a logo that captured her complex argument in one fell—and vivid—swoop: a line drawing of a mother bear and her cub. The bear has survived the ups and downs of CUB's history.

The front page of every *CUB Communicator* displays the drawing. An image of a mother bear nuzzling her cub incorporates traits conventionally ascribed to the good parent: loving concern and tender affection. A mother-bear suits the mythologies of motherhood in the United States; she does not suit the stereotype of the relinquishing mother that guides adoption policy. On the cover of the *Communicator*, the logo tells readers that birthparents *are good not bad parents*.

The logo condenses CUB's critique of American adoption culture. Plain and unadorned, the drawing exposes the hypocrisy of a culture that denies expressions of parental love to a person whose parental role has taken an unconventional course. Birthparent concern for a child that results in an adoption plan receives a sentence of stigma and secrecy. The logo also demonstrates the power of nature: the maternal figure and her cub stand strong against any "papers" the state sanctifies. An instinctual attachment, the logo asserts, cannot be erased by state fiat. Under Lee's leadership, the argument did not end with instinct and nature, with the assertion of birth bonds the bear and cub illustrate. Lee extended the imagery of the bear in a crucial way.

The bear became Artemis, goddess and hunter—hunting, one might say, for the pieces of her life she had lost. She grew fierce, her stance bold, and her gestures those of the warrior. "In Greek mythology, there was a Bear Goddess called Artemis. Artemis represented the wild self, the power to be your own person, free, uncaged, with permission to growl and to protect. As the myth went, those who invoked Artemis awakened the integrity of self that upholds the right to be different, to be the people we are and to walk the path we do," wrote Lee in a 1983 issue of the *Communicator*.[27] Echo of Lee's own story, the bear-as-Artemis advocates self-confidence and a bold assertion of identity. Under Lee's leadership, that was first and foremost the goal: "hunting" for the status of parent the state withheld. The story of Artemis adds the crucial dimensions of self-assertion and of a quest for personal autonomy; the hunt is for hidden parts of one's identity along with social acknowledgment. Lee's daring appropriation of the "coming out" metaphor from a gay rights movement emphasized the significance of a claim to self, unfettered by the conventions and the sanctions of a mainstream society.

The logo brought together the fierceness, the ferocious presentation of self, with the nurturing, loving aspects of parenthood. The image remains in the group's acronym as well as in its visual imagery; cubs, mother bears, and that American icon, the teddy bear, form the bulk of the products the organization markets. In all its manifestations, on t-shirts, in toys, and on banners, the logo reminds members and observers of the love a birthparent never relinquishes.

Effective at condensing complicated ideas and combining the antithetical traits of fierceness and nurturance, the logo preserves the personal thrust of CUB's position. The logo is about *self*, about a status denied and a sentiment distorted by the surrounding society. In that guise, the logo triumphs over the external forces that have determined "surrender" in the United States since laws were passed in the mid-nineteenth century. Insistence on an assertion of self and on the recognition of parental status redeemed the individual birthparent and, as Lee anticipated in her references to civil rights and women's liberation, the birthparent cause rode into public on the crest of a wave of identity politics.

New members, with new agendas, filled the membership rolls of CUB in the decade after its founding. By the end of the 1980s, Lee decided to withdraw from the organization and to deal with adoption in other contexts. Although she had embraced the logo of a mother bear and its counterpart in the myth of Artemis, she did not take a feminist stance. Lee's focus remained on birthparents, a category created and caught by conflicting messages in American culture; her focus lay less on the *mother* who relinquished than on the *person* who was not free to make decisions about when and how to have a child.

Other members of CUB had another vantage point. For them, birthparenthood was above all a woman's issue. After all, these voices argued, in the United States it is mothers who sign the surrender papers and it is women who most often are measured against high standards of parental performance. Upon the social and economic weakness of an unwed or unprepared mother, the argument continues, rests the structure of twentieth-century American adoption. The argument accurately reflects the history and the existing culture of adoption in the United States. The figure of a bad mother apears in one guise or another in adoption policy, in public discourse, and, enduringly, in popular responses to the parent who gives (up) her child. Fathers who surrender children do not interest policy-makers or the public as much as woemn who relinquish—or men who neglect or abandon children.[28] Even today, with visible changes in American adoption practice, those who relinquish are referred to in the feminine, and the *bad parent* is almost always the *unloving mother*.[29] The argument that relinquishment is a feminist issue, however, avoids the fact that those who relinquish by-and-large lack the social support and the economic resources for making another decision. A feminist perspective can obscure the moralism and the material ginequities that lead to a surrender. "Surrender" reflects the unequal distribution of moral and material resources. In her tenure at CUB, Lee advocated analyzing the conditions that lead to relinquishment in any of its configurations.

The stories I heard, in the 1980s and early 1990s, covered both sides of the fence: some had a feminist cast and some dwelt on the lack of leverage that in every instance leads to relinquishment. Those who rejected what they considered a narrow feminism dwelt on the importance of age, of economic position, and of marital status in determining a relinquishment. These factors, in this view, led to relinquishment and, as well, set the terms for a re-delegation of parenthood. In stories of "giving up" framed that way, birthparents explicitly compare themselves with the prototypical adoptive parent: individuals who are well into adulthood, with good jobs and material advantages. Although these differences had often entered into a birthparent's original acceptance of adoption as best for the child, in retrospect the comparison also constituted a criticism of cultural criteria for a good parent.

Turning the spotlight on material conditions and demographic traits illuminates the categorical dimensions of the delegation of parenthood in the United States. The power of categorical dimensions is evident in the interpretive framework birthparents apply to their experiences, despite the fact that a majority of birthparents in the United States (and in CUB) share the characteristics of the presumptive adoptive family:

middle class, white, and educated.[30] The framework reflects the moralistic side of American adoption. In placement decisions, the designation of a good parent legitimizes the traits of a bad parent. Presumably objective measures, like stability and economic wherewithal, obscure the underlying judgment of character that guides these decisions Birthparent narratives expose the hypocrisy in a presumed objectivity by dwelling on the attribution of "sinful" they experience.

As long as the birthparent is considered evil, these narratives imply, the onus is taken off society. Stigmatizing the relinquishing parent takes the blame off a society that fails to provide resources for those who lack the means of caring for a child. From this perspective, adoption compensates for inadequate welfare and community services.

When CUB members demand contact with the child, they also assert the "goodness" of their characters; a request for information about a child cleanses the "evil" by indicating the commitment to a child. Moreover, in offering that commitment as justification for a search, birthparents present the emotional dimension of parenthood as equivalent (if not superior) to the material resources they recall as determining fit parenthood in the original arrangement. Search stories are a reminder of the significance of enduring solidarity to notions of parenthood in the United States.

After she came out of the closet, Lee located the son she had relinquished twenty years earlier. She did not, however, consider her own quest a guide for all birthparents: some, she knew, would claim parental status while remaining childless and some would simply request information about a relinquished child. CUB, in her view, was primarily a support group and secondarily an "educational" organization. "CUB is a M.A.S.H. unit (mutual aid, self help)" and "has been able to educate the public to the trauma of family separation by adoption," new members read in a brochure.[31] At the same time, the appeal of Lee's reunion was irresistible; her story created a demand for contact not just data. By the end of the 1980s, CUB communications frankly supported searching. Scenes of reunion in the *Communicator* constituted a strong argument against secrecy and sealed records.

"The most wonderful, unashamed tears ... "

"Like a little two-year old," Molly told me about her relinquishment, pleased to discover later that she had put up a fight. She
had joined CUB only to discover that she was not done with
fighting and that she might even locate the twins she had surrendered when she was sixteen. Molly told me her story in a
crowded kitchen, inhabited intermittently by one or another of
her four children. Full of emotion, her story was also self-con-
sciously critical of American adoption.

She began her search by visiting the agency that had placed
the children. Sitting in front of the desk talking with a social
worker, she told me, brought back the feelings of vulnerability
and childishness she had worked so hard to suppress. But the
social worker was sympathetic and told Molly the name of the
adoptive parents. That made it easy for Molly to find their
house. "I drove around and around. It was a big house, with a
big front lawn, a beautiful house." Still, actually getting in touch
with the family daunted Molly for months. She worried about
her looks, her life, and her likelihood of pleasing the adoptive
parents—let alone the girls she had relinquished. Encouraged
by members of CUB, Molly one day picked up the telephone and
identified herself. "The mother invited me to come and visit the
girls," who were about to leave for college.

In talking with me, she recalled how worried she was about
what to wear. "I could not decide what to wear, the house was so
elegant. Would they be all dressed up?" The twins, she knew,
had gone to private school and taken horse-back riding lessons.
Their "privileges" seemed so much more than she could offer
them, she confessed, still squirming at the differences. Yet, like
most members of CUB, Molly had asked that her children be
placed with well-off, stable, and financially secure parents.
Nearly twenty years later, the choice of material comforts struck
a note of discomfort in Molly's narrative. And she revised the
balance as she went on with her search story.

She drove up the large driveway, and walked into the "formal living room." Two young women greeted her, accompanied
by their mother. In words I heard in other search narratives,

Molly told me, "their mother was very polite, calm, cold even." "And one twin was the same way," she continued. The other, Beth, "was emotional like me." The importance of the contrast came home to me after several interviews. The birthparent search story claims her (or his) emotionality and attributes "coldness" to the adoptive parents. The birthparent claims a love that is natural and attributes to the adoptive parents a caring that is calculated. The contrast reflects a cultural dichotomy between impulse and intention that influences judgments about the placement in an adoption.

Molly's story exposes some other aspects of placement practice. Meeting her daughters in their stable, two-parent family prompted her to phone the birthfather. (She also told her current husband, father of the four children I met, about the twins.) "Buddy was as thrilled as I was," she said. They had a "four-way" reunion, and began a pattern of meeting for dinner from time to time, "just like a real family," she concluded. In the regular reunion dinners she had with Buddy and the twins, Molly replicated the traits she had originally chosen for an adoptive family: father and mother, with the luxury of being able to spend time at family dinners.

Molly's narrative displays the significance of class in child placement decisions. Although she, like most birthparents of her era, chose a well-off and stable married couple as the ideal adoptive family, she subsequently defined these signs of good parenthood as inadequate and incomplete.[32] Nearly twenty years after the relinquishment, Molly rejected the appeal of material well-being by summoning up a cultural interpretation of parental love: expressive, emotional, and spontaneous. By that measure, in her narrative she clearly won over the adoptive parents.

Molly's search reverses the surrender and redeems her character. She had reclaimed her own past and, in CUB's vocabulary, *unfrozen* her memories. Those who search and find, as Molly did, similarly report feelings of release and of redemption. These feelings arise even when the meeting is cool and the adoptee response indifferent. Regardless of its content, a meeting turns the signature on a piece of paper into a purely formal act; the power of the state to reassign kinship vanishes in the face of an actual encounter. Moreover, a meeting erases the stigma attached to relinquishing a child and undermines the power of a cultural stereotype.

Reunions between birthparent and child challenge the bearing of American adoption law on notions of parenthood and on ideologies of family. As described, such reunions install the "real" parent into the child's life, whatever the behavior and the interactions that ensue. This interpretation is reiterated in language that often resembles the words used to describe birth—a rush of spontaneous and overwhelming love. It is reiterated in the detailing of remarkable resemblances between parent and child. And it is reiterated in the sense of contentment birthparents report result from a meeting. In reunion stories told by birthparents, it is as if nature has been awakened and the "bad" parent redeemed.

"I went home," a woman told me about her first meeting with a relinquished child, "and I was crying, I was laughing, I was screaming in the car. It was just too good to be true!"[33] Sometimes the reference to a day of birth is explicit: "I was filled with joy only equal to the day I gave birth to him," one parent began her description of a reunion.[34] Do these descriptions mean the parent "has the child" again? For some birthparents, that is the case. In our conversations, a birthmother told me: "I feel like I am her mom. I mean, I *know* I'm her mom. I mean, for God's sake I gave birth to her and I don't want to be called anything else."[35] In a quieter version, another birthparent stated: "But I will not look back as I thank God I now have my child back again."[36]

Love and excitement do not provide roles for a parent and a child who have been strangers for years.[37] Birthparents who maintain contact—and not all do—have a hard time finding a model for *behavior* in the relationship. Day to day interaction often gives way to participation in life-stage ceremonies, a high school graduation, for instance, or a wedding. These are the extended kinship models that do not demand more than presence. One Sunday, the *New York Times* featured a wedding story that turned out to be an adoption story. Bride and groom had known each other in college, had then relinquished a child, and lost touch with each other for twenty-five years. Reunited, their next step was to find the daughter—and there, at the wedding, stood all three looking like any "ordinary" family. Intentionally or not, the *Times* story also reminds readers that birthparents are not necessarily the poor and vulnerable of popular stereotype.

A photograph of birthparents with a relinquished child, like the exhilaration portrayed at CUB meetings, evokes the "real" in cultural constructions of kinship. Evidence of *flesh-and-blood* contrasts with the dry story of adoption official state documents tell. One vivid scene of a reunion is enough to call up the cultural assumption that birth bonds persist beneath the legal maneuvers of adoption. A birthparent I interviewed conveyed the gist of this, the anecdote of her first encounter with a relinquished child making clear the banishment of interfering "others." The two met at an airport. "And when I got off the plane we, neither of us had any problem recognizing each other. And she [the daughter] stood in the middle of the aisle, all the people are still trying to get—you know, the aisle just as you get out the gate. And people had to go around us. And we stood there and cried, for a long time. With our arms around each other. And it was the most wonderful tears I ever shed in my life. The most wonderful, unashamed ..."[38]

Unashamed. The word addresses several levels of the American adoption experience. A reunion is the moment a birthparent triumphs over the stigma and the secrecy surrounding her surrender. A reunion banishes the invisibility and the shame relinquishment imposes, asserting the rights to parenthood birth supposedly provides. The instant recognition and attachment Rhoda describes counteract the prescription to forget she, like others, heard in the 1960s and 1970s. In many ways, a reunion initiated by a birthparent brings the "giving" of a child into public light, out of the shadows of the closet. Stories of reunions change the meaning of the original decision for the birthparent, if not in the eyes of others.

The reversal and the redemption are not complete. The very dilemma a birthparent in the United States faces is that reunions do not remove shame and stigma from the birthparent experience. Often, in fact, reunions increase the condemnation of society—for a person who goes back on a contract, changes

her mind and imperils another person (the adoptee), and follows her whims rather than her "reason."

Not all birthparents want a reunion with a child. Many
reject the activism of CUB and many fear the granting of legal
rights to adult adoptees to unseal adoption records. "When I go
to Chicago," an adoptee told me about her reunion with a birthparent, "if she meets someone she knows down the street, she'll
introduce me as her friend from Colorado because she's not able
to face it."[39] A number of birthparents are outspoken against
reunions and the intrusion on their privacy a search by an
adoptee represents. "Dear Abby," wrote a birthmother, "I placed
my child for adoption 27 years ago with the understanding that
the adoption records would be sealed forever—and the 'forever'
was underlined. I was told that I would never see my child again.
That is exactly the way I wanted it, as it was the most traumatic
incident of my entire life."[40]

In May 2000, when the state of Oregon granted adoptees
the right to open the original birth certificate, it was against the
protests of a group of birthparents. The adoptee cause prevailed,
for reasons that are familiar in American adoption history: the
child is viewed as *subject of* not actor in the arrangement; the
child, now adult, should gain the resources of any "full citizen,"
and records are resources in American society. The child is the
valued figure, as evident in the "best interests of the child" principle that pervades adoption policy. The "child" persists even
when, as in the case of opening records, the adoptee constituency is an adult population.

No more than there is a consensus among birthparents is
there a consensus among the two million or so adoptees in the
United States about sealed records, anonymity, privacy, and confidentiality. But the adopted person who goes to court to request
records has a winning card as the *child* in the transaction. A
"child's" request for information, for the facts of life, and for a
meeting with a birth relative seems just in American society, in a
way that birthparent claims do not. The adoptee "in need"
prompts a positive response on the part of judges, lawyers, social
workers, and the public. How do adoptees construct the claims
that now receive a sympathetic hearing in courts and agencies?

How do adoptees handle the initial discovery of facts on unsealed documents? What do adoptee stories of moving from "information" to reunion add to a cultural account of American adoption?

II. Adoptee Experiences of Searching

"A face with genes like mine ..."

As a group, ASG turned to searching more quickly than CUB. Members of an adoptee search group did not have to deal with enforced silence and social stigma. By the mid-1970s, officially—if not in every single instance—being adopted was rarely a dark family secret. Advice to adopting parents included: "tell the child and talk about adoption as often as is comfortable." The background information adoptive parents received contained more than birth date, weight, and birthparent health and hobbies. While many members of ASG had horror stories of family secrets, all joined the group at a time when it was "right" to know. This meant, the accumulation of stories at meetings revealed, that the information packaged by an agency, a social worker, or a judge was *not enough*.

For adoptees in support groups, the acquisition of "facts" is insufficient. A summary of birth data, a careful description of the birth family, a paragraph or two about the birthmother's personality seem as thin as they would to anyone who discovers his or her life in an official document. At ASG, adoptees question the records that compose a life made by social agencies and they question the role of the state in enforcing that "biography" for the whole of an adopted person's life. Karen recalled her own search at almost every meeting I attended: her movement from vague feelings of dissatisfaction to getting information to needing to find a birth relative. With the energy and commitment Karen conveyed, the "right to know" changed into the "need to see." Papers were not the *flesh-and-blood* that dominates the symbolism of American kinship.

"I want to see a face with genes like mine," Nancy explained to me. "Mostly all my cousins looked like their sisters and brothers. You know, I can *see* who looks like who," was Heather's version. Urging a search for a replica of oneself, Lifton told her readers: the adopted person "looks in the mirror and wonders whose eyes are looking back at him."[41] The Eriksonian emphasis on biological ancestry as crucial to identity formation enters adoptee discourse, first through Lifton and then through memoirs and media presentations. "When you have biological relatives," another adoptee told me, "you are a whole person. That part is missing [for the adoptee]. There's a basic physical aspect of our lives that's missing. ... There is some relation that pumps through a blood line and that is gone, completely gone."[42]

Phrased in terms of identity, of deprivation of crucial facts, and of the importance of hereditary factors, adoptee searches fit late twentieth-century American culture. Unlike birthparent searches, adoptee searches do not threaten the structures of adoption; rhetorically, they pull away from adoption and take on issues of personal growth and development.[43] Add to this the "best interests" principle, and it is not surprising that an adoptee's quest to know her or his birth relatives gains a sympathetic hearing in state after state. And even where state laws maintain closed records, a sympathetic social worker can circumvent the law. "She pushed the files all around on her desk," an adoptee told me about discovering the name of his birthmother. "She shoved this one particular folder right in my face."[44]

In the past two or three years, several states have bowed to the demands of adoptees and the professional opinions of (some) social workers. Tennessee, Alabama, and Oregon have recently granted adult adoptees the right to "unseal" sealed records. Whether that means the adoptees who learn names will make contact—the irresistible impulse described by Karen and others in ASG—remains to be seen. "I do see her [birthmother] point of view," said Mr. Price, who was raised an only child. "Maybe she never, ever, wanted her husband or her children to know about this. But what about me? I've apparently got a bunch of half siblings out there, and I'd like to meet them. It would be nice to be able to see somebody that resembles me physically. Maybe they'd get a kick out of meeting me."[45]

Opponents, including birthparents, claim the right of privacy. "We made life decisions based on those assurances [of privacy]. Now, we are being left with our trust shattered, our hearts broken and the threat of our lives being changed forever without our consent."[46] When the Maryland legislature debated granting rights to adoptees, William Pierce of the National Council for Adoption, compared opening adoption records to allowing a third party to review the private records of a physician or a psychologist.[47] While the right of privacy certainly complicates the case enormously, the real point may be a fear of new family arrangements—kinship ties that stretch the American kinship grid even further than it is already stretched by divorce, single parenthood, and adoption itself.

No one knows whether thousands of Oregon adoptees will actually search for "someone who looks like me." Experts estimate that two-thirds of adoptees never search for a birthparent.[48] Adoptees (and birthparents) in support groups dispute these findings: searching, they claim, has so many meanings that no count is possible. Members of search groups also claim that once factual information is handed over, in the tedious language of an official document, it is hard not to take the next step. Moreover, increasing cultural emphasis on genetic factors in the health and well-being of a person pushes even the shy adoptees further along the track to making that first phone call. "My name is Helen, and I'm calling about a very personal matter. I was born on March 24, 1955, in Kansas City." So the reunion began for the woman who spearheaded the Oregon initiative. As in Lee Campbell's case, the reunion ended in friendship and not in a parent-child relationship. But that is not always the case.

"It ain't as easy as it sounds. ..."

"Reunion," not meeting or encounter, is the preferred word for adoptees and for birthparents. The term captures the special quality of families-come-together, a gathering of kin who find striking similarities with one another and who spread the myths of "you are just like your Uncle Bob." For the participants, reunions activate bonds between "flesh and blood," the real relatives of American cultural interpretations of kinship.

In initiating a reunion, birthparents struggle with the meanings of parenthood and family. Adoptees bring forward other ideas when they embark on their quests for kin, focusing on equal rights and personal autonomy. The conceptual differences disappear in action, but they are important for understanding the impact of reunions on adoption and on family in the United States.

"The year our minister wrote to Michigan for my original names, I was 38," wrote Karen in the *ASG Newsletter*, remembering back over twenty years. "He didn't know how to go on from there and I didn't either so I carried the paper around in my wallet for years." She continued: "June of 1977 [two years later], my husband Ted and I went to Michigan, searched and found my cousin, Sally. Sally led me to my sister, Mary and the rest is history."[49] The history involves finding her birthmother and then creating a relationship between her adoptive and her birthmother. Karen's is a triumphant origin story. "My search was the best thing I ever did." And she added, "I love getting birthday cards from two mothers."

Karen's story also reveals the incompatibility between demands to "know" facts and the actual desire to meet a parent. The gulf between demanding a document and discovering a "remarkable intimacy" with a stranger appears in virtually all adoptee narratives. A quest for identity ends up in an encounter with relatives, persons with their own lives and expectations. The adoptee is faced with the chore of charting kinship terms and behaviors in addition to assessing an agency's report or a doctor's case files. "Birthday cards from two mothers" is the tip of a story whose impact on policy is not yet clear.

Currently, in all states, the adoptee can get information on a "good cause" plea; a psychological or medical need for information persuades most judges in most states of the union to provide documents. Moreover, the articulated adoptee position that an adopted person is subject to a contract he did not make evokes the spirit of the United States constitution. At the same time, in many states information is anonymous and confidentiality rules the day. An adoptee who decides to make contact finds her or himself in the realm of the unlawful, the surreptitious, and the culturally "wrong." He opens a social worker's file folder, for instance, or lies to the driver's license bureau; he claims to be an old friend or someone with an inheritance to offer. In reunion stories I heard, adoptees cite a higher law, justify a secular wrong by appealing to a spiritual right. "Searching may be unethical but it's not immoral," an adoptee explained to me. "When you know that there's a piece of paper in a courthouse concerning you," Mr. Price said, "concerning an event that took place between you and another party, your birthmother, and you're not even allowed to see it, I just think that's wrong."[50] Still, these (often elaborate) rationales do not provide a pattern for interacting with found kin.

The reunion transforms "finding facts" into feelings—of love, attachment, recognition, and obligation, the elements of kinship as defined in American culture. "And if that's there and my [adoptive] parents don't drink a thing I still may be an alcoholic or a foodaholic," an adoptee explained his quest to find his birthparents. "Plus the fact your tendency to heart disease, your tendency to diabetes, you know, it's in your genes and no one can change that environment." He met his mother and described the encounter in terms that had little to do with the medical reasons he cited for searching. "We stayed up all night talking. Her love for me was unconditional, so much so that she loved me without ever having seen me."[51] The medical and constitutional grounds for locating a birth relative evaporate under the cultural script for a flesh-and-blood relationship.

Conventional expectations involving love, loyalty, attachment, and concern determine the adoptee's assessment of the reunion, and often lead to a revised interpretation of searching. Narratives refer to the obligations and duties American kinship patterns prescribe, and to the attention a child owes a parent that reciprocates the love a parent ideally promises a child. "So my adoptive mother is also needy and I can't do everything for her [birthmother] that ideally she would like a daughter to do and ideally that somebody could do. But at some point I just have to recognize my limitations and I have more responsibility to her than I do to my natural mother." Another adoptee complained about the competing demands he experienced from birth and adoptive parents. "So you don't want to neglect one for the other and it's, you know, it ain't as easy as it sounds." (personal communication)

No one I met actually deemed a reunion *bad*. When the relationship failed to meet expectations, when one or the other or both struggled with the "map" for further interactions, still the adoptees, like birthparents, cited the satisfactions: knowing a relinquished child was "OK" and, in the adoptee case, knowing the facts of one's past. Karen never gave up on any relationship reported by a member of ASG. Reflecting a good American value, she advised a person to "work" at it. "Some people's relationships go by the wayside. But you have to work at them. If you don't work at it, if both of you don't work at it, it's going to fall apart. If everybody doesn't work at being a family, then that's going to fall apart too."[52]

Do the references to feelings and emotions, and to the *work* of maintaining a relationship, indicate that adoptees who search are looking for another family? That is a conclusion critics of searching voice, fearful that "another family" destroys the foundation of American adoption. Does an articulated curiosity about "someone with genes like mine" suggest that adoptees are bereft of significant ties? Adoptees who search answer these objections by insisting that "reunions" are only part of the story, and that contacts with birth relatives only a small part of the overall goal. Searches and reunions symbolize the more important task of challenging laws of confidentiality and anonymity.

The challenge occurs at a time, and in a culture, in which the principle of a *right* to information and a *wrong* in state mandated secrets about an individual has wide support. The adoption reform movement also shows that support is measured: the children who search for information receive more sympathy and quicker judicial responses than the parents who search. Ultimately, behind the talk of medical cause and legal rights, *children* gain access to information that may violate a parent's right to privacy. Not every adoptee who sees her or his original records makes contact with a member of the birth family. Alarm that granting an individual access to her or his original birth certificate will open the floodgates to reunions reveals how threatening reunions are, not the likelihood that the flood will happen.

The drama of reunions, played out fully at meetings and in the media, leaves the importance of statistics far behind. Too, the drama of that first meeting, relished by participants and by journalists, focuses attention on particular aspects of adoption culture in the United States: the perceived "loss" of blood ties, the perceived "lack" of "faces like mine," and the perceived disadvantage of not knowing biological roots. These thoroughly cultural responses to adoption now receive backing in recent attention to genetics and to inherited capacities. In contemporary American society, the danger in reunions is not that adoptees will have "too many parents" or that birthparents will "ruin" the adoptive family. The danger lies in the emphasis on "blood" and "biology" that could well strengthen already-existing doubts about the endurance and solidarity of a "chosen" parent-child relationship.

Moreover, reunions suggest that individuals can make and remake their own relationships. Reunions suggest that individuals can interpret the significant symbols of American adoption in their own ways. Reunions are linked to other changes in adoption that follow the same path, especially the move to banish confidentiality at the very outset of an adoptive arrangement. For some these changes represent chaos. For others, these changes represent the *choice* that adoption can be about—in the United States as in other societies of the world.

III. New Allies in Adoption Reform

"Opening, in some respects …"

No one knows how many reunions occur between adoptees and a birthparent or other birth relative. And no one knows the subsequent course of these meetings. There are no statistics on the number of adoptees or birthparents who make an effort to unseal a document or who try unsuccessfully to locate a "missing person" in their lives. Finally, as some scholars of the search phenomenon note, there is no way of knowing how many adoptees and birthparents think about "finding out" but do not try.

At the beginning of the twenty-first century, adoption searches and reunions are well known. The import of these events on adoption law is less well-known, and the impact of changes in law on conceptualizations of family and kinship is even more obscure. The words search and reunion do not have fixed meanings in adoption circles, implying everything from a phone call to a continuing relationship. The most distinct (agreed-upon) outcome of searches is the move toward opening adoption at the outset.

On Sunday, October 25, 1998, *The New York Times* placed a picture of "two mothers sharing one child" on the front page of the first section. "The intimacy between these two families [birth and adoptive] would have been rare just a few years ago and unthinkable a generation ago," the article stated. "But such open contact between adoptive parents and biological parents is one of the many ways that adoption has evolved from a secretive, closed process weighed down by dark stigmas and painful misconceptions into an infinitely more transparent experience."[53]

Had American adoption come so far in so short a time? A shift in one generation would be remarkable, given that the history of adoption in the United States is one of resistance to change. A shift from "dark stigmas" to "open contact" sounds good—but what, one might ask, does "open contact" really mean? And, if adoption is truly no longer "closed," what might that mean for the future of adoption in the United States?

The two mothers on the front page tell a long tale, and they fail to tell some part of that tale. They tell of changes in agency policies that came on the heels of dramatic (and well-dramatized) reunions between adoptees and their birthparents. They tell, too, of agency reactions to the loss of clients as potential adoptive and birthparents turn increasingly to non-agency placements.[54] The two mothers in the *Times*, with their tiny, sweet infant, do not tell of changes in the adoptable population; they do not tell of the neglected and abandoned children filling the category of "available." Nor, as they cuddle the child they share, do these mothers hint at the disagreements, disputes, and hostility to openness that fill the pages of journals, books, and newspaper stories.

Instances in which birth and adoptive parents meet one another and exchange information are not rare. Such arrangements recognize the importance of "knowing" to individuals involved in an adoption, and the pressure against secrecy searches inspire. The attack on sealed records has been going on for decades; adoption could not continue in its old ways. Still, open adoption is not, as it is sometimes portrayed, an *opening* in response to *closed adoption* or a full disclosure in response to the thin, disguised background information conventionally characteristic of American adoption.

The boat has not been rocked quite as thoroughly as *The New York Times* photograph suggests. A close look reveals that the new adoption bears clear marks of the old, in its ruling principles and in its interpretations of kinship. Contact between birth and adoptive parents, however established, upholds the significance of "blood" to the adopted child's identity. Contact also is presumed to protect the adoptive parents from the unwanted and unexpected intrusion of a birthparent. These ideas shore up traditional views of adoption in the United States.

Opponents uncover the radical aspects of this new form of adoption. They are fierce in their opposition to meetings between birth and adoptive parents, to the disclosure of identifying information, and to "opening" a sealed arrangement. Objections delineate the conservative side of American adoption in claims that open adoption "confuses" a child with too many parents, that non-confidential adoptions encourage women to abort rather than place children, and that open adoption makes "facts" more important than "caring" in a person's decision to adopt. Each of the objections reiterates the importance of traditional adoption for upholding traditional family values.

As early as 1980, when open adoption was barely a glimmer in anyone's eye, Senator Gordon Humphrey proclaimed his view that non-confidential adoptions encourage abortion. The individual who cannot be assured of secrecy, he said, will abort rather than place her baby. "It just seems to me if all of a sudden now you're going to tell such a woman that her choice is to place the child up for adoption and she cannot be assured of any secrecy," Humphrey told a congressional hearing. "It just seems to me that a great many, because they are so immature and so subject to various kinds of parental pressures, it just seems to me a lot of them are going to choose abortion rather than going through with adoption."[55]

With no cited evidence to support the point, Humphrey took the rhetoric around the country, stirring up a pro-life audience. The use of adoption to argue against abortion is as inflammatory now as it was twenty years ago. It is distinct from the other attack on open adoption, which claims that non-confidential adoption poses a risk to the child.

This position against open adoption falls within the province of "the best interests of the child." Opponents of opening adoption who warn of risks to the child do not review birthparent decisions but rather outline concerns about the child's security and well-being. The child will be confused by too many parents, critics say, or the parents will quarrel over what the child should know about adoption or, finally, the child will be torn in her or his loyalties and love. Each point assumes that a nuclear family is best for a child. From that perspective, opening adoption strikes yet another blow against "family values" in the United States.

The *Times* photograph of two mothers sharing a child represents a dramatic vision of non-confidentiality. It also isolates the fact of "two mothers" in an adoption from all other instances of two mothers in a society with high divorce rates. A birth and an adoptive mother are not the same, in the American imagination, as the first and second wives of one husband. Culturally, a birth and an adoptive mother are at two ends of a moral continuum, one the bad and one the good mother.[56] This persistent moralistic reading of adoption has another effect: the child disappears from the assessment of secrecy and of openness. Debate about the relationship among the parents ignores the resilience of children and the interpretations children make of family.

Assessments of closed and open adoption focus on the *interests* of adults. A calculation of adult interests guides the degree to which openness is sanctioned by state law, by agency policy, and by participants in an adoption. Adults who arrange an open adoption may, for example, withhold information from a child; they may decide on the terms of contact, especially when a child is very young.[57] They may find that "knowing" other parents solidifies the bonds with a child or that such familiarity intrudes on the parent-child relationship. In adoption, studies of a change in practice ask about the results for a child. This kind of outcome study does not yet exist for the "new" openness. Paradoxically, inasmuch as the arrangement is still unconventional, many instances of openness are themselves hidden.

Participants in non-confidential adoptions have various reasons for entering the arrangement; few of the stated reasons challenge American cultural understandings of family, kinship, and identity. Unlike traditional adoptions, however, *these new arrangements are controlled and designed by the participants in diverse ways.*

The diversity is important, reflecting the choices birthparents make about the parents of their children, the demands adoptive parents make for information, and the insistence by adult adoptees that they need "facts." Agencies jumped on the bandwagon of adoption's redesign, not the first but not the last either. By 1990, one scholar estimates, over 80 percent of adoption agencies in the United States encouraged an exchange of information between birth and adoptive parents. About 20 percent had families participating in adoptions where birth and adoptive parents knew one another.[58] Something new is happening in American adoption and, like every other change in that institution, this one reflects a tug between individual interpretations, state policies, and the cultural norms guiding kinship.

A California agency was the first to publicize its practices of permitting contact and an exchange of identifying information. In the mid-1970s, the Children's Home Society of California held meetings between birthparents and adoptive parents; a small number of participants in these meetings actually identified themselves to one another.[59] But the dent had been made. In Texas, several years later, two social workers decided that complete disclosure and contact between birth and adoptive parents was best for the child, and publicized their policies as well.[60] Policy-makers and legislators did not then see the woods behind these apparently scattered trees.

In the mid-1990s, I worked with an agency that was introducing new forms of stranger adoption. The agency currently offers three arrangements: fully disclosed adoptions, semi-open, and traditional closed adoption. "Traditional" refers to anonymous, sealed-record adoption. In semi-open adoption, participants exchange letters and photos without any identifying information. In fully-disclosed adoption, the participants meet one another at the agency and exchange names, though not, I discovered, addresses. "Fully-disclosed" is not prescriptive; the phrase not only means something different to each participant but also changes over the course of the adoptee's childhood.

Marilyn and David were among the clients of that agency who agreed to a fully-disclosed adoption.[61] They met the young mother and exchanged information about themselves with her. "We felt comfortable with her," they told me, and were overjoyed when, five months later, she handed a baby boy to them. All three parents promised to stay in touch while Danny grew up. Marilyn and David sent Sally letters; Sally phoned them, at first regularly and then more and more sporadically. When Danny was two years old, Sally moved out of the state and eventually stopped phoning. Marilyn and David still have contact with Sally's mother and are pleased that Danny knows a "birth grandmother." They also told me they were glad that "Sally wants to move on with her own life."

The story is typical. "For all studies," a writer on open adoption notes, "the actual amount of contact ... is in the range of two to four contacts a year."[62] The number itself is an estimate. Moreover, the place, the duration, and the texture of "contact" is as various as it would be for any group of individuals.[63] By and large, then, the meanings of contact and of disclosure are negotiated by the participants—and secrecy can creep back in at any moment. Like Marilyn, David, and Sally, participants in open adoption get tired of sending news, impatient with deciding what to tell and what to keep silent. A birthparent I knew, who had been promised an open adoption, stopped hearing from the adoptive parents when her child was two years old. "Why can't they just send me a picture," she said to me. "A picture of him standing against a blank, white wall?"[64]

Adoptive parents confess to annoyance at the questions a birthmother asks. Visits can be uncomfortable. "Sometimes I think I'm tired of sharing. It's getting ready for the visits. The kids will fight and punch each other and you say, 'Oh Lord, please don't do this in front of them [birthparents].' When they leave, I say, "Whew, that's another visit over with."[65] Lincoln Caplan ends his narrative in *An Open Adoption* with the voice of the birthfather on an answering machine and silence on the part of the birthmother—who had instituted "openness" in the first place. *The New York Times* article concludes with a quotation from a birthmother: "At least our lives won't be entirely separate, but I really can't imagine how it will all be in a month or a year from now."[66]

In the end, the facts are not fully disclosed but carefully distributed by participants. Sally was happy to know where Danny was living. Marilyn and David enjoyed the facts Sally told them about her own childhood, dreams, and ambitions. The information she provided, they assured me, helped them be better parents of Danny. And, they added, Sally's awareness of how they lived eased her uncertainties about the decision to relinquish; she would not change her mind. The story of Marilyn, David, and Sally reveals more about open adoption than the *Times* photo or the vivid controversies in the media. In so-called open adoption, *the exchange of information does not create a new family or form new threads of kinship.*

The exchange of information *does* alter interpretations of giving and receiving a child. With the disclosure of information, as well as the possibility of communication and contact over time, participants take over the terms of the arrangement. The parent-child relationship becomes less a matter of state delegation than of individual decisions about the resources a child needs in order to thrive. Disclosing information is an important shift, not in kinship or family, but in the interpretations and the practices of adopting.

"Open adoption" has been most successful among two groups of people: intellectuals and the strongly religious. On the face of it different, these two groups share a willingness to ignore mainstream definitions of adoption and to circumvent the laws that enforce these definitions.

"As happens in any innovation, the pioneers of open adoptions are a very select group of parents: highly educated, liberal, open-minded, nondefensive, experimental individuals who are not tied to traditional mores and lifestyles," claims a recent book on American adoption.[67] The practices these pioneers try out signal less a breakdown in family ideology than a challenge to the discrimination against birthparents exclusion from the adoptive family implies. Parents who embark upon a disclosed adoption bridge the categorical gap between birth and adoptive parents, and they dismantle the markers of difference that have structured placement for decades. They do not necessarily invite new members into the family or alter a view of family that includes interested and loving others. "Liberals," they protest the inequities in traditional measures of good and bad parenting, but the protest may have little or nothing to do with an understanding of family.

An acceptance of the "equality" of a giving and a receiving parent recalls forms of adoption in non-industrialized societies. The recall is even stronger for the other segment of the American population known for its support of opening adoption. Members of religious communities have embraced open adoption and have readily translated "disclosure" into face to face contact. Like the prototypical non-industrialized society, these communities are relatively homogenous, sharing not only religious beliefs but also secular values and life-styles. Furthermore, the significance of *faith* in such transactions alters the meaning of openness and, as well, influences interpretations of the motives for relinquishing and for adopting a child.

"I think a big part of our decision-making and being able to cope with whatever happens is that we are Christian and we know the Lord is in control."[68] The quotation from a parent in a disclosed adoption turns the motive for adopting into a spiritual gesture. The child is considered "a gift from God" and the exchange is an act of love *and* faith. This viewpoint vitiates the "child of one's own" premise of adoption and accentuates the altruistic dimension of adoption. Too, as in non-industrialized societies, in religious communities the exchange of the child at once "succors" the child and solidifies the bonds among the adults. Protected by homogeneity, by shared convictions, and by religious beliefs, participants perceive few risks in an open adoption.

In either case, the open arrangement is undertaken by individuals who are not the "average members of a community" adoption literature describes. And, whether they are religious or liberal, the pioneers of open adoption may still be regarded as renegades. A parent who rejected disclosure put it: "Some liberal people think that they can handle all this but I personally wouldn't want to."[69]

Different as the documented participants in open adoption are, publicity about their decisions increasingly influences anyone who participates in an adoption—even if that influence results in an "I wouldn't want to." For the analyst of adoption in the United States, the cited supporters of open adoption expose two strands of recent changes in policy: the emphasis on "altruism" in the exchange of a child and the recognition of the support secrecy lends to categorical discriminations in the delegation of parenthood.

Any open adoption, whatever its locus or its enactment, undermines the wall of secrecy that has been with American adoption for at least half a century. At the same time, the diversity of forms of open adoption reflect a general shift: participants in adoptive families are more diverse in motive and in interpretation than ever before in American history. The old dichotomy of "rational" versus "emotional" bases for choosing an adoptive arrangement has multiple new forms. Some individuals choose open adoption for "intellectual" reasons, assuming the more that is known, the better a parent-child relationship will be. This sets no limits on *what* is known, and *how*. Other individuals choose open adoption in order to be "close" to the other parents of the child. But this sets no limits on the nature of that closeness or its frequency.

Still, the data that exist suggest there are limits on open adoption. The individuals who are willing to "share" a child, as the *Times* put it, tend to occupy similar socio-economic niches. Sally grew up in the same region as Marilyn and David, and her educational background was not radically different from theirs. Fully disclosed adoptions, with or without ongoing contact, are breaking down the interpretations of adopting, and of having a family. They do not yet break down the social and economic parameters surrounding child placement in the United States.

From "fictive" to "functional" kinship

Non-confidential adoption, face to face contact, full disclosure are all part of current vocabulary, and none means exactly the same thing to those who use the concepts. Partly, as members of CUB and ASG articulated, it is a matter of "information" or what one knows and how. Partly, as professionals and policy-makers claim, it is a matter of asking what adoption really accomplishes in the United States in the new century. There is little agreement on either of those matters.

The debate over opening adoption increasingly leaves behind the adult adoptees and the birthparents who request information and, often, reunions. In Oregon the adoptees who won the case for access to their original birth certificates did not address the policies and practices guiding the adoptions then being instituted. Their fight was against *past* secrecy. CUB is bolder in its reach, establishing a connection between birthpar-ent searches and the rules governing the making of fictive kin-ship in the twenty-first century. "Closed adoption harms all parties by denying choices and by imposing secrecy on people who do not want it. We encourage openness, honesty, and coop-eration in adoption."[70] CUB's reach suggests how radical open adoption could be: *no secrecy at any point along the way.*

Still, "disclosure" refers not to intimacy or love but to data—files, case records, government documents. In that sense, full dis-closure has little to do with the open exchange of children that characterizes, for instance, Polynesian societies. Disclosure has little to do with the social bonds, the ties of affection, an exchange of children establishes in such societies. *Facts* are exchanged, and selected facts at that. A social worker described open adoption to a *New York Times* reporter as "being a pen-pal."[71]

That remark captures the conservative nature of the arrangement: *open adoption does not establish a new kind of family.* As interpreted in American culture at the moment, open adoption does not create diffuse and enduring solidarity between the adults who exchange a child. As long as contact depends on letters and not on face to face meetings, open adoption does not meet cultural criteria for kinship; the behaviors that tell a per-son she or he is interacting with a relative are missing. In addi-tion, terms of address and of reference are idiosyncratic and not part of a "system." A birthparent may be a "tummy mummy," an "Aunt Sue," or "my good friend." Adoptive parents may be "like parents," "good to my child," or "good friends." As Tom said to me, when talking about his newly met birthparents: "Sometimes I call them Mom and Dad and sometimes I call them Mr. and Mrs. Blackman."

The failure of open adoption to create kinship has its roots in the inequities that shape American adoption practices. As long as the delegation of parenthood is based on a judgment of "fitness," differences between birth and adoptive parent prevail. Even when parents are said to "share" a child, their capacities as parents are considered different, and the distinction creates a wedge in the relationship. As long as the birthparent's decision to relinquish carries a moral sanction, she does not meet adoptive parents on the equal grounds kinship ties assume. In American culture, adoptive parents occupy a higher moral ground than birthparents. The moral difference persists, preserving a perceived distance between birth and adoptive parents despite the closing of the gap that open adoptions imply.

Until the inequalities disappear—until external judgments of stability and of fitness fall out of the delegation parenthood—, open adoption cannot approach the model of exchange and disclosure that exists in non-Western societies. Open adoption is far more conservative than its critics and its supporters claim. However defined, open adoption preserves the values that adoption has historically upheld: family members should be alike; a child's interests are best served in a nuclear family; knowledge of her or his background is good for a child's "adjustment." Open adoption implies that the legal relationship created by adoption is not enough to ensure a child's well-being. With its implication that there is something essential about a birth relationship and that knowledge of genetics helps a child move into the future, open adoption follows the dictum, "blood is thicker than water." But, as always in adoption history, practice dents the wall that ideology makes. While a disclosed adoption upholds the importance of "genetics," the exchange of knowledge, of communication, and often of concern about a child between adults who once were totally separated from and anonymous to one another marks a crucial change in the transaction.

Freed from old divisions between the "giving" and the "receiving" parent, adoption can embrace a wider range of functions and forms—for instance, caring for abandoned children, broadening the definition of "parent," and providing children who are in danger with safe homes. Overall, too, open adoption recognizes the significance of participant *choice* in the transaction of a child; beyond the range and diversity of practices, all attend to the particular and idiosyncratic ideas a person has about "having a child." Open adoption accepts the selfish interest that underlies decisions that are geared toward caring for another, in this case a child.

Critics condemn open adoption for going against the grain of the "natural" family and therefore putting children at risk. The condemnation looks more and more like a whistle against the wind, given the number of children already living in "non-natural" families. The trajectory in fact fuels the protests against open adoption, an arrangement that critics regard as turning adoption into an additional alternative family form. From another point of view, however, openness "normalizes" the adoptive relationship which, like any other relationship in a post-modern society, is subject to change, breakdown, and modification. The adopted person, like anyone else, has the ability to cope with crisis and to respond to new situations.

But what about the children who are at risk and especially vulnerable? These children form a large group, perhaps the majority of those children available for adoption in American society. Their life-histories are substantially different from the life-histories of children who are part of open adoptions. The children who swell the category of "available" are those whose need for placement exposes the class, race, and gender biases that still pervade official American adoption policy.

Looking at these children shifts the focus away from the triad to the policy-makers and the officials who define and implement child welfare policies in the United States in the twenty-first century.

Notes

1. Wayne Carp, in *Family Matters*, details the history of record closing in American adoption. It was not until the mid-1930s that virtually all states "sealed" stranger adoptions. Carp 1998.
2. By the mid-1970s, there were around two million adoptees in the United States, according to best guesses. Anyone who writes about adoption is confronted by the chaos, not to say non-existence, of figures on adoption in the United States: no single agency counts and no census forms ask for that status.
3. I am talking about the impact of its rules and regulations, not about the motives of individuals involved in adoption in any particular instance.
4. "Sunshine" laws require an exposure of business practices.
5. Lifton 1975: 3.
6. The registry still exists and remains an important institution.
7. *ASG Newsletter* Spring 1999: 1.
8. I deal with the significance of the word "surrender" at greater length below.
9. Lifton 1975: 4.
10. Personal communication.
11. Personal communication.
12. Lifton 1979: 64.
13. Sorosky, Baran, Pannor 1979: 227.
14. Personal communication.
15. Personal communication.
16. "Although it is commonly imagined that adoption records are a single, tangible, entity ... the reality is much more complicated," writes Wayne Carp. "There are in fact three sources of family information about an adopted child: the records of the court that approved the final adoption.., the state repository for birth certificates, and the case files of the adoption agency"; Carp 1998: 36.
17. *ASG Newsletter* 5/86: 4-5.
18. *ASG Newsletter* Spring 1999: 2.
19. Personal communication.
20. Lifton, Betty Jean. *The New York Times* 3/1/86: 27.
21. Feigelman, William. *The New York Times* 3/11/86: 23.
22. Birthparents do not insist on a distinction between voluntary and involuntary relinquishment; for those who speak out, any relinquishment of a child is coerced.
23. For instance, Inglis 1984; Gediman and Brown 1989; Gritter 2000.
24. Campbell 1979: 26.
25. Personal communication.
26. In the 1990s, efforts were made to replace "surrender" with the phrase "make an adoption plan." Besides the clumsiness of the phrase, it fails to capture the element of coercion most outspoken birthparents claim is part of the relinquishment experience.
27. *CUB Communicator* 6/83: 23.

28. Some of the most vivid recent controversies involve men claiming the rights to a child that they did not know—and were not informed—the mother had relinquished. Although in all states, the putative father is supposed to be notified when his child is freed for adoption, not all states implement the policy effectively.
29. In a recent edited volume (1998), Nancy Scheper-Hughes and Carolyn Sargent offer a demonstration of the pervasiveness of "maternalizing" the unfit parent.
30. Bachrach 1990; Gritter 2000.
31. *CUB New Member Information* n.d.: 5.
32. Among others, Gritter [2000] shows that the qualities birthmothers choose match the indicators agencies tend to use in selecting good parents.
33. Personal communication.
34. Rillera 1982: 48.
35. Personal communication.
36. *CUB Communicator* 6/83: 9.
37. Most reunions occur between birthparents and adult adoptees, since the norm against intruding in a child's life remains fairly strong inside as well as outside CUB.
38. Personal communication.
39. Personal communication.
40. *The Waterville Sentinel* 5/1/84: 24.
41. Lifton 1979: 72.
42. Personal communication.
43. This was something Lee promulgated in CUB, but she lost out to birthparents who vented their anger at the institution of adoption.
44. Personal communication.
45. Verhovek, Sam Howe. *The New York Times* 4/5/00: 14.
46. Ibid.
47. Personal communication via e-mail.
48. Verhovek, Sam Howe. *The New York Times* 5/31/00: 7. See also Verhovek, *The New York Times* 6/3/00.
49. *ASG Newsletter* Spring 1999: 1-2.
50. Verhovek, Sam Howe. *The New York Times* 4/5/00: 14.
51. Personal communication.
52. Personal communication.
53. Fein, Esther B. *The New York Times* 10/25/98: 19.
54. See Chapter Four, below.
55. *Oversight on Adoption Reform Act* 1980: 61.
56. Existing literature, both professional and popular, scrupulously distinguishes a birthmother from an adoptive mother.
57. In pioneering research on openness in adoption, McRoy and her colleagues discovered that children often have no access to the information or to the contact the adults have; McRoy, Grotevant, and White 1988.
58. McRoy 1991: 100.
59. The Children's Home Society of Los Angeles, California. Mss. in author's possession.

60. Silber and Dorner 1990.
61. Names and details have been changed to protect confidentiality.
62. Gross 1993: 273.
63. In a cautious approval of open adoption, the CWLA advises professional counseling for all participants.
64. Personal communication.
65. Quoted in McRoy, Grotevant, and White 1988: 89.
66. Fein, Esther B. *The New York Times* 10/25/98: 19.
67. Brodzinsky, Schechter, and Henig 1992: 190.
68. Lindsay 1987: 91.
69. McRoy, Grotevant, and White 1988: 77.
70. President's Message to Members of Concerned United Birthparents 9/15/2000. http://www. cubirthparents.org/presidents.htm.
71. Fein, Esther B. *The New York Times* 10/25/98: 19.

Chapter 3

From "Drifting" to "Permanency"—Adoption Policy and Practice

The Clinton Initiative

On November 19, 1997, President Clinton signed the Adoption and Safe Families Act, which became Public Law 105-89. This was a significant federal initiative, claiming that all children in the United States deserve permanency and a family that will last forever. The subtitle of the act reveals its specific focus: "to promote the adoption of children in foster care."[1] The act addresses a world of parents and children that had changed substantially in the past quarter century. Huge numbers of children in foster care told of an increase in the population of parents unable to care for children; the numbers told as well of the failure of social services to help such parents. A crisis had swept the United States, and the 1997 act proposed adoption as the solution.

Adoption has a more prominent role in Public Law 105-89 than in any preceding federal guideline for child placement. This prominence has implications for the meanings of adopting given by those who participate in and by those who arrange transactions in parenthood. The act marks an appropriation of adoption as an institution by the federal government that is unprecedented; under its aegis, adoption absorbs new functions and new tasks, as well as new significances. The appropriation parallels the rapid change in adoption practices brought about by individuals, often outside the parameters of government guidelines and agency policies—individuals like the members of CUB and ASG who out of personal concerns alter the customs of "moving" children in the United States. How do the initiatives of adoption reform movements and of federal guidelines come together? Is the wave of change more cataclysmic than commentators describe, so that ultimately the meaning of adoption will bear *no* connections with anything practiced before in American society? Will we discover that sealed records and confidentiality are only the slightest of issues and that the implications—and history—of secrecy have to be reconsidered?

Under Public Law 105-89, adoption explicitly replaces foster care as the "best" solution for children at risk and in trouble. "While foster care offers these children a safe and nurturing temporary haven in their time of greatest need, as many as 100,000 foster care kids will need permanent homes in the next few years," noted President Clinton when he signed the bill. "Many of these children have special needs and require the security and stability of an adoptive family to develop their full potential. Adoption allows these and other children to have the permanent homes they deserve, and it enables many dedicated adults to experience the joys and rewards of parenting."[2] *The New York Times* photograph accompanying the news story offers a pleasing, untroubling view of adoption: a young, energetic boy hopping around the Oval Office on a broom-stick horse. The text of the Adoption and Safe Families Act offers quite another interpretation of adoption.

The act transforms adoption from a family-building into a child-rescuing operation. A solution to the "crisis" of foster care, adoption in Public Law 105-89 bears little resemblance to American adoption as it has existed in law since the 1850s. It bears even less resemblance to the stereotypical version of adoption, which features a couple and children who could be "their own."

The children for whom the act prescribes adoption are troubled and troublesome, the danger they pose more vivid and more encompassing than the dangers Charles Loring Brace perceived in the "street urchins" he brought to "kindly mid-western farm families" in the late nineteenth century. While the word "adoption" runs through the 1997 act, in context it acquires meanings that stray from the common understandings honed into place over the course of the twentieth century. At the same time, the word is crucial to selling the plan to the American public.

Throughout, the act draws on the popular and the professional interpretations of adoption available in the 1990s. No child, announced Clinton in one of several speeches preceding the act, "should be uncertain about what the word 'family' or 'parent' or 'home' means, particularly when there are open arms waiting to welcome these children into safe and strong households where they can build good, caring lives."[3] Adoption, in this familiar formulation, gives a child a "real" family and adults the opportunity to be parents. On the November day he signed the bill, the president declared National Adoption Month. "As we observe National Adoption Month, we reaffirm our commitment to adoption as a new beginning for thousands of children, and we celebrate the many American families who have embraced these children by accepting the rewards and responsibilities of adoption."[4]

The day Clinton signed the bill the number of children in foster care topped the five hundred thousand mark. The same day the number of children adopted from foster care was at the level it had been for a decade. These hundreds of thousands of children are not babies or infants. They are older children, who have spent weeks, months, or even years in foster care homes or who have been removed from a home in which their lives were daily threatened. Can these children readily find the "open arm," Clinton anticipates? Who are the adults who embrace such vulnerable and at risk children? Is the "rescue mission" Clinton outlines anything like the *adoption* he describes?

Ostensibly about children, the act actually addresses the adults who can or cannot care for children. First, there are the adults who put children at risk and who do not provide safety and security for a child. Second, there are adults who take on the care of children without legal sanction but, often, with long-term emotional commitments. Third, there are the adults who qualify to have a child and can be granted permanent parenthood in a court of law. The 1997 Adoption and Safe Families Act distinguishes one group of adults from another, perpetuating the distinctions that have underlain American adoption through most of its history. Provisions of the act formalize the distinctions and place the *kinds* of parents and transfers of children under the close supervising eye of the state. At the same time, the child welfare policy is presented in a language of family-building, love, and concern. These contradictions hinder the implementation of the act.

Implementation is assigned to the Department of Health and Human Services (DHHS). At the start of the twenty-first century, programs are in place and publicized across all fifty states. In the end, the success of such programs depends on the interpretations given to adoption by individuals directly involved in the transactions: the parents who lose children, the parents who gain children, and the professionals who mediate the transfers.

These interpretations are constrained by the provisions of the act. Under the framework of "permanency," transferring a child into an adoptive family becomes a priority; adoption becomes the solution to an array of problems. Furthermore, with permanency a priority the act speeds up the procedures for removing a child from the parent who cannot or does not provide safety and security. In instances where relinquishment would be cumbersome or is resisted by an individual, the 1997 Adoption and Safe Families Act draws on termination proceedings as an expedient mechanism. Finally, the provisions of the act create a new group of available children. The children who become "adoptable" are not the thriving infants of an idealized adoption but children who have been abused, are at risk, require special care, and often refuse the affection of adults. The 1997 act responds to a crisis in the care of children and addresses a moment in American history when a generation of children fails to thrive without the intervention of outsiders in their lives. The crisis described in the act impinges on all three members of the adoption triad, affecting practices and views of adopting. Stark as the situation is, there are also continuities with old patterns of adoption in the United States, including definitions of a bad and a good parent, the gendered aspect of those definitions, and the class and race biases they contain.

The federal response to the existence of half a million at risk children is not surprising. Dependence on adoption as the solution *is* surprising. Increasing the number of adoptions requires a substantial shift in policy and in practice. The outcome the act proposes turns attention away from the reunification policies that sustain a biological family and towards the formal re-delegation of parenthood that creates adoptive families. Moreover, the act emphasizes legal, court approved relationships over informal, communal or kin-based arrangements for taking care of a child who is in danger. The act places faith in adoption, ignoring the controversies swirling around that form of family-building. In its leap of faith, the act carries onto a new plane the challenges posed by those who argue for non-confidentiality, full information, and the banishment of all secrets from adoption.

Foster care itself challenges interpretations of adoption that have developed in the United States since the middle of the twentieth century. Condemnation of foster care as a method for taking care of children reaches a high pitch exactly when adoption is lavishly praised. Why is one form of socially-designated parenthood so different from the other?

I. Foster Care as the Ultimate Evil

The checkered history of American foster care

The 1997 act advocates the movement of children out of foster care into adoptive families. Behind the prescription lie decades of concern about foster families, the adults who foster children, and the institutions that supervise children in the "system." In essence, the Adoption and Safe Families Act dismisses foster care as worn out, imperfect, and unsuitable for children. Foster care, to put it bluntly, has a *bad reputation* in American policy, practice, and popular opinion, and the act reflects this viewpoint. Yet, while pushing children out of foster families, the 1997 act does not phase out foster care, in part, as I show, because foster care is economically, politically, and ideologically necessary to the survival of adoption.

Once foster care and adoption were close cousins, the thin line of legal permanency not a crucial factor. Enduring solidarity and commitment counted in assessing the well-being of the child. Early in the twentieth century, social workers and participants still might blur the two, less interested in the difference between foster care and adoption than in the fact that both represent a removal of the child from her or his biological parents. Concern then, as now, lay with "how the child fared" or the *outcome* of being brought up by a delegated rather than a birthparent.

In a pioneering study in the mid-1920s, Sophie van Senden Theis (of the State Charities Aid Association of New York) studied the "adjustment" of adults who had been raised by substitute parents. She discovered that individuals raised by a non-biological parent fared well as adults; she did not distinguish between foster care and adoption. Over the course of the next seventy-five years, the lines between the two grew firmer and now the distinction between a foster and an adoptive parent is unmistakable. The distinction influences the studies of adult adjustment that continue to be a major method of assessing placement decisions; while recognizing that both represent a "removal" from the biological parent, few scholars any longer blur foster care with adoption. Rather, surveys of the outcomes of placement draw fine distinctions among types of (so-called) substitute care, separating temporary care from the informal exchange of a child, and both of these from a legal and permanent assumption of parenthood. The distinctions contribute to the growing inclination to juxtapose informal adoption as well as foster care against formalized, adoptive relationships. The juxtaposition highlights the effectively marks the cultural conventions for a good parent, a properly composed family, and a solid and enduring parent-child tie.

By the beginning of the 1990s, no one confused foster care with adoption. The media, participants in both kinds of families, and professionals keep the distinction clear and public. Besieged by cultural messages, children who are fostered learn to wish for adoption and individuals who foster either hide their status or make efforts to change it—trying, in many cases, to become adoptive parents. Overall, secrecy surrounds the experience of foster care and pushes the arrangement into the "closets" of privacy. While members of adoptive families grapple with the issue of sealed records, members of foster families grapple with a secret kind of family. Foster care as an institution may be on the public stage, but the parents and children who belong to foster families hide the facts of their lives. "When you are little," a twenty-year-old former foster child said, "you don't want people to know you are in the system."[5]

How has foster care become a *system* while adoption is a version of *family*? The United States extends the difference further than other Western nations and further than societies in which the circulation of children is casual and informal. Federal guidelines over the past quarter century add to the negative views of foster care by representing adoption as a "better" way of caring for children and, in complement, by locating safety and permanency in certain kinds of families. In the process, not only the officially designated category of "fostering" but also an array of practices involving the informal care of children falls by the wayside. Mentions of kin-care, of extended family arrangements, and of other versions of "swapping" appear as second-best options not as the cultural choices they are. Kin-care has a place in the implementation of the 1997 act, thoroughly hedged in by qualifications. "The Department [of Health and Human Services] intends to fund projects in the future under this authority to improve our knowledge of the use of kinship care for ensuring children's safety and permanency. Examples of topics that might be addressed under this demonstration authority include the development of best practices for licensing and approval of relatives' homes...."[6]

Rules for the formal approval and licensing of relatives' homes diminish the value of customary kin care. Such provisions indicate concern about the effectiveness of kin care arrangements designed by the relatives themselves, a practice followed by not a few groups in the United States.[7] Beneath the concern lies a prevailing discomfort about *any* non-legal arrangement for the assumption of parental care. That discomfort in turn speaks to the race and class biases that pervade placement decisions in the United States.

Like kin care, foster care is a strategy for those who choose not to bring a new (or "substitute") parent-child relationship to court. Like kin care, too, foster care is described in the press and in literature on child placement as an alternative that lacks the stability and the structure of a conventional, mainstream American family. This portrayal neglects the positive dimensions of foster care and in doing so emphasizes a white, middle-class norm for caring for children. In comparison with adoptive parents, foster parents come out as less committed, less able to provide unconditional love, and less capable of enduring solidarity. Descriptions of foster care reiterate the characteristics, and they take on a negative patina. Foster parents are a "refuge," a help in time of crisis, and a temporary solution. Foster parents are the "fall back" compared with the adoptive parent's "pillar of the community" role. Foster parents are employees of the state and its agencies, without the privacy an adoptive family is granted after legalization. And, in a final source of stigma, foster parents are *paid for* caring for children, while adoptive parents are not—recent *tax breaks* for adoptive families only underline the difference.[8]

At the same time, foster parents fill a crucial role in the child welfare system in the United States. Over the course of the twentieth century, the role has reflected and reproduced the characterization of individuals who foster. The temporary and expedient, impermanent and necessary, aspects of a fostering role take precedence over the parental aspects. Foster care becomes primarily a stepping stone towards permanence somewhere else, either in the biological family or in an adoptive home. Combined with the prejudice against informal fosterage customs in a bureaucratized society, the role of foster parents as emergency caretakers has damned the institution even more severely. Licensing is a blow against rather than a redemption of foster parent status, inasmuch as it excludes the affectional and the (possible) relational components of the arrangement. By the end of the twentieth century, the "parent" in foster parent is a legacy from the past not an indication of status or of role.

The 1997 Adoption and Safe Families Act at once upholds and undermines the value of foster care. By maintaining a category of temporary caretakers, the act values fosterage as a crucial way of caring for at-risk children. By designating the relationship as temporary, the act contributes to the negative stereotype of those who take on the role. The ambiguity continues in the domain of "value" that becomes monetary. Foster parents are paid by the state, but at costs that are much less than those for institutional care, another option for children at risk.

Compared with orphanages or other public or private institutions, foster families are a good cost-benefit value. In 1990, to prove the point, *USA Today* published an interview with the director of the North American Council on Adoptable Children (NACAC). "If you look at the number of new kids coming into care in a given year—say we have an increase of 20,000 kids— and if we put those kids into institutional placements at $100 a day, you're talking about $720 million in new money. If we put them into foster families, ... we're talking about $150 million. So there's a big range in between there to pay for these 20,000 new kids."[9] In November 2000, *Time* magazine reported: "It costs at least $7 billion a year, or about $13,000 a child, to care for America's foster kids."[10] And the expenses keep going up. Foster care, *The Washington Post* reported, is the country's fastest growing entitlement program.[11]

There is another way of looking at the economics of foster care. Individuals who become foster parents are cheap labor; foster parents are low paid and they lack collective bargaining rights. "In most states [in 1998] regular foster care payment rates .... lagged behind the United States Department of Agriculture's (USDA) estimated expenditures for raising a child..."[12] Few foster parents can manage on the state subsidy alone, and fewer still make a profit from caring for children. Low paid, foster parents require more work to make ends meet; in this case, with reimbursement per child, more work means taking in more children. The option of taking in more children does not increase respect for the foster parent but instead distances her or him further from cultural conceptualizations of the "natural" (adoptive or biological) parent.

Foster parents have virtually no bargaining power. Nominally designated "parents," they are actually servants of the state and they have no control over the fair and equitable distribution of resources. Putting it differently, in the United States foster parents succumb to the decisions of others about the fate of the children in their care; they may be asked at the last minute to take a child or told at the last moment that a child is leaving their household. All across the country, "foster parents were viewed as 'clients' of the agency or as paraprofessionals, and were expected to accept the removal of a child from their home on very little notice," write William Meezan and Joan Shireman, reporting on a nation-wide study of foster care.[13] Not much has changed in the fifteen years since that survey. Total dependence on state bureaucracies characterizes a group called "parents" and treated as employees. In 1990, a foster child provided her account of these swift and unexpected transfers: "outsiders can come in any time and take me away."[14]

In June 2000, *The New York Times* published one of many stories about the foster care system in New York City. This time the story was about a child who had been abruptly removed from the household while his foster mother was on an errand. The mother, Mrs. Rodriquez, had left Andrew home with an older boy and when she returned after a brief trip, she found him gone. No one had notified her of the removal. A feisty person, and a committed parent, Mrs. Rodriquez demanded a public hearing. She had the right to such a hearing after the 1977 Supreme Court case, *Smith v. Offer*, but it was four months before her request was granted.[15] Upon that delay, she brought suit, claiming she had a right to notification and to a prompt hearing. The United States Court of Appeal, Second Circuit, decided against her. Nicholas Scoppetta, commissioner of the New York City child welfare agency, once a foster child himself, agreed with the Court. "The court, he added, properly distinguished between the rights of a parent, who is entitled to a hearing within 24 hours of an emergency removal and the rights of 'someone who is potentially a parent.'"[16]

Mrs. Rodriquez defined herself as Andrew's parent, with nothing "potential" about it. She is unusual in fighting for that definition. For most foster parents, demanding a hearing that acknowledges their parenthood means risking their jobs. "Unless a foster parent is strongly invested in the child and willing to risk the long-term wrath of an agency (particularly the possibility of not getting future placements)," comments legal historian Robert Mnookin, "the foster parent may view the cost of the hearing as too great."[17]

Like birthparents, foster parents are part of a history in which placement policy has been guided by the cultural assumption that a "family" best serves the best interests of a child. "If there is one certainty, it is this," intoned a late nineteenth-century home finder, sounding like many a late twentieth-century politician, "that the family is the direct outcome of nature's own plan to secure the safety and growth of the child."[18] Birthparents and foster parents are also part of a history in which policy reflects a hegemonic view of the family, stable and anchored by a married couple. In a contrast that justifies the "re-placement" of children, birthparents and foster parents are reputed to lack these characteristics. However, unlike birthparents who in recent years have achieved leverage through the "product" they have, foster parents in the same period have lost leverage. At the beginning of the twenty-first century, the media and federal guidelines equally portray foster parents as providing a last-ditch solution, one that is detrimental to a child's best interests. Class action suits brought by foster parents make little dent on the cultural, economic, and political factors that keep them in a marginal, vulnerable, and scorned position.

In the fall of 1990, Senator John Heinz of Pennsylvania received a letter from one of his constituents suggesting that he do away with foster parents. The writer informed Heinz that, in her experience, foster families were all "dysfunctional" and the children in them unlikely to grow up well-adjusted. The letter remained in his files, representing both a view held by many of the state's voters and a position that did not lend itself to obvious action. Heinz left the foster care system in place in Pennsylvania, where it serves the same function of expedient or emergency caretaking that it does in every other state.

Foster parents are vilified as a class for the abuses committed by a few. Reports of mistreated and neglected foster children focus on the individuals who perpetrate the crimes not on the culture that sustains a group of underpaid "parents" in order to rescue at-risk children. The circle grows vicious, as the blame for flaws in a system falls on individuals and the connotations of "foster" turn increasingly negative. The roots of the word in nurture and in sustenance are missing for the participants in the process. Children who are fostered are not seen to be blessed with a generous and nurturing environment. Instead, "foster" evokes provisional maintenance, detrimental to the child.

Children in limbo

"This is a class action brought on behalf of children who are in foster care under the supervision of the District of Columbia Department of Human Services (DHS)," began a district judge opinion in the spring of 1991. "It is about the failures of an ineptly managed child welfare system, the indifference of the administration of the former mayor of the District of Columbia, Marion Berry, and the resultant tragedies for District children relegated to entire childhoods spent in foster care drift. Unfortunately, it is about a lost generation of children whose tragic plight is being repeated every day."[19] This puts the blame where it ought to go—on a system, on institutional negligence, on misplaced political attention. Unfortunately, that is the rare response; more common are headlines like the one in a recent issue of *Time*: "Fifteen years in foster hell."[20]

In August 1997, *The New York Times* published the results of a study of foster care done by a national organization. The prognosis was dire: "Children in foster homes were far more likely to end up on welfare or in jail later in life than children raised in the more stable atmosphere of an adoptive home."[21] The study, the *Times* noted, utilized anecdotal evidence rather than hard data. Yet the paper published the study on its first page, part of a continual critique of fostering. Foster care, according to the *Times*, places children in dire risk, lives interrupted and unfulfilled.

There are data to draw on for the newspaper or magazine determined to condemn the nation's foster care system. Outcome studies continue, assessing the impact on a person's development of an upbringing by a foster parent. "[A] child who is neither living with his own family nor adopted ... may come to think of himself as being less than first rate, or an unwanted human being," write two experts on foster care.[22] Assessments of foster care, then, rely on measures of individual responses to the situation. The assessments are psychological in approach, ignoring or minimizing the cultural assumptions that turn fostering into a source of low self-esteem and troubled adulthood.

Few foster children in the United States brag about or relish the status, and most remember feeling lousy, marginal, and strange. "It is a measure of its [foster care] toll that Scoppetta, though one of New York's more respected lawyers, a confidant of mayors, and a man with friends, money, and a loving family, still feels ashamed of his past. 'You never really get over being in foster care,' Scoppetta once told a small group of teen-age foster children—abuse and abandonment victims, children of addicts—who wondered how this man in an expensive suit could feel the way they did."[23] In Pittsburgh, a twelve-year old who could have been a member of Scoppetta's audience, admitted: "No one knows in my school that I'm a foster child, except two people and they didn't spread it. I don't tell anyone. Because if they know that I'm a foster child—I think I'm the only foster child in the whole thing—if they know, they won't want to be friends with me."[24]

The shame and stigma described by Nicholas Scoppetta, and by a twelve-year old in Pittsburgh is only part of the story. The other part is the *why:* the cultural reasons for foster care's bad name and reported ill effects. That fostering should have dire consequences is not self-evident; nor is the sharp separation between fostering and adopting a universal phenomenon. The history of foster care in the United States has seen the construction of a diatribe against fostering that completely vitiates the notions of nurture the word implies. Not generous or loving, foster care is viewed as the opposite and, recently, as cruel and unforgiving. Commentaries followed by surveys obscure the function of the criticism: the imposition of a model of family on all segments of the population.

The history of a diatribe against foster care begins in the late nineteenth century, when charity workers called those parents who chose to cope with poverty or crisis lazy and irresponsible. Placing a child with someone else has, in the United States, rarely had the positive connotations that fostering has in other cultures of the world. The emergence of a profession of social work, replacing the charitable workers of an earlier era, intensified the condemnation by adding the rhetoric of expertise to judgments of the custom. By the time I did my own fieldwork in Hawaii in the 1980s, the customary (non-legal) form of adoption, *hanai*, was designated aberrant within the American child placement system. In virtually all fifty states, individuals who choose fostering rather than an institutionalized and legalized mechanism for responding to family difficulties are considered "marginal" in one way or another. Condemnation of foster care is a way of insisting on the *rightness* of certain kinds of family and of certain interpretations of parental behavior.[25]

The alarm spent on the "widows" and "indigents" who depended on foster care in the nineteenth century has transformed today into the blame placed on "irresponsible" and "self-interested" parents who are said to casually exchange children. With an echo of the birthparent situation, blaming the person avoids the circumstances, either the poverty that makes "placing out" a necessity or the cultural customs that make fostering the basis of bonds between adults. For much of the twentieth century, the parent who left the care of her child to others was accused of lacking love, despite the fact that she was more likely to lack resources. She might equally be blamed for "generosity" in giving her child to a friend or relative, a disregard of the segments of the American population for whom that is a traditional value. In Hawaii, for instance, individuals who lovingly give children face sanctions and often censure in an American state. The association of foster care with "cultural difference" may further damn the practice.

By the second half of the twentieth century, formulations of alarm and of condemnation appear under new guises; class and race biases are subsumed under (or disguised by) a sharp focus on the children who experience foster care arrangements. In the nineteenth century do-gooders certainly wrung their hands over the fate of the children in foster care, but their philosophical stances bore down hard on adults. In the twentieth century, though much of the rhetoric and many of the actions directed at foster care echo back a century, a substantial literature on child development supports the case against "temporary" care. Theories of child development on the one hand lift the discussion from stern moralizing about parental behavior and, on the other hand, reduce the problem of fosterage to an individual event rather than a social issue. In addition, theories of child development tend to be linked to a particular cultural and historical moment.

The central principle of contemporary North American child placement policy, in the best interests of the child, has a clear articulation in a small book published in the early 1970s. *Beyond the Best Interests of the Child*, written by a lawyer and two child psychiatrists, sets guidelines for any rearrangement of a parent-child relationship that involves the state. While focusing on the needs of children, the book scrupulously reminds its readers that these needs come to public attention when the state intervenes in family. At the same time, the voices of the psychiatrists tend to overwhelm the voice of the lawyer, and theories of child development tend to obscure the historical and the cultural dimensions of American child placement policy.

"Everything must be done for an imperfect being, which as yet does nothing for itself," the authors begin their analysis of the conditions for a child's growth and well-being.[26] In her or his best interests, the book argues, a child should experience permanent care over the course of childhood. The dangers of moving from household to household, and of not knowing the security of one family, are framed in psychological terms. "Physical, emotional, intellectual, social, and moral growth does not happen without causing the child inevitable internal difficulties. The instability of all mental processes during the period of development needs to be offset by stability and uninterrupted support from external sources. Smooth growth is arrested or disrupted when upheavals and changes in the external world are added to the internal ones," the three experts write.[27] A persuasive and empathetic template for child welfare policy, the theory lends itself to diverse interpretations as a guideline for practice. The meanings of "stability" and of "uninterrupted support" are open to negotiation, and the concepts can become weapons in a battle against styles of parenting that has quite other bases. They can, and have, become weapons in a fight against foster—or non-legalized—parenthood.

In addition, the theory of child development in the *Best Interests* volume bears a close relation to notions of the mature adult personality. "Where continuity of such relationships is interrupted more than once, as happens due to multiple placements in the early years, the children's emotional attachments become increasingly shallow and indiscriminate," write the authors. "They tend to grow up as persons who lack warmth in their contacts with fellow beings."[28] The statement naturalizes a *type* of person, just as other passages in the book naturalize a kind of family. As anthropologists show, naturalization quickly becomes normalization, with complementary prescriptive norms. In Polynesian cultures, where fosterage and informal adoption continue, an adult personality of low intensity and "coolness" is valued.[29] In both instances, the links between child rearing and adult personality are naturalized and the perceived "naturalness" influences the decisions made in a child's best interests. When these decisions come into the public domain, under the eye of the state, a notion of adult personality is used to exclude types of family that are seen to threaten values, social order, and moral standards.

Without meaning to condemn fosterage, *Beyond the Best Interests of the Child* plays a role in the exclusion of foster care from the category of "good" parenting that shapes North American child placement policy. The emphasis on stability and on continuous care in cultural theories of childrearing provides state officials with a rationale for replacing foster care with other arrangements. At the same time, application of the theory has closed the door onto forms of fosterage that do provide security, safety, and permanence. It is not because foster care is bad that fostered children grow up recognizing the truth in what Scoppetta said, that you never really get over it. It is because foster care is considered less than satisfactory and less than *parental* that children and parents suffer in the system.

This is not to deny the evidence and the dangers of mistreatment and of abuse. These now well-publicized aspects of foster care, however, cannot be extracted from a cultural and historical context in which fostering is unrewarded.

From foster care to adoptive families

Andrew was removed from the home of Mrs. Rodriquez because she left the eight-year old alone with a twelve-year old. In the eyes of child protective personnel, that made her a "bad" parent. Granted a hearing after the four-month delay, she ultimately won the return of Andrew to her household. As the New York state court indicated, however, she remained in the status of foster parent. The state court's opinion is based on an interpretation of the 1977 Supreme Court case that granted rights to foster parents, and shows the limitation of those rights. *Smith v. Offer* distinguishes foster parents from biological and from adoptive parents. Foster parents, the opinion reads, have a right to be notified of the removal of a child only when that child is to re-placed in another foster home. They have no right to a hearing when the child is to be reunified with a biological parent or placed in an adoptive home. This in effect creates a distinct category of *foster parent*. Furthermore, foster parents do not have a right to an immediate hearing, as do adoptive or biological parents threatened by the removal of a child.

The Supreme Court decision grants limited legal recourse to the foster parent. A reminder that fostering is not the same as adopting is implicit throughout the opinion and echoes the views a foster parent encounters when she or he approaches an agency in order to adopt. Clients of an agency and paid for the duties they do, foster parents almost universally elicit concern when they apply to be adoptive parents. The process of becoming a foster parent and the criteria that qualify a person as a foster parent seem to constitute the very grounds for refusing a petition for adoptive parenthood. Foster parents in the United

States find themselves in a bind: the characteristics and the circumstances they present in order to be accepted in the role of foster parent disqualify them from adoptive parenthood. The terms of disqualification are not entirely open. Some, like unmarried status, may be articulated; others, like an ability to take and give a child, evoke an unarticulated discomfort.

As foster care diverged from adoption, the rules for foster care became more rigorous. Left out of the "just like" category adoptive parents occupy, foster parents are constrained by rules that keep the boundaries around that category clear. Foster families are not just like biological families; nor are foster parents conceptualized as just like biological parents. The behaviors they are asked to demonstrate and the relationship they bear to an agency throw the fence between them and biological and adoptive parents high. A break down of the boundaries and the re-qualification of foster parents as adoptive parents occur only against a resistance that is remarkable given the connotations of "foster" and given the five hundred thousand children who need homes.

Foster parents are parents who are not supposed to act parental. Foster care manuals warn foster parents against loving a child too much and becoming so "attached" that the removal of the child is painful. Parents who are stigmatized for being "temporary" are penalized for establishing enduring bonds with the children in their care. "In another sense, fostering fails in cases where the adults transgress the role assigned to them, i.e., where their feelings become totally involved with the child in their care."[30] Comments like that push the foster parent further from cultural conceptions of a parent and pull them back into the category of client or of paraprofessional or of paid worker. Foster parents fail when they fall in love with a child. Adoptive parents are reminded that falling in love is the basis for a sturdy relationship.

The expectation that a good foster parent restrains her love dovetailed with the reunification practices of the 1960s and 1970s. The foster child ideally was expected to return "home" and to break ties with the fostering family easily, smoothly, and absolutely. Foster parents (like members of CUB) discuss love for a child in other terms, not a rope that keeps a child tethered but an emotion that helps a child thrive. As one foster mother said to me, "I know I have to let the children go. That does not mean I can't love them until they leave me"—in her case, to be placed in an adoptive family. Sarah had had three biological children as well and she made an analogy: "Of course I loved them, but when they were teen-agers, I had to let them go."[31] The warning against love in foster care manuals reminds foster parents that they are part of a professional team and necessarily on call.

The contradictions in interpretations of love that stem from categorizing *kinds* of parent pervade foster care. The adoption reform movement brings these contradictions out of the closet, claiming a definition of "love" that transcends the rules of an agency, the provisions of state law, and the shibboleths of policy. But members of the adoption reform movement, including birthparents, stand on a stronger foundation than do the foster parents whose cultural image remains negative. There have been moves to break down the boundaries separating foster from adoptive parents. The practices that banish boundaries, however, are short circuited by ideologies of the family.

In the early 1990s, I participated in a training group at a local adoption agency. The group included both potential adoptive parents and potential foster care parents. Just at that moment, throughout the country agencies were instituting programs called *fostadopt*. The precipitating factors were two-fold: one, the need for more foster parents as the number of children needing homes began its upward spiral; two, the need to alter expectations about adoption and to encourage individuals to try fostering on the way to adopting. My group included some individuals who only wanted to foster, some who only wanted to adopt, and some who were willing to step through foster care on the way towards adoption. As in earlier periods of American history, in fostadopt programs the line between fostering and adopting faded while the line between biological and non-biological parenting thickened. The social workers articulated this perspective. Week by week, during discussions and skits, it became clear to me that fostering and adopting could not yet be considered one kind of substitute parenthood.

The skits and discussions confronted the issue of "falling in love" and forming an attachment. With a profession behind them and the literature of child development at their finger tips, the social workers conveyed the fine difference between foster care and adoption: restraint of love on the part of a foster parent contrasted with the rush of love expected of an adoptive parent. "In regard to the role and responsibilities of foster parents on the foster care team, the agency's expectations are very clear," stated the manual we received. The sentence left little doubt that as foster parents we were "helping" the agency. When it came to the child, need—not love—was the operating concept. "As a foster parent," the section continued, "you are expected to provide for the child's basic needs as well as any special needs the child may have by virtue of his past experiences or his status as a foster child."[32]

Like the manual, the social workers kept the distinctive traits of foster parenting before our eyes. In the process, they separated fostering from the cultural ideal of good parenting, which we had been asked to describe on in-take forms. In line with early 1990s policy, too, the agency was alert to the rights of the biological parents, to the pressures for "reunification," and to the lively possibility that the foster child would go home. Unlike adopting parents, foster parents could expect regular visits from the biological parents and eventually a relinquishment of the foster child to a permanent home. "Foster parents should be aware that while a child is in foster care, the child's natural parents retain certain rights with regard to the child, unless those rights are terminated by a Court action."[33] In contrast with adoption, the foster child was never "one's own."

And so I found myself sharing the betwixt and between that is American foster care: designated a parent, yet instructed to "transgress" cultural constructions of good parenting.[34] In the role of foster parent, I was told *not* to demonstrate unconditional and absolute love, and to regard the child less as a "relative" than as a vulnerable being with special needs. As the eight of us sat together in the classes, we also learned what a good parent meant—and the traits expected of an adopting parent: permanent, unconditional, and absolute love, as if the child were "one's own." To cross the bridge from one to another, to move from the status of foster to the status of adoptive parent, did not seem an easy journey, though it was the journey half the participants undertook.

The agency is forward-looking in permitting the journey. It is still the case in the United States that foster parents are more often disqualified from than considered to be qualified for adoptive parenthood.

"Many foster parents are not 'typical' adoptive parents," write foster care experts Meezan and Shireman. "Some are older; others have low incomes or limited education. Many were not initially motivated to adopt when they applied to the agency." So deeply embedded is the cultural distinction between foster and adoptive parents that even the growing number of available children barely alters policy. "Even with repeated evidence that many children never return to their biological homes from foster care, many [professionals] did not see adoption by foster parents as a viable alternative to foster care 'drift.'"[35]

Under the 1997 Adoption and Safe Families Act, fewer children will be returned to their biological homes. More will remain in the swelling foster care system. And more of those in the system will become part of a drifting population, not only temporary "visitors" in one foster home after another, but denied the possibility of permanence as long as the parents who want them are denied the possibility of adopting them. The crisis of foster care is further exacerbated to the extent that those who are granted the possibility of adopting do not choose children who have been in the system. The adult most quickly and easily approved by an agency may be the very adult who searches outside an agency, and outside the United States, for a child of his or her own.

II. The New Birthparent

Severing the ties that bind

The 1997 Adoption and Safe Families Act supports adoption rather than foster care. The act also supports adoption rather than reunification with a biological parent. The second is far more extraordinary than the first provision. Reunification suits an American culture of kinship, in which blood is (still) thicker than water. Reunification also suits an American culture of child rearing, in which being brought up by a birthparent is, under most circumstances, seen to be in the best interests of the child. For most of the second half of the twentieth century, reunification guided agency decisions about child placement. It was the promise of reunification that led to the advice we heard in the fostadopt training group, that we not grow "too attached" to a foster child.

Reunification has dropped out of public discourse and, as the 1997 act signifies, out of placement policy. This is the case for several reasons, but the primary one may be the failure of social services to meet the needs of parents in trouble. Parents who are unable to cope find minimal resources for carrying them through the crisis. Moreover, the recent insistence on "family values" works against the vulnerable parent and against any parent-child relationship that does not resemble mainstream interpretations of family. A call to place children in adoptive homes is at once a move against foster care and a move against efforts at rehabilitating collapsing birth families. There is nothing wrong with a call for adoption. In contemporary American culture, however, the call gets entangled in an ideology that blames the victim and in a welfare policy based on cost-benefit calculations rather than on an extension of the meaning of permanency for a child. American child welfare policy prefers the cost efficient adoptive family to the financial costs of rehabilitating a birthparent and the ideological costs of re-evaluating foster care and the persons who undertake fosterage.

The Adoption and Safe Families Act draws the state further into intervention in parent-child relationships. Its provisions permit the swift and final termination of parental rights, a situation that is categorically different from relinquishment. And while the claims of CUB that surrender is always coerced and involuntary are valid, the experiences CUB members report are of a different kind from those outlined by the termination proceedings in the 1997 act.

For decades, child placement policy in the United States favored reunification. Birthparents in CUB noted this ironically, claiming they had not benefited from an emphasis on reunification. Several told me they had "never heard of" foster care being used as a temporary expedient until the birthparent could get on her own feet. Others remarked that biological parents whose children were placed in foster homes had a far better chance of seeing and being with their children than did parents who gave a child to an adopting family. At the same time, there is some irony in the history of American attitudes toward forms of placement. Developments at the beginning of the twenty-first century are shifting the weight of moral stigma from the birthparent who relinquishes to the parent whose rights are terminated. Under the pressure of CUB and of the adoption reform movement, the birthparent who surrenders stands in a brighter light than she has in earlier decades. By contrast, the parent who is subjected to termination proceedings accumulates the "evil" once thrust upon the unprepared parent.

Up until the 1980s, birthparents who surrendered a child fell out of discussion as a "public problem." They *vanished* from the scene. By comparison, parents in trouble and with troubled relations to their children garnered attention from policy makers and social workers. In 1980, one of the first federal acts dealing with adoption also emphasized the importance of efforts to keep biological parent and child together. Only after such efforts failed, the act proclaimed, could adoption be considered. The Child Welfare Reform and Adoption Assistance Act of 1980 (Public Law 96-272) specifies that the "concept of permanency planning refers to efforts to maintain a child's birthfamily whenever possible, to return a child to his birthfamily as soon as possible, and failing either, to establish for him legally the permanent nurturant relationships with caring adults preferably through adoption."[36] Suiting a cultural ideology in which birth ties are central to notions of parenthood, the effort required money for training and rehabilitation programs. That requirement was to be the Achilles heel in the policy.

In 1990, Senator John Heinz of Pennsylvania received a congressional memo asking him to support further funding of Public Law 96-272 provisions. "Current evidence shows that intensive family preservation programs are effective in preventing foster placement for the vast majority of families served, and that parents can make substantial gains in parenting skills and environmental conditions for the family. Given that services to families in their own homes are less costly than out-of-home care, advocates agree that funding for additional and extended at-home services should be a priority." In Missouri, where the program had been working well, "of the 90 families served so far, nearly all of them are still together. Without this emergency program, children from these families would be in foster care. The annual cost is $4,000 to $5,000 per family, less than half the cost of foster care for each child."[37] With two large urban centers in his state, Heinz may have viewed 90 families as a tiny drop in a big bucket.

Still, based on his staff's recommendation, the senator from Pennsylvania gave his support to the bill. In Pennsylvania, his staff reported: "These programs are cost-effective as well—compare $2,000 per family for 6 weeks of support services provided by a case manager in a family's home to $10,000 for foster care for one child for 18 months."[38] That assumes that six weeks works. At-home programs represent short-term intervention, an optimistically "quick fix," whereas foster care support extends over months and years.

The congressional memo hinted at the precariousness of short-term intervention even as it advocated increased services for families in trouble. But only hinted: faith in being able to "fix" a family remained in the memo alongside mention of the spread of drug addiction and the rise in child abuse cases. "Chemical abuse is a significant factor in over 70 percent of all cases investigated. Cocaine and crack use have become increasingly common among families in the child protective system."[39] The days of family services and reunification programs were numbered. Cost-benefit calculations did not hold when drug-addicted parents required long term care, prolonged services, and intensive counseling. Federal money for reunification and rehabilitation programs was not enough to carry states like Pennsylvania through the crisis.

Almost simultaneously with the memo he received, John Heinz learned of a new federal initiative. According to this initiative, money was to be transferred from reunification and rehabilitation programs to adoption. The 1990 Adoption Opportunities Act doubled federal funding for adoption. Anticipating its 1997 successor, the 1990 act treats adoption as the response to a crisis, in which a generation of children is in dire danger. Closing the gap between children *in danger* and children *freed* for adoption fell to the departments and agencies that are assigned to implement federal guidelines. That is, in order for a child to be adopted, he or she must be released forever from a biological parent. Parents who endanger their children may not be in a position or in a state of mind to sign surrender papers. The state must intervene in the best interests of the child and terminate the rights of the parent.

The concept of termination is a far cry from surrender, relinquishment, and even "giving up" a child. A look back at the portrayals of the mother who gives up her child reveals how radically the picture of the unfit parent has changed in the past five decades. A look back, as always in history, reveals continuities as well.

The history of American child placement policy is a story of designating some parents as unfit. From the Puritan fathers to contemporary congressmen, pointing to the bad parent has been a popular way of regulating families. Only the traits have changed. In the 1950s, the crimes Senator Estes Kefauver depicted in his hearings on juvenile delinquency seem benign in the world of 2000 and 2001: petty thievery, breaking curfews, an unplanned pregnancy here and there. The greatest danger Kefauver saw was that the children of irresponsible teenage girls would grow up to be irresponsible in turn. The solutions he proposed include increased community services and help for the girl who, basically a good girl, had gone astray. The threads of a persistent sexist imagery were there as well: the obligations of a *woman* to be a responsible and well-timed parent, the duty of the community to help a *mother* through her mistakes. These threads attained darker hues in the next two decades.

In the 1980s, Senator Gordon Humphrey of New Hampshire took up the issue of the girl-gone-astray. Testimony at the hearings he conducted, as well as his own statements and letters, reveal that "straying" was the least of the matter.

Humphrey had other evils on his mind, among them abortion. In *Roe v. Wade* years he drew on the image not only of the "bad girl" but also of the girl who could make her mistakes worse by aborting a baby. From his perspective, to contemplate abortion after falling prey to seduction deepened the woman's "evil." He proposed adoption instead.

In the spring of 1985, Humphrey announced the formation of a bicameral, bipartisan Congressional Coalition on Adoption. "The Coalition was formed," he explained, "in response to a growing awareness of the tragedy that leads over a million women a year to terminate their pregnancies in abortion, while many couples unsuccessfully seek an infant to adopt." He dismissed foster care, a costly and inefficient system. "Equally tragic are the large numbers of children remaining in foster care, and our society's failure to find a permanent home for these children." Rather than aborting or placing a child in foster care, Humphrey proposes, the unprepared mother should give her child to a "worthy couple."[40]

This assumes the unprepared mother perceives "worth" in the same way Humphrey does. And as my interviews with members of CUB showed, many birthparents do share what is, after all, a cultural convention about good families. Like the senator, birthparents who relinquish a child choose a "worthy couple"— a married couple with resources and a stable home life. Retrospective framing of the decision to give up a child resonates with the adoption policy Humphrey advocates. Despite second thoughts and afterthoughts, most members of CUB talked of the surrender in terms of what they were giving the child by placing her or him with a worthy couple.

Humphrey also directed his comments toward the person who had not yet contemplated adoption as the solution to an unplanned or untimely pregnancy. Where his program parts company from CUB is in its insistence that pregnant women be advised about the advantages of adoption. CUB members might describe the goal of adoption in the same terms Humphrey uses, but their narratives of signing a surrender paper speak of failed resistance to the social pressure counseling can incorporate. Humphrey turns the advocacy of counseling on the wheel of family values, the lodestar of social pressure in child placement policy. Federal funds appropriated to family planning, he argues, should be transferred to counseling programs. "For too long, our image of family planning has been exclusively family planning through the prevention of pregnancy, the limiting of family size, or the spacing of pregnancies. It is time to recognize the importance of positive family planning, that is the formation of families through adoption, for those who would otherwise not be able to establish a family."[41]

Narratives at CUB indicate how close to coercion counseling can seem to be. Though it would be unfair to accuse Humphrey of intending to coerce girls into giving up their babies, the end result of the policy he proposes is a restriction on options for women with unplanned pregnancies. In its worst reading, Humphrey's position results in practices that move babies from the disadvantaged individual to the advantaged couple, a possibility that is emphasized in literature critical of adoption in the United States.[42] Humphrey recognizes the tightrope he is walking. "Even if a single woman considers adoption she may dismiss it prematurely as too expensive or too difficult, and instead choose to have an abortion or raise her child out-of-wedlock. No pregnant woman should ever be coerced into releasing her child for adoption, but she should be helped to make an informed decision, after considering all of her alternatives."[43]

Humphrey's position evolves into the current "adoption not abortion" view of the Christian right. His position also reflects the family-values ideology that continues nearly twenty years later to discriminate among classes of parents, measuring a good parent against mainstream standards like marriage and income. The same standards narrow the pool of adoptive parents, even as professionals call for the adoption of all unplanned, abused, and abandoned children.[44] Most significantly, however, Humphrey's advocacy of counseling for unprepared mothers creates a dichotomy between "couples" who are worthy of having children and "mothers" who cannot care for children, and are therefore unworthy of being parents. The story Molly told in the last chapter about her reunion indicates both the weight of the dichotomy and the efforts birthparents make to reverse it.

In Molly's narrative, her demonstration of parental love made her as worthy as the adoptive couple, with their "grand" house in the suburbs.

Not a new theme in the history of American child placement policy, by the mid-1990s the class of "unworthy mother" had expanded beyond the imagination of even an alarmist like Gordon Humphrey. The reality of drug addiction and the scandals of abandoned "crack babies" drove politicians and professionals into approaching placement as a *necessary* intervention on the part of the state. Adoption became one of a set of punitive measures designed to control individuals whose perceived sins far exceed those of the "girl gone astray." No longer simply unprepared, these are mothers who are accused of abusing their babies by taking drugs during pregnancy, of being unable to raise a child because cocaine "killed" the maternal instinct, and of endangering others through their own actions. As always in American child placement history, the discourse of alarm centers on individuals, not on a social and economic system that produces individuals who can not safely care for a child. Nor did policy-makers who, like Humphrey, vituperated against "bad mothers," demand increased social services for the persons who became, in their views, bad. National guidelines that influence state and local programs have only reduced the possibilities for rehabilitation and for alternative forms of "parenting." Reunification policies fade on all levels and, despite a cultural theorem that blood is thicker than water, the state currently carries on a policy of efficiently severing the ties that bind.

By the end of the 1980s, any newspaper and any news program was likely at some time or other to feature an article on the "crack-baby epidemic." Stories of babies left on doorsteps, children abandoned in rat-infested apartments, and teenagers whose behavior reflected the addiction of their parents entered the public discourse on adoption and foster care. Reactions to such stories range from the establishment of vital protective programs for at-risk children to the formulation of questionable plans for the parents of these children.

"Simply, we cannot allow the stranglehold drugs have on addicted mothers to further tighten and constrict the lives of our children," wrote Pete Wilson of California to fellow senators in 1989. "The wasted potential both of the abusing mother and especially of the abused and innocent child compels a humane society to act."[45] But how act? Like Humphrey, Wilson offers adoption as an answer, with termination of the mother's rights occurring as quickly as possible. Setting the needs of the child against those of the mother, Wilson argues that speedy termination is in the best interests of the child. He found a responsive audience. "We should do this [termination] not as punishment, nor as vengeance, nor even for deterrence, but purely for the protection of the soon-to-be-born child. Taking custody of the child unfortunately but necessarily means taking custody of the mother." And he found imaginative interpretations of his position by others: "We can pass laws saying that any pregnant woman who takes cocaine during pregnancy will be sent until delivery to some not uncomfortable, secure location (boot camp, county jail, house arrest—the details are a purely technical matter) where she will be allowed everything except the liberty to leave or take drugs."[46]

The position draws on an accepted principle of American child welfare practice: removal of a child whose safety and security the parent threatens. And while few would disagree with the principle, the specific program Wilson (and not Wilson alone) proposes ultimately sets *child against parent*. The proposal ignores the rights and the circumstances of the drug-addicted parent in the interests of rescuing her child. It is the most recent, and perhaps the starkest, representation of the conflict between parent and child interests that plagues American policy.[47] In the United States, state intervention in parent-child relations has often resulted in accentuating the competing interests of parent and child: the child is rescued and the parent is forgotten. Drug-addiction, while a real danger to a child, also serves as a convenient rationale for policy-makers who advocate a strict and absolute termination policy. "Cocaine may be the most effective destroyer of the maternal instinct ever found."[48]

In 1998, Wisconsin attempted to establish a policy of incarcerating drug-addicted pregnant women. "The Governor of Wisconsin, Tommy G. Thompson, is expected to sign a bill on

Tuesday that would permit the state to take into custody pregnant women who exhibit a serious and habitual 'lack of self-control' in the use of alcohol or drugs." In his column in *The New York Times*, Bob Herbert responded to the proposal. "Already the rights and bodily integrity of women are being eroded in ways that are alarming. Under the Wisconsin legislation, a legal guardian could be appointed to represent the interests of the fetus of a woman taken into custody for abusing drugs or alcohol. Thus, an adversarial situation is established. The woman suddenly finds herself at war with her own body."[49] And with her own child. Rightly defending the integrity of women, Herbert does not concern himself with a further problem of the policy: where do these children go?

Positions like that taken by Wilson, by Thompson, and by others violate the freedom and integrity of women. Such positions also ignore the fate of the children whose very well-being is the ostensible goal of "controlling" (if not incarcerating) mothers. Rather like President Clinton in the mid-1990s, advocates of these positions harbor the optimistic view that there will be "open arms" to accept the children removed from drug-addicted parents. Moreover, given the pressure of permanency planning, the expectation is that adoption will be the outcome for this newest batch of "available" children. The reality is that babies of drug-addicted parents are not first on the lists of those adults who are qualified for adoptive parenthood by most agencies in the country. Nor are they the first chosen by those who adopt independently.

The problem of drug-addicted parents recalls another theme in American adoption. Children "released" from parents with addictions offer potential parents a reminder of the nature versus nurture pairing that never quite disappears from discussion of "taking in" a stranger child. Although adoptive parents do not dwell explicitly on the "bad seed" myth, still concern about what the child may carry does not vanish from decisions about becoming a parent. Adoption argues a belief in nurture and in environment. American culture argues for a search of the "background" of the child as a way of preparing the soil for her or his best growth. A child who is born in a "boot camp," his mother incarcerated for addiction, challenges adoption practices that reflect the "as-if-begotten" of adoption laws. The known pasts of these available children separate them sharply from the adoptive parents, pushing considerations of as-if-begotten aside. Adopting parents who accept a child from a (perhaps metaphorical) boot camp must rely on nurture and on environment. Yet this reliance wavers under recent publicity about genetic predilections and, a modern version of the bad seed, inherited traits.

Termination of parental rights, (TPR), under civil or custodial proceedings, is not the same as the surrender of a child. The word "surrender" carries connotations of coercion for all three members of the triad but surrender is mild compared with termination. "Termination" does not let anyone forget the punitive side of adoption customs in the United States. The parent whose rights are terminated takes the role of the "evil" mother who never totally disappears from the culture of child placement.

At the beginning of the twenty-first century, termination of parental rights has become a necessary strategy in many parts of the country. Drug addiction, abuse, and abandonment threaten the lives of many more than the five hundred thousand children mentioned in Clinton's 1996 and 1997 speeches. To rescue and to ensure the safety of a generation of threatened children requires swift measures; termination has taken a place in the public discourse as an especially effective measure. Emphasis on permanency in child welfare policies adds to the appeal of termination proceedings, which are more absolute and final than the relinquishment papers signed in days of opening adoption. The parent whose rights are terminated faces a life sentence. A lawyer described TPR as the "capital punishment" of family law, adding that it might be a life sentence for children.[50]

As always in child placement affairs, public discourse displays contrary positions. For those who support TPR, there are those who resist imposing a "death sentence" on vulnerable, addicted, or abusive parents. That position requires a supplementary one: an argument for increased funding for community-based family services. The position wars against federal policy—inscribed in the 1997 Adoption and Safe Families Act—

which mandates adoption rather than rehabilitation and reunification. At the same time, an argument in favor of increased community services pulls on another strand of child welfare policy, the historical dependence on states to respond to the breakdown of parent-child relations.

The issue is ideological as well as budgetary. A decision to reunify families rather than to re-place a child draws on cultural views of parenthood and of family that are clearly not homogenous across the country. Expensive in a purely fiscal sense, reunification policies are also "expensive" in a cultural sense: that is, they often involve the shoring up of non-conventional families—for instance, a sixty-three-year-old woman caring for three generations of her children, in a case of family reunification I observed. After the issuance of Public Law 105-89, states had the option of resisting the plea for permanency through adoption. Next door to Washington, D.C., in Baltimore, Maryland, the local authorities tried out alternatives to terminating parental rights and placing children in adoptive homes.

The Washington Post took issue with a TPR policy in a series of articles. The series featured Tammy, a drug-addicted mother of three who lived in Baltimore. Arrested several times, Tammy appeared before judges more than once. Once, to her good fortune, her children wept in despair as she was sentenced to a term in prison. Moved by the children's tears, the judge prescribed rehabilitation as part of the prison term and Tammy came to the attention of interested social workers. Her time in jail pushed her over the line into a commitment to the rehabilitation programs: she joined AA, a Christian church, and attended training programs sponsored by a Baltimore social service organization. Eventually Tammy's children were returned to her custody and a family reunification policy seemed justified.

An argument against swift termination proceedings, the series also argues for increased social services and funding for community programs. This has not happened. The story across the country continues to be the other one, termination of parental rights combined with pleas for more adoption. Pleas are supported by an increase in the funding provided to states for adoptive placements, subsidies to adults who adopt children, and publicity about the benefits of adopting for child and parents. The pleas are not, however, supported by changes in standards for the acceptability of adoptive parents, ideologies of the "good" adoptive family, and definitions of the sources of safety, permanence, and enduring solidarity.

Adoption dominates the scene

With the Adoption and Safe Families Act of 1997, adoption dominates child placement policy in the United States. Foster care had long ago lost its value as a refuge for children, and after the 1980s, family preservation and reunification programs came under equally severe criticism. As *The New York Times* put it the day the bill was signed: "The new legislation marks a fundamental shift in child-welfare philosophy, away from a presumption that everything should be done to reunite children with their birthparents."[51]

At the beginning of the twenty-first century in the United States, adoption dominates not only child welfare but also other policy arenas: the war on drugs, the fight to uphold family values, and the struggle to cut federal government spending. The transaction has come to bear many burdens on a national level, replacing weak social welfare systems and upholding an ideology of the family. Simultaneously, those who participate in adoptions accord other, diverse meanings to the transaction; it is the individuals who arrange adoptions and who are personally enmeshed in this form of kinship that are crucial to the implementation of Public Law 105-89. Behind the programs institutionalized by the Department of Health and Human Services are the people who adopt, or do not adopt, children.

In 1996, President Clinton responded to the reports of thousands of abandoned and abused children in one of the wealthiest nations of the world. He drafted an executive order, Adoption 2002, that preceded the Adoption and Safe Families Act. In it, the president proclaimed "that every child deserves a safe, permanent family; that the child's health and safety should be the paramount consideration in all placement and permanency planning decisions; and that foster care is a temporary situation—it is not an appropriate place for children to grow up.

Adoption 2002 establishes unequivocally that the Federal goals for children in the child welfare system are safety, permanency, and well-being."[52]

In what became Public Law 105-89, adoption unequivocally constitutes the best route to safety, permanency, and well-being for children who are at risk. Throughout the many sections, a legally structured and court-approved arrangement takes precedence over casual, kin-based, and informal means of caring for children. In its outline of programs for implementing the Adoption and Safe Families Act, the Department of Health and Human Services reiterates the goal. "The concept of permanence is best defined as a stable, legally-sanctioned relationship with caring, protective adults. This may be achieved in a child's birth family, but, for many children in foster care, it may occur through adoption or [legal] guardianship."[53]

The act, then, restricts the notion of permanency to a *legal* relationship between parent and child. Emotional attachments, loyalties, obligations and exchanges between adults—none is considered a guarantee of the child's safety and security over time. The wording in the act excludes, too, the attachments that develop between foster parents and children. The openness to various long-term arrangements in the 1973 *Beyond the Best Interests of the Child* is missing from the 1997 act. Goldstein, Freud, and Solnit write: "Even though their [foster parent] applications for legal adoption may be denied in court, in fact what they may have become are parents by 'common law adoption,' which, we would argue, deserves recognition."[54]

"Common law" bespeaks a commitment to the child that lasts without court sanction. Yet recent federal guidelines give short shrift to virtually all parental arrangements that have not been approved by an agency or legalized in a courtroom. Appropriation of parental duties by individuals who (for whatever reasons) would not pass public tests for a "fit parent" comes under stern and, often, suffocating, regulation. A woman I knew in Hawaii kept her role as a foster parent a secret from neighbors and visitors. She feared she might be denied the status if the arrangement became public, even though she assumed permanent responsibility for the well-being of the children.[55] Mistrust of parent-child relationships that are not legalized stems from the perception of "crisis" in the transfer of a child from a biological to a social parent. The courts, in this view, provide a foundation for permanency and safety.

Individuals, like my friend in Hawaii, who are parents without a legal designation bear the brunt of the poor state of the foster system in the United States. Foster care arrangements *do* collapse, and children float from home to home in a limbo of insecurity and danger. The fault does not lie with the informality of the arrangement, however, but with a stringent budget, an overworked social work staff, and the criticism foster families experience from the public and from the professionals who appoint them. The criticism speaks explicitly to the very real abuses reported of foster parents. On a deeper level, criticism of foster care represents a condemnation of alternative means of "parenting" a child and wariness of the assumption of parental duties that is not sanctioned by an agency or a court. Perhaps, too, the criticism of foster care reveals a doubt about the endurance of a spontaneous commitment to a child in need. Criticism of the foster care system ultimately beats the dying horse without confronting the reasons for its problems. Individual foster families receive the blame for a negligent society. As a Washington, D.C. judge remarked: "The court can only wonder how an agency that cannot track the location of the children in its custody can possibly comply with the remaining requirements of federal and district law, much less with reasonable professional standards."[56]

The 1997 Adoption and Safe Families Act treats the problem of foster care by replacing it with adoption. By mid-century, adoption stood for all that foster care was not: stable, regulated, and with definite legal boundaries. The broader the chaos in foster care, the more appealing the much tidier institution of adoption became. Nearly twenty years before Clinton's initiative, the federal government was already pushing adoption into the holes the foster system left in providing for the safety of children. In 1980, congressional hearings conducted by the subcommittee on child and human development persuaded legislators of both parties, and in both houses, to grant increased funding for "adoption opportunities." One witness testified:

"The benefits of adoption are difficult to measure simply on a monetary scale in that children who are placed in adoption are offered some sense of permanency and stabilization within one family unit."[57] Ten years later, in 1990, federal spending on adoption opportunities doubled.

Moves toward encouraging adoption continued, through budgetary allotments as well as less materialistic rewards. In 1996, Congress granted adopting families an income-based tax subsidy of $5000. Two years later, the Adoption and Safe Families Act offered states $4000 for every new adoption, and $6000 for every new special needs adoption. On the day the bill was signed, Hillary Clinton presented thirteen *Adoption 2002* Excellence Awards. "The winners are dedicated individuals and organizations, both large and small, who have worked to move children out of the foster care system into permanent, loving homes."[58] The Excellence Awards indicate the variety of mechanisms utilized to increase the number of adoptions in state after state. Besides the monetary prize, the publicity surrounding the awards makes adoption unmistakably a good thing. States vie for recognition for having an abundance of "loving homes" within their jurisdictions. Like her husband, Hillary Clinton covers over the fact that states are being paid for each adoption with the reminder that adoption is a loving gesture towards a child.

President Clinton was a master of the rhetoric. When he signed the bill, he stated: "We have put in place …. the building blocks of giving all of our children what should be their fundamental right, a chance at a decent safe home; an honorable, orderly, positive upbringing; a chance to live out their dreams and their God-given capacities."[59]

Effective rhetoric places an audience in the position of having to accept the argument. This Clinton's language clearly does, with its reference to the secular and the sacred symbols of American culture that few would reject. The rhetoric is further persuasive since it is accompanied by the promise of financial rewards. Under the 1997 act, each state receives money for successful adoptions. In response, public and private agencies, as well as officials of the court, work together to increase the number of adoptions. Pennsylvania is one example. "The Adoption

Legal Services Project is based on a unique and ongoing local public/private sector partnership involving state, county, and judiciary entities and the private law firm of Reed Smith Shaw & McClay. Created in 1996, the project addresses a critical problem in the Allegheny County child welfare system: the large numbers of dependent children languishing in foster care due to stalled or blocked adoption proceedings."[60] In New York City, Nicholas Scoppetta reported that a "record 11,000 children have been adopted [from foster care] in the last three years alone."[61] Between 1996 and 1999, the number of children adopted from foster care went from 28,000 to 40,000, but this is still only a dent in the 550,000 in foster care.[62]

In the fall of 1999, the state of Pennsylvania received an Excellence Award for its success in placing foster children in adoptive homes. "Adoption of foster care children nearly tripled under the Ridge Administration, jumping from 676 to 1,795. Pennsylvania now ranks sixth in the nation for placing children in permanent homes."[63] The children pictured in honor of Pennsylvania's receipt of the award contrast with the boy on the hobby horse in the White House the November day Clinton signed the Adoption and Safe Families Act. The children in the picture are "special needs," and one died within a year of her adoption.

Using the familiar concept of adoption, the act asks the institution to do something different from what it has done, and been, for at least seventy-five years of American history. It asks individuals to adopt children who are not the stereotypical, sweet babies once composing the (fairy-tale) story of adoption in the United States. "While not the only explanation for mounting foster-care rolls, drugs—especially crack cocaine—are the heart of the problem. . . . Despite reported declines in crack use, they continue arriving today, and staying—children whose parents remain lost to drugs and whose own emotional scars inhibit adoption."[64]

Throughout the 1997 act, the term "special needs" clusters these tormented and abused children into a category shared by children whose problems are benign, whose special traits are racial, and whose dilemma is that they are siblings.

"Special needs" came into use during the 1980s. Two streams conjoined to produce the terminological change: an increasing demand on the part of potential parents that could not be met with the existing supply of available children and the public despair at how many children languished in unsafe conditions. The older term, "hard to place," damned the very end it served, discouraging potential adopters. The new label, special needs, seemed to remove the stigma through the positive connotations of "special." Perhaps potential parents might see the appeal of such adoptions and shift their desires away from the increasingly rare healthy white infant. But "special" covers a wide gamut, and the phrase unintentionally redefines family in the process of intentionally reclassifying children.

"Special needs" includes children with severe medical and psychological problems, children who are older, children who are in sibling groups, and children of minority background. As much as telling anything about the children, these categories tell something about the course of adoption in the United States—the desire for infants, the expectations of a "good" child, and the difficulty of placing minority children. Inasmuch as Public Law 105-89 concentrates on special needs children, its goals run up against the conventions of adoption practice. "The median age of children who are legally free and awaiting adoption is almost nine years old," DHHS reported in 1996, in response to Clinton's executive memorandum. "Slightly over half of the children are of minority heritage. Two-thirds of the children in the special needs category have medical problems, developmental delays and disabilities, and/or behavioral and psychological problems."[65] Four years later, in 2000, nothing had changed. Of "available" children, "more than half (54%) are African-American, 31% are white, and 9% are Hispanic/Latino, with the remainder generally being Native American, Asian, or multi-racial. Roughly two-thirds of the registered children are boys. Nearly one half of them are in a sibling group that needs to be adopted together."[66] A high proportion had been in foster care for between three and five years, adding to the "needs" they already may have had.

The figures repeat the fitful history of American adoption. Individuals who want to be parents, broadly defined, are stymied by standards for adoptive placement that are narrowly defined. The generosity, open arms, and loving homes that constitute the rhetoric of adoption policy fall down before the expectations parents and professionals have about *family*. A biological model continues to influence those expectations, so that infants and young children are most readily adopted 48 percent of all adoptions are of children under five years old.[67] Furthermore, the same model means that minority children remain out of the loop as long as minority applicants are discouraged from adopting—discouraged by costs as well as by criteria. Patterns of same race placement join with ideologies of the family to limit the impact of presenting children as "special" rather than as "hard to place."

The Adoption and Safe Families Act anticipates "open arms" for all adoptable children, but these are arms of a special sort. While using "adoption" in a conventional sense, the act extracts meanings that lean away from family building and towards charity or altruism. Oddly disconnected in American culture, charitable rather than "child-having" adoption is the requirement of the new federal initiative. The shift from child-having to charity alters interpretations of the family—in practice charitable adopting deviates from the biological model and the matching policies that have accompanied that model. The challenge of "special needs" adoption lies less in the inability of potential parents to extend their understandings of adoption to an altruistic act than in the weight of racial especially, but also ethnic and religious, matching on the decisions made about child placement by participants as well as professionals.

A further obstacle to the kind of adopting the act requires are the hardships involved in devoting one's life to a child who has psychological or medical problems or both. Children who have suffered severe abuse and cannot express love and affection put a strain on even the most generous individuals.[68]

In 1991, I spent an intense three hours with Emily, who had adopted three special needs children. Her story was full of pain, reflection, courage, and uncertainty. The door closed, the university quiet in the late afternoon and early evening, my office provided exactly the privacy she needed to be as honest as she was.

Emily and her husband Tom had entered the domain of special needs adoption somewhat involuntarily. They were disqualified from a conventional adoption because they were not infertile; they had raised three biological children. So they found themselves forced to decide among a range of "special" children. "We were told that often the sibling groups were younger, healthier children than many of the other kids who were special needs adoption who had considerably more problems," she remembered. Defining themselves as ordinary parents, Emily and Tom opted for children for whom love, attention, care, and protection would be enough. And, she added, the two sisters looked adorable in their photos.

The placement immediately hit rough spots. "Dora really started giving us a hard time. Um, to the point of extreme temper tantrums where she would bang her body against the walls or lay down on the floor and kick her feet," Emily continued, in her conversation with me. "She started trying to control the situation in the house. Um, and using food as a weapon. She would—she could sit and not eat for two hours or she could sit and totally gorge herself and then throw it all up. And she got really good at that, that was her, I think that was her big test." The story got worse, as the still distressed mother reported an accusation of sexual abuse. Dora told around school that her adoptive father had "climbed in the sleeping bag with her and did something to her." Alerted, social workers removed both girls from the household. But Emily and Tom were persistent and, after prescribed counseling, the adoptive family was reunited. Remarkably enough, Tom and Emily then adopted a special needs boy. "We're blessed with a lot," Emily told me, "and so I have a lot to give back."

Emily's is not a unique narrative. In 1998, for instance, Ann Kimble Loux published an account of similar troubles, of challenges to "ordinary" love and to cultural interpretations of parenthood. Like Emily (and others I met), Loux reconsiders the meaning of adoption and of "having" a child. Her difficulties being a parent to the girls she adopted separated that experience from her behavior as the parent of biological children. What, she asks, does that difference reveal about love, attachment, and the content of parent-child relationships variously formed? Love, affection, concern, and care take on new meanings under the circumstances of the kinds of adoption Emily and Annie Loux describe. Furthermore, such revisions, a constant in the history of American adoption, bear closely on the motivations for adopting in the first place. The reasons a person accepts the care of a "stranger" child forever and (presumably) unconditionally no longer conforms to earlier theoretical distinctions between "wanting a child" and "wanting to help a child."[69] Differences between adopting out of necessity, that is, infertility, or out of desire—the altruistic adoptions of the 1960s and 1970s—disappear.

Adoptions like the ones described by Emily and by Ann Loux, too, stretch the meaning of "rescue" in adoption discourse. Not a new motive, adopting in order to provide a child with safety and security changes under the goal the federal act sets: to save over 500,000 children, all of whom are "special."

The difficulties of implementing the 1997 Adoption and Safe Families Act are legion. They include convincing those who contemplate adoptive parenthood that adoption can fulfill charitable as well as (or instead of) "child-having" purposes. They include answering the charge that granting subsidies and financial support to adoptive parents creates a (new) market in children. Difficulties include breaking down the entrenched state prerogatives in the distribution of children that accompanied the passage of adoption laws in the nineteenth century. And they include revising the criteria for good parents and for stable families that have been in place for over seventy-five years.

Crossing boundaries

"Jurisdictional barriers between State child welfare systems may also result in delays in implementing permanent plans for children. At times, there is an unwillingness to effectively coordinate services to families and share limited resources across state agencies."[70] The barriers referred to by this Department of Health and Human Services report are deeply embedded in American child placement history. In the tradition of domestic and family law, laws regarding the welfare of children come under state jurisdiction, a privilege carefully protected. Within states, too, public and private agencies carefully guard their prerogatives, insisting on the right to make their own decisions about qualifications for parents, appropriate homes for children, and measures of success in placement. These privileges and pre-rogatives hinder adoptions across state lines and, often, from one part of a state to another.

Success rates for placement of special needs children reveal something about the cultural, ethnic, and racial diversity of a state. North Dakota, for example, has the highest success rate of any state for the placement of foster children into adoptive homes. In 1997, the state reported that nearly 97 percent of its foster children were adopted. By contrast, in the same year only 15 percent of Pennsylvania's foster children were adopted, the second lowest percentage in the country. The relative homo-geneity of the population in North Dakota may be one element in its successful adoption rates, though obviously other factors enter the picture (for instance, the rates of subsidies for adopt-ing families). In Pennsylvania, not simply the state's racial and ethnic diversity but also the distinctions between urban and rural areas affect placement rates; to diversity as a possible fac-tor in slowing down the rates of placement must be added geo-graphical segregation and the conservative welfare policies of the state. California, by contrast, crowded with diverse ethnic groups, has a higher rate of adoption from foster care, as much because of residential integration as of state policies that are favorable toward the placement of children in "mixed" homes.

Pragmatic considerations and ideological convictions obstruct efforts to establish a national adoption exchange. In the mid-1990s, Congress asked the Department of Health and Human Services to "maintain a national adoption information exchange system to bring together children who would benefit from adop-tion and qualified prospective parents who are seeking such chil-dren, and conduct national recruitment efforts in order to reach prospective parents for children awaiting adoption."[71] In its 1998 response to President Clinton's adoption initiative, DHHS noted the failure of such efforts. "Despite the requirement in title IV-B to recruit potential foster/adoptive families to meet the needs of children requiring out-of-home placement, the pool of permanent families for children of minority heritage, older children, mem-bers of sibling groups, and children with emotional, developmen-tal, or physical challenges remains insufficient."[72]

States protect the population of children and families within their boundaries. They guard the relatively small budget allotments they have for foster care and adoptions. The result is often a closing of boundaries, so that the movement of children from state to state vanishes from the landscape of special needs adoptions. In some states, too, the movement of children across county borders may be stymied as well. The combination of maintaining traditional family composition and of guarding budgets has the (partially unintended) consequence of upholding racial and ethnic barriers to the proposed full-scale adoption of foster children. While foster children reputedly move from house to house with shocking frequency, they are moved from state to state with surprising infrequency.

The intricate connection between a policy of matching and a cultural convention about family composition severely limits the free movement of children in the United States. To put it differently, the connection intrudes upon placement decisions made by individuals who contemplate or who arrange the adoptions of foster children. Resistance to the "open distribution" of foster children also reveals the extent to which arranged families represent the "sameness" that is valued by wider family ideologies. The DHHS report points this out. "Further, some workers and agencies have delayed or denied adoptive placements because their priority was to seek families with backgrounds similar to those of the children needing permanent homes, even though this practice is illegal."[73]

Matching is an arena where the legal succumbs to the customary; the language of law cannot compete with cultural, and individual, views of a good and an enduring placement. The law itself is ambiguous. In 1994, the federal government proscribed the use of race or ethnicity in placement decisions. The Multiethnic Placement Act "prohibits delaying or denying the placement of any child on the basis of race, color or national origin" at the same time as it "requires States to diligently recruit prospective adoptive and foster care families who reflect the ethnic and racial diversity of children in the state for whom foster and adoptive homes are needed."[74]

The contradiction affects all aspects of adopting in the United States. On an individual level, the goal of a "match" may well disappear; evidence for this abounds in the many international adoptions in which Caucasian parents adopt non-Caucasian children. But matching persists on an institutional level, when rules are made about placing children who need homes, who are at risk and in danger. Then matching holds sway, reflecting a cultural assumption that a child will be "better off" where he fits in and that a sense of belonging comes from a perception of sameness. Justified by psychological theory, matching also justifies racial policies in American adoption. This is perhaps the most complex issue raised by the 1997 act, inasmuch as it draws on two sharply opposing positions: the argument that black children ought to remain in the black community, exposed to black cultural experiences; and the argument that all children deserve a home and that placements should be color-blind.

Throughout the 1990s, African-American children constituted half the population in the "special needs" category. The percentage of African-American children in foster care is consistently out of proportion to the number of blacks in the total population. And the proportion of minority children who remain in foster care, never adopted, exceeds that of other special needs categories. In New York City, for every one African-American child adopted, four children await adoption. Where, for these children, are the "open arms" President Clinton confidently anticipated?

They are there, untapped by agencies and unacceptable by old-fashioned criteria for adoptive applicants. They are there, but caught by the high costs of adopting and by the reluctance of practitioners to place children into (presumably) unconventional families. A revision of the criteria for adopting families would facilitate the placement of more children of minority background, but would still leave the knotty issue of same-race versus transracial placements. A plea to give all children permanent homes sidesteps the central issue of what kind of homes and on what bases.

For three decades, practitioners and participants in adoption have recognized both the significance and the drawbacks in the strong position taken by the National Association of

Black Social Workers (NABSW). In 1972, the group voiced an opposition to transracial placements and, thirty years later, maintains the position. Defense of the position reflects a long history of exploitation of the black community—depriving blacks of resources, including children—and the black pride movement of the 1960s. Far from being an attack on adoption, the position recognizes that adoption is not only the making of a family but the reiteration of distinctions and differentials that structure the wider society. Support of same-race placements borrowed from a politics of cultural identity and, too, from the perception that black parents regularly lose out in delegations of parenthood.

The conditions under which a black parent surrenders a child, in this perspective, reflect the failure of society to provide financial support to such parents, not norms against single parenthood.[75] Moreover, the circumstances leading to a termination of parental rights fall heavily on members of the black population: poverty and addiction. But the position of the NABSW makes another point as well: given the large number of black children floating through the foster care system, recruitment of black adopting parents must be rigorously encouraged. Like adoptive parents I met, who bitterly remember the restrictions on agency approval, members of the NABSW delineate the biases in placement practices, which effectively exclude larger numbers of black than white applicants.

The NABSW shares with adoption reform groups the exposure of long-kept secrets in American adoption customs. These are not the secrets of sealed records, but the secrets of cultural assumptions and, for the NABSW, of a relentless racism in the direction adoption takes in the United States. While over five hundred thousand children languish in foster care, and over half of these children are black, waiting for new recruitment of black parents may not serve the best interests principle. Recognition of the undercurrents of placement practice, however, comes out with the foster care crisis as it has not in earlier decades of adoption history, and that does serve the interests of children—and adults. The meaning of "race" in family composition follows on the heels of questions about the role of race in placing children.

As of today, over half the minority children freed for adoption are still waiting for open arms.

In any society, the terms of adoption reflect and reinforce dominant social divisions and cultural values. In American society, race and class play a part in adoption decisions commensurate with the part they play in other policy arenas and in everyday discourse. The dismantling of race and class structures in child placement is not a straightforward matter. The argument of the NABSW concerns losses to the black community, exploitation of the vulnerable, and breakdowns of black cultural coherence that cannot be easily ignored. Arguments in favor transracial placement, appealing on the one hand, on the other have been viewed as using children for a "social experiment" in integration. Even the plea to expand the pool of acceptable adoptive parents, widely made, comes up against cultural assumptions about the sources of permanency and safety for a child in an American cultural milieu. Here the fiscal issue appears as well, inasmuch as a link is presumed to exist between financial security and the well-being of a child. But offering financial help to those who adopt prompts as much resistance as proposals to banish race and income from the consideration of an adoptive placement. If race-based placements follow a biological model that implies sameness in families, resistance to income supplements for adoptive families has the same root in a conceptualization of the "natural" family.

Distant from the precincts of congress and the corridors of agencies, individuals alter the culture and the customs of adoption. The history of American adoption is one in which change occurs because individuals make choices about "family" that disturb, topple, or adjust the accepted shibboleths of successful placement. Every social worker who places a black foster child in a white family makes a change. Every time a single black adult is approved as an adoptive parent, the conventions wobble. *Adoption 2002* requires more of those "wobblings," and yet the wording of the text respects family ideologies that keep old policies entrenched in a new era. At the beginning of the twenty-first century, evidence of a swelling in the "pool" of potential adoptive parents is unmistakable. The next question is: will the expanded pool be large—and open—enough to absorb a population of abandoned and abused children that grows not just annually but day by day?

Notes

1. Adoption and Safe Families Act, Public Law 105-89.
2. Seelye, Katharine Q. *The New York Times* 11/17/97: 14.
3. Mitchell, Alison. *The New York Times* 12/15/96: 1.
4. The Evan B. Donaldson Adoption Institute. http://www.adoptioninstitute.org/research/ressta.html.
5. *Time* 11/13/00: 79.
6. DHHS Response to Clinton's *Executive Memorandum: Adoption 2002.*
7. The DHHS response refers specifically to Native American tribes.
8. During the 1990s, tax breaks and subsidies were proposed for adopting parents. These "payments" are controversial, not least because they muddy the distinction between foster parents and adoptive parents; see below.
9. Quoted in *Adoptalk* 1990: 10.
10. *Time* 11/13/00: 75-76.
11. Russakoff, Dale. *The Washington Post* 2/23/98: 6.
12. *Adoption Advocates*. File://jm%27s%20harddisk/destop%20Folder/.
13. Meezan and Shireman 1985: 13.
14. Quoted in Triseliotis and Hill 1990: 113.
15. According to *Smith v. Offer*, a foster parent is only entitled to notification if the child is going to be placed in another foster home, not if she or he is returning to a biological parent or has been freed for adoption.
16. Bernstein, Nina. *The New York Times* 6/9/00: 29.
17. Mnookin 1985: 115.
18. Quoted in Tiffin 1982: 93.
19. *LaShawn et al v. Sharon Pratt Dixon* (Mayor of Washington, D.C.) 1991.
20. *Time* 11/13/00.
21. Molotsky, Irvin. *The New York Times* 8/8/97: 16.
22. Triseliotis and Hill 1990: 120.
23. Russakoff, Dale. "The Protector," *The New Yorker* 4/21/97: 65.
24. *Developments* 1996: 1.
25. In a series of articles, Bruce Bellingham has described both the necessity of fosterage as a coping strategy for the poor and disadvantaged and the role fostering plays in hegemonic control of family and parent-child relationships. See bibliography.

26. Goldstein, Freud, Solnit 1973: 13.
27. Ibid: 32.
28. Ibid: 33.
29. The best account of the links between child rearing and adult personality in a Polynesian culture remains Robert Levy's *The Tahitians* (1973).
30. Goldstein, Freud, Solnit 1973: 26.
31. Personal communication.
32. *Manual for Foster Care*, in author's possession.
33. Ibid.
34. In fact, the manual contained a large number of specific instructions, reminding us that we were "workers" for the state and not "real" parents.
35. Meezan and Shireman 1985: 13.
36. Cole and Donley 1990: 278.
37. H. John Heinz III Archives (10/2/90).
38. Ibid.
39. Ibid.
40. Humphrey to colleagues 6/3/85. H. John Heinz III Archives.
41. Humphrey to colleagues 7/29/85. H. John Heinz III Archives.
42. There is now especially true in literature critical of international adoptions; e.g., Barrett and Aubin 1990; Solinger 1992.
43. Humphrey to colleagues 7/19/85. H. John Heinz III Archives.
44. See below on how these restrictions are handled in the 1997 Adoption and Safe Families Act.
45. Memo from the office of Pete Wilson. H. John Heinz III Archives.
46. Reprinted in *Congressional Record* 8/1/89: 3.
47. The conflict again comes up, when birthparents claim that adoptee searches violate their privacy rights.
48. *Congressional Record* 8/1/89: 3.
49. Herbert, Bob. *The New York Times* 6/14/98: 15. In an odd postscript, in January 2001 newly elected President Bush nominated Thompson to be Secretary of the Department of Health and Human Services.
50. Herring, 1998: 5
51. Seelye, Katharine Q. *The New York Times* 11/17/97: 14.
52. *Executive Memorandum: Adoption 2002.*
53. DHHS Response to Clinton's *Executive Memorandum: Adoption 2002.* A shift between "permanency" and "permanence" occurs throughout writings on child placement policy. I prefer the term permanency.
54. Goldstein, Freud, Solnit 1973: 26.
55. She would not have been approved because she was the mother of the drug-addicted father whose children she "fostered" when I met her.
56. *LaShawn et al v. Sharon Pratt Dixon* 1991.
57. *Congressional Hearings, Adoption Assistance and Child Welfare,* 1980: 260.
58. http://www.adoptioninstitute.org/research/ressta.html.

59. Clinton speech 11/27/97.
60. *Redesigning Human Services in Allegheny County* 1998: 10.
61. Sengupta, Samini. *The New York Times* 12/6/99: 36. This is out of approximately 35,000 children in foster care.
62. http://www.adoptioninstitute.org/research/ressta.html.
63. *Network News* 1999: 1. The piece mentions that nationwide adoptions of children who were in foster care increased from 28,000 in 1996 to 36,000 in 1998.
64. Herbert, Bob. *The New York Times* 6/14/98: 15.
65. DHHS Response to Clinton's *Executive Memorandum: Adoption 2002.*
66. http://www.ggw.org/cap/aboutkids/html.
67. http://www.adoptioninstitute.org/research/ressta.html.
68. In my training group, the video of an autistic girl brought strong reaction: as she failed, repeatedly, to respond to loving gestures, several people in the room said "I could never manage a child like that"—despite the fact that the girl was utterly adorable.
69. William Feigleman and Arnold Silverman make the distinction in a fine study of adoption, *Chosen Children* (1983).
70. DHHS Response to Clinton's *Executive Memorandum: Adoption 2002.*
71. http://www.adoptioninstitute.org/research/ressta.html.
72. DHHS Response to Clinton's *Executive Memorandum: Adoption 2002.*
73. Ibid.
74. *The Multiethnic Placement Act of 1994.*
75. In general, the literature shows that black parents relinquish less frequently than white parents; the percentage remains under 1 percent for blacks and, currently, nearly 2 percent for whites.

Chapter 4

Taking (Care of) the Children—Adoptive Parents in the Twenty-first Century

A stable marriage and a white picket fence

By the end of the twentieth century, adoption had affected millions of individuals in the United States. By then, too, adoptive families looked very different from one another. A diversification of adoption practices and of interpretations of an adoptive family characterized adoption in virtually every community in the country. At the same time, federal policy and state legislation continue to operate with traditional assumptions and concepts. Provisions in adoption law and the programs for implementation assume adoption is *only* what it always has been: adding a child to a family. Such official documents also assume a particular definition of the family: mother, father, and children. By the end of the twentieth century, these assumptions fit fewer and fewer of the adoptive families in the United States, yet they still run through policy statements and state programs.

The discrepancy between child placement policy and adoption practice has several consequences. First, caught in traditional notions of adoption and of the family, federal and state policies cannot take advantage of new cultural interpretations of parenthood that are inspired by new adoptive arrangements. Second, in embracing an inherited idea of the "parent," federal and state policies severely limit the pool of adoptive applicants. And third, inasmuch as American adoption policy comes clothed in a language of sentiment and love, practices that acknowledge the significance of "consumer" choice are totally ignored. Shy of a language that implies a market, federal acts nevertheless operate in a context of highly volatile relationships between supply (of children) and demand (by adults). Accepting the role of a market in child placement practices may well serve not sacrifice the best interests of the children. On the ground, and in the strategies used by agencies and by independent mediators, market forces increasingly hold the day in the form of advertisements and of sliding fee scales. Remaining behind, policy loses the opportunity to regulate and to benefit from these forces.

Reluctance to face the "new" in adoption practices puts the federal initiatives of the mid-1990s in a precarious position. In a move that is without precedent in American history, the 1997 Adoption and Safe Families Act creates a vast supply of adoptable children.[1] The act urges that all at-risk and vulnerable children be freed for adoption. At the same time, the wording of the act leaves intact a picture of the adoptive family that comes from at least half a century ago. With an inconsistency that does have precedent in American history, the act radically alters one side of the equation—a definition of the "adoptable" child—while barely modifying the other side—criteria for the "qualified" parent. Provisions of the act uphold cultural norms and respect the "uniform" standards for placement that have existed since the 1920s, but the act ultimately is at war with itself. An expansion of the supply goes hand in hand with a constraint on demand. Fortunately, participants in adoption have begun to make the changes that are necessary if the act is to succeed in its stated goals. This penultimate chapter, then, is in many ways the beginning of the story of adoption in the twenty-first century, for it is upon a *new supply of adoptive parents* that modern "fictive kinship" depends.

The stereotypical image of the adoptive family is as familiar as apple pie. Recent advertisements for the large discount store, Ikea, show just how familiar it is: a tumble of little children in a well-furnished bedroom; sometimes a mother appears to control the pillow fights and sometimes a father appears (home from work) to add his jokingly stern voice to the melee. In manuals, these are the at-home mother, the bread-winning father, and the several children of a "typical family." These are the mother, father, and children that influence applicants for adoptive parenthood even before they embark on the (not easy) journey to adoption. Caucasian or, at least, racially the same, financially secure, living in a suburban house, with a big backyard and a white picket fence, the ideal American adoptive family sets a high standard for family. The familiar picture also reveals one of the primary functions of American adoption policy: to keep that high standard of family in front of the American public.

In the mid-1990s, President Clinton made adoption one of his administration's causes. In speeches, presentations of awards, and finally in the 1997 act, Clinton spoke of the failings in America's concern for a generation of children. His answer was adoption; precisely, the act advocates the swift "freeing" of children who are in trouble from the parents who abuse or neglect them. The act also advocates adoption as the route to safety and security for these children. The Department of Health and Human Services received the task of putting the lofty goals and the fine rhetoric—as well as the real benefits of an adoption program—into action. Immediately, the DHHS recognized the difficulties of its assigned chore. While every state might accept the charge in the federal act, every state had (and would maintain) control over the justification for terminating parental rights, the criteria for adoptive families, and the vision of the "proper" adoptive family within its borders.

"Many different factors can serve as a barrier to permanency," the DHHS response to Clinton's adoption initiative notes, "ranging from worker decision-making, to the lack of availability of needed services for families, to court delays, to the supply of adoptive families."[2] The DHHS report concentrates on programmatic solutions, through retraining social workers, expanding family services, and speeding up court actions. Behind all of those, however, lie inherited principles for the terms under which a child can be permanently placed away from her or his biological parent. These terms are *cultural*, with the many complexities of meaning and value that the anthropological concept implies. The DHHS report, like the 1997 act itself, winds its way out of the morass of meanings by simplifying a notion of "parenthood." Although simplification may be the most expedient strategy for policy-makers, in this case the result is an obstruction of the goals of the policy.

Throughout the act and the DHHS report, adoptive parenthood is considered a distinct category. Adoptive parenthood differs from any other form of permanency, including long-term foster care and legal guardianship. The wording of the act and the report distinguishes adoptive parents from other permanent caretakers of a child, and accords adoptive parents a special niche. Adoption provides safety and security—and the "orderly" upbringing every standard manual prescribes. On the day he signed the bill that became public law, Clinton proclaimed (perhaps with tears in his eyes) that every child should know the meaning of the words "mother" and "father," and that all children have the right to "an honorable, orderly, positive upbringing."[3]

The sentiment is, of course, neither wrong nor inappropriate to American culture. The danger lies in the links between rhetorical statements and interpretations of adoption by those who participate in the transaction—whether as parent, social worker, lawyer, or mediator. Taken literally and combined with long-standing expectations, the wording of the act excludes single-parent families, individuals whose motives may be charitable and not (necessarily) familial, and adults who are drawn by the social emergency rather than by an attraction to a particular child. Put into the context of American child placement history, the act excludes many individuals already caring for the children upon whom the act focuses: kin, for instance, and, not surprisingly, foster parents.

It might be said that the 1997 Adoption and Safe Families Act constitutes a final blow against foster care. Brewing for several decades, condemnation of the foster care system and, with it, of those who foster, is evident in the act. On the day Clinton signed the bill, he designated November National Adoption Month. Adoption, he said, allows "foster children and other children to have the permanent homes they deserve, and it enables many dedicated adults to experience the jobs and rewards of parenting."[4] Foster children will be moved into adoptive homes with all deliberate speed. The implication of the act is a *move*, not a redefinition of the foster as the adoptive parent. Such a redefinition meets resistance, given the cultural emphasis on the *special* character of an adoptive parent who is, not only a facsimile but in some renderings an epitome of the "natural" parent. Redefinition meets resistance, too, in the face of the need to maintain a service class of parents until either adoption successfully opens arms for all children or other forms of permanent care receive social and political (and fiscal) support.

Ultimately, however, the act blurs the distinction between foster and adoptive parent. For one, the children who are advertised as adoptable are children with traumatic pasts, difficult childhoods, and often unpleasant character traits. They are not the cute infants that go with a picket-fence family but rather the needy children who end up in foster families. For another, the "open arms" called for will be rewarded not just with praise and gratification, but with income subsidies. Adoptive parents will be paid for taking on at risk children.

At the same time, even these provisions simultaneously accentuate the deep rifts in the American adopting population. Those who answer the call to adopt "troubled" children occupy a particular niche in the panoply of potential parents, distant from the niche occupied by the potential parents who search for babies through independent brokers or in the orphanages of countries around the world. The real problem at the moment is that the 1997 act leans on the second niche, the potential parents who meet the old criteria for a good adoptive applicant, while ignoring occupants of the first niche. In virtually every section, the act calls for a population willing to take a chance on a child. In very few sections does the act offer ways of taking a chance on the adopting population in the United States.

A model of adoption based on the stereotypical family sits heavily on a kind of adoption that stretches far from family into the realms of charity, community, and social responsibility.

I. Assuming Adoptive Parenthood

All those checks and all those hoops

Over the past two or three decades, the number of individuals who apply to be adoptive parents has risen exponentially.[5] The reasons are several: higher rates of infertility; later marriages; more frequent divorce and remarriage. Those are demographic factors. Cultural factors also enter the picture, in the form of changing understandings of family and of parenthood. The result is not only a large number but also a diverse array of adoptive parents.

Still, a conservative strain pervades the increase in adoption, evident in decisions made by participants in the transaction. When parenthood goes "public," it seems, inherited prejudices and presumptions rear their heads. The decision to adopt a child, for instance, reflects a cultural assumption that a "real" family contains more than adult members. In the early twenty-first century, too, the *kind* of adoption individuals choose carries references to as-if-begotten, even when the concept of "matching" is radically transformed. And, last but not least, the "hoops" and "checks" adoptive parents vividly and uniformly remember enforce traditional interpretations of what a parent, a parent-child relation, and a family should be.

In remembering the qualifying tests they took, adoptive parents talk of "everyone else" who "just has babies." The implication that there is a *natural* way of having children relegates adoption to another category; the comparison with nature, in an American context, suggests there is something less good about adoption, despite the growing prevalence in practice. In surveys of the population, a majority of respondents admit they consider adoption a "second best" way of having children.[6] Second best, it goes without saying, because "just having" or "giving birth" is first best. The journey to adoption is a journey away from just having. From the first phone call to an agency, through the subsequent question-and-answer phase, to being "handed" a child, adoption is a process of *petitioning* and *succeeding*. Regulations and criteria enlarge in memory because cultural images present a different model of becoming a parent.

In the early 1990s, Alan, a single father, told me the story of his efforts to adopt. His was a familiar tale of red tape, police checks, agency concern and social worker investigations. "I mean, if they put every parent, if they put every mother and father through that before they had their first child, there would be a lot less loose children in the world," he concluded. "But they actually put, they put adoptive parents—I can understand now why a lot of people say the heck with it and don't do it."[7] As his narrative suggests, the experience of applying for a child is unforgettable. And, too, the experience severely distinguishes the adoptive parent from the parents who, as he implies, "just have children."

Once the state is involved in the process of having children, public concern for the permanent security of a child comes into play. Methods for ensuring security vary over time, but always reflect the current ideal for a family, for a parent, and for the relationship between parent and child. Moreover, as I discovered in my conversations, these methods invariably frame the self-perceptions of applicants for adoptive parenthood. Predictions about a child's development, and her or his ability to thrive, are a mine field of uncertainties.[8] In the United States, since the Progressive Era, the solution has been close scrutiny of parents and of applicants for parenthood. The hope is that adult character and stability offer some insurance of a child's well-being. Behind the hope lie the tests and the trials, the hoops and the checks, through which an adult's character and stability are measured.

"Demand," then, is monitored by the ideologies and the practices of child placement in the United States. The supply side does not remain steady either, changing in quantity and in composition from decade to decade. In 1997, when Congress approved the Adoption and Safe Families Act, something new happened in American adoption history: an abundance of children were deemed candidates for adoption. Suddenly the supply changed in a remarkable manner. Not only does the act extend the meaning of "adoptable," but its provisions back this up with detailed provisions for freeing a child for adoption (or, to put it differently, for *terminating* a parent's rights). The provisions of the act are not so detailed when it comes to the demand side; the thorough description of new categories of available children is not matched by an equally thorough penetration into the categories of "adopting" individuals. The adopting parent remains a simplified if admirable figure who stands in for a complex process of applying for and choosing a child. The act does not confront the hoops and checks that exclude certain individuals and that make a person like Alan think more than twice about initiating the steps toward adoptive parenthood. Alan persisted and became the father of an eleven-year-old Hispanic orphan, a boy who could well have been in Clinton's mind when he conceptualized the child at risk and in danger.

The 1997 Adoption and Safe Families Act turns the "pool" of adoptable children into a veritable ocean. In the face of this well-publicized proclamation of the availability of adoptable children, the tightness of restrictions on adopting parents creates a loud dissonance. The result is one of the least defensible contradictions in American adoption history. Ostensibly to ensure the *safe* permanency of a placement, restrictions not only check a family but hold petitioners up to high standards. An adoptive mother expressed the same view as the single father I quoted above; her situation was quite different: she was a lawyer and married to a professional. But partly because she was not a stay-at-home Mom, the hoops were high for them. "This is very extraordinary," she said to me. "You get two horrible people who can produce a child naturally and there's no restrictions whatever on them. Then you get two people that probably are going to be great parents and they've got to subject themselves to all this, all this stuff, and it just doesn't seem right sometimes."[9]

Questions about subjects, like sex and money, that are ordinarily not discussed among strangers can especially enrage applicants for adoptive parenthood. Besides intruding into the culturally *private*, they seem to have little to do with cultural constructions of a parent. Yet, in a world of few proven tests of good parenting, inquiries like these constitute the "science" of placement.[10] A few adoptive parents I met remarked that the doctors and the fertility specialists of their pre-adoption experiences did not probe so deeply or so relentlessly into the intimate details of a relationship. Adoption "wasn't as depressing as the medical part," one adoptive father told me, "but it was, I always called it 'jumping through hoops' for somebody. You jump through the hoop and you could be rewarded by jumping through the next one."[11] Like surrender papers for the birthparent and closed birth certificates for the adoptee, in-take procedures signify the experience of adoption for adoptive parents. For all three members of the triad, "papers" represent the heavy, and the disenfranchising, arm of the state.

"Papers" also represent a history of *individualizing* adoption, characteristic of American policy and custom. For practitioners and participants adoption is "bowling alone," despite the fact that recent federal initiatives convey a message of concern for a society that is sacrificing a generation of its children.[12] There, however, lies the point: adoption focuses on individuals—children and adults—and not on the circumstances that create a supply of available children. Nor do adoption policies consider the cultural ideologies that determine the value of a person, child or adult. Consistent with this individualization, criteria for adoptive parenthood focus on personal traits, including social position. These criteria move the transaction a far distance from the communitarian impulse that pervades every section of an act pleading for safety and security for "all America's children."

Uniform standards for adoptive placement

Tests of character and "hoops" of discomforting questions pertain particularly to agency adoptions. Following the passage of adoption laws in the mid-nineteenth century, agencies became crucial to the transaction of children, gradually developing uniform criteria for good placements. The involvement of agencies distinguishes adoption in Western nations and, as well, restricts the forms a permanent transfer of parenthood can take. By the early twentieth century in the United States, the fate of children who needed homes was fully in the hands of trained professionals. A familial and domestic event fell under the supervising eye and the objective evaluations of non-family members. But the professionalization of child placement is rife with inconsistencies, inasmuch as states control agency policies, individuals within agencies make decisions on the basis of personal contacts, and participants in an adoption withdraw into the privacy of family life after the transfer is completed.

Professionalization stands in for the lack of federal laws regulating adoption and foster care practices. The growth of a profession of child welfare provided an opportunity for imposing uniform standards on a disparate set of practices and, perhaps, establishing standards for adoption that transcended particular decisions.

In 1921, the Child Welfare League of America (CWLA) came into being, an umbrella organization for child welfare agencies throughout the country. Since that time, the CWLA has monitored and assessed numerous issues that apply to children and to the family, from juvenile delinquency to adoption. Advocates for children, the CWLA has special significance in decades in which the federal government secedes from such issues. Whatever the political regime, however, the CWLA pursues a task the federal government does not consistently perform: systematizing child placement practices for all fifty states. The manuals the organization publishes are a barometer of changes in psychological theory, in the politics of welfare, and in notions of the family. The manuals also reveal the tension between cultural values, particularly the strain between the *privacy* of domestic matters and the *publicity* of children at risk and in trouble.

Every decade or so, the CWLA issues new or updated manuals on adoption and foster care. These small, readable booklets outline contemporaneous standards for gauging the "best interests of children" and for dealing appropriately with relevant adults. Criteria for good families and enduring parent-child relationships recognize the case-by-case basis of all social work practice. At the same time, the criteria create a picture of the American family that reflects mainstream, white, and middle-class values. Diffused through state agencies, CWLA criteria narrow the funnel for acceptable adopting parents considerably.

The criteria for an adoptive parent have changed little over the past seventy-five years. An adoption social worker can measure an applicant against the following list: "total personality functioning, emotional maturity, quality of marital relationship, feeling about children, feeling about childlessness and readiness to adopt, and motivation." After the list come paragraphs that elaborate each of the indicators. Under "emotional maturity," for instance, the manual explains: "flexibility and ability to change in relation to the needs of others; a capacity for relationships; self-respect; an ability to cope with problems, disappointments and frustrations."[13] A bit abstract and clearly idealistic, such a guideline does little to ease the encounter between a potential parent and a careful social worker.

The CWLA *Standards for Adoption Service* also outlines appropriate motives for adopting. A social worker is advised to judge motivation in the following way: "The desire to adopt should be based on emotionally healthy needs, such as the desire to have a more nearly complete life, to accept parental responsibility, to help children, to extend themselves to another child, to contribute to the development of another human being, to love and be loved."[14] Like the criteria, the motivations assume personal capacities of a special sort; love comes only at the end of the list. Like the criteria, too, the outline of motivations creates an exclusive applicant pool. Echo of the fairy-tale adoptive family presented in the media, the adoptive family that emerges from CWLA literature holds no surprises: stable, steady, and able to provide a child with "advantages," an acceptable adoptive parent shows no unusual traits and makes no outlandish requests. The mold is strong, and presumed to be a reliable measure for a child's security; the mold persists, despite demographic changes in the population that adopts through agencies and despite the CWLA's efforts to open the door to a wider range of adoptive applicants.

The standards imposed by individual agencies can be even more stringent, especially in the face of a shortage of desirable babies. Here and there, agencies treat adoptive parenthood as a privilege to be attained by a few. "Dr. Lorna Forbes, psychiatric consultant to the Los Angeles Department of Adoptions, has suggested eight adoptive-parent characteristics important to a successful adoptive placement. They are ability to work with an agency, to express tenderness, to arbitrate, to be tolerant, to live nonisolated lives, to be resilient, to have a healthy ego that enables them to defer gratification, and a life style reciprocal to that of the child to be placed. The ideal adoptive family is therefore one that is healthy, outgoing, tender, tolerant, flexible, resilient, cooperative and social." This is one agency's adaptation of the CWLA instructions and it is, as the author of an article noted, a "heady combination."[15] The Los Angeles prescription *is* heady, and it exemplifies a transformation of the adoptive parent from "kindly neighbor" into "above-average person."

The shift is not new. State intervention in parent-child relations tends to produce a tightening of standards for the *good* parent; this is true in custody cases, in placement cases, in any cases in which an official judges the best interests of a child. At the same time as criteria came into being, studies of adoptive families presented an alternative view. Sophie van Senden Theis, in her pioneering study, argued that adoptive parents were just like everyone else, not particularly outstanding or unusual. Thirty years later, in the 1950s, two scholars of adoption reached the same conclusion: adoptive parents are the *kindly neighbors* in any town.[16] And in 1983, a book on "new patterns of adoptive relationships" asked: "What are the common features of today's adoptive parents?" and answered: "They are not greatly distinguishable from most other American parents."[17] And in the 1990s, the picture of "average folks" persists, warring with the criteria agencies continue to set.

Perhaps there is a resolution to the discrepancy. Criteria select parents, but once the child is placed and living in the household, parents do become "ordinary," with nothing special to distinguish them from neighbors. Once the hoops are jumped, a parent settles into the regular tasks of raising a child. Adoptive parents are especially indistinguishable from everyone else when the child who is placed resembles them in features and is of the right age to be their biological child.[18] It is also possible that passing the tests gives adoptive parents the confidence to be "ordinary" parents. Or, perhaps, only individuals who know they can pass the tests apply to an agency in the first place.

But agencies are not the only route to adopting in the United States. A large number of individuals in the 1990s and in the early years of the new century by-pass agencies altogether.

Independent adoptions: leaving the agency behind

"Thousands of Americans over 40 do adopt healthy white infants every year through private channels, said Ms. Stocker, by hiring a lawyer to do the search or placing their own classified ads in small-town newspapers. ('Loving Christian couple wants to make a home for your special baby: large white house, cat, big sister. Call 1-800 ...')." Even in their big white house, *The New York Times* op-ed piece suggests the Clintons would not be accepted by an adoption agency in the United States. They are, for one, too old, and for another, too busy. "Inquiring Americans want to know: how much time off would the First Father take?"[19] Now that Hillary Clinton is senator from New York, she is a working mother—a further disqualification.

Had Bill and Hillary pursued the plan of adopting, they could have left agencies behind. More and more individuals in the United States turn elsewhere in the quest to adopt a child; approximately 40 percent of all adoptions now are handled outside of agencies.[20] Whether this is because applicants are disqualified by agency criteria or decide they want something different from what an agency offers, many individuals look for alternative modes of adopting. Some people simply find agency procedures too "snoopy" and intrusive. Others know they will be disqualified by marital status, sexual preference, social position, or material resources. Still others are aware that in entering an agency, they are entering a competition with other petitioners for a child; they refuse to "race" for a child. The race is even tighter for individuals who have specific demands, for instance, for a healthy white infant, sometimes referred to as *dwi's:* "domestic white infants."

Overall, and most significantly, adopting without an agency reflects a long-standing cultural presumption that child-having should be individual and private, and a matter of free choice.[21]

Adopting independently is not new in the history of adoption. For centuries, in the West as in virtually every other part of the globe, individuals have simply taken children in, caring for them permanently and assuming all the rights and obligations of a parent. In the United States, laws of adoption changed that, and changed it radically. Informal arrangements fell into the category of illegal or of immoral; legal adoption took its place as the "right" way of taking in a child, a view that persists into the 1997 Adoption and Safe Families Act. Transfers of a child that occur outside an agency, and that often do not go to court, intrigue and alarm observers, evoking the vision of an illicit trade in children and of nefarious brokers of babies. Reasons for the alarm are clear. The situation is intriguing exactly because free choice is an ideal in American interpretations of becoming a parent.

The line between "choosing" a child and entering a market in children can be thin. In a conversation with me, an adoptee pictured his parents walking up and down the "aisles," looking for a baby that suited them particularly well. He had grown up with the story of a chosen child, a popular way in which parents in the 1950s and 1960s presented adoption for an adopted child. As his picture conveys, however, the negative connotations of a market can take precedence over the positive connotations of being wanted, desirable, and appealing. The metaphor of a market and of *preferences* for particular items lurks at the sidelines of discussions of adoption, and becomes an effective strategy for condemning adoptions that do not go through agencies. To breathe a word of selling and buying babies is enough, in American culture at any period, to damn the transaction in parenthood. While independent adoptions especially fall prey to the metaphorical construct, references to a market suggest that adoption borders on the exchange of children in the American imagination, uncomfortably. Add to the dread of a market in children the notion that adoption responds to crisis—the crisis of infertility or of high rates of unplanned pregnancy or, now, of huge numbers of at-risk children—and the ground is set for both alarm and surveillance.

In 1985, the Senate Sub-Committee on Security and Terrorism put independent adoption on the agenda.[22] One congressman explained why: "Many [non-agency] adoptions involve people who prey on the emotions and frustrations of couples longing for children and on confused and distraught birthmothers. Those unscrupulous people perpetuate their fraud with complete disregard for the welfare of the subject of the adoptive efforts—the children."[23] Placement on the agenda of this sub-committee shows that, despite a rhetoric focusing on the feelings of individuals, independent adoption is perceived as posing a far greater threat than fraud and exploitation. Portraying independent adoption as a national security risk suggests the arrangement endangers the institutional structures of American society. In the perspective presented at the hearings, independent adoptions undermine the authority of child welfare agencies and, in addition, precipitate the end of the American family. "Adoption is one of the most charitable and loving acts in our Nation. With public and private agencies acting as a catalyst, adoption unites prospective parents and adoptable children into a permanent family unit."[24]

The congressional hearings came on top of a generally expressed alarm at the rising number of non-agency adoptions in the United States.[25] These arrangements seemed to policy-makers, to professionals, and to the press to reek of a blatant commercializing of adoption in the United States. The attribution took the onus off commercialization inside agencies. "The review of state laws and regulations revealed disturbing facts regarding adoptions for profit and other legally questionable activities in the area of independent adoptions," wrote three scholars of adoption in the late 1970s.[26] The study reported a widespread perception on the part of social workers that in independent adoptions money not best interests determined the placement of a baby. "Ten percent [of those interviewed] believed that nearly all independent adoption activity in their area could be classified as 'for profit.' Over half thought that organized rings specializing in these activities were in operation."[27] Ten years after the sub-committee hearings on security and terrorism, in the mid-1990s, alarms intensified. Not only had the number of independent adoptions continued to rise, constituting almost half of all adoptions, but also stories of fraud, exploitation, and baby-brokers dominated newspaper headlines.[28] Media stories and professional evaluations expose a fact of American adoption: depicted in a language of love and of high moral standards, adoption has always been regulated by supply and demand and by the ideal of a "desirable" adoptive child. In agencies, the differential that allows some people to attain the ideal is veiled; outside of agencies, the differentials are hard to hide.

Had the Clintons pursued the plan of adoption, they would have found several routes to a "good baby" or a child of their choosing. Like other applicants who are disqualified by agencies on the basis of criteria that can seem arbitrary and unrelated to parental traits, the Clintons might well have turned to a lawyer or mediator and adopted *independently*. They might then have chosen a baby who fit perfectly into their family. Independent adoptions in the United States are likely to maintain the fairy-tale picture of adoption: non-agency adoptions have risen in number at least partly because that is a way in which applicants for adoptive parenthood can find a child who will be as-if-begotten. One study of independent adoption concludes: "89% of the children were placed before they were 2 weeks old and almost all (95%) were placed before the age of 3 months."[29] Ironically, then, the very arrangement that is vilified as a threat to security and to family values as often as not upholds the traditional parameters of adoption in American society.

Adoptive parents who adopt independently are probably not the parents the 1997 Adoption and Safe Families Act requires. Adoptive parents who adopt independently are in the majority middle class, white, and mainstream, or at least able to afford the high costs of adopting outside an agency these days. The 1997 act addresses an adopting population that is far more split along class and race lines than the wording acknowledges.

"Clearly, the primary factor encouraging prospective adoptive couples to seek children independently is the shortage of white, healthy infants available through agencies."[30] This was

1978, and the "shortage" has intensified in the ensuing decades. "Before 1973, the year that abortion was legalized, about 9 percent of births to unmarried women in the United States resulted in adoptions. By 1981 that percentage dropped to 4 percent, and by 1988 to 2.3 percent."[31] The shortage is more severe in some categories than others: at the end of the 1990s, only 2 percent of white parents with unwanted pregnancies relinquished a child.[32]

Competition for dwi's outside of agencies brings the monetary factors that are historically part of American adoption practice into the open. "If you have 40 white couples chasing every white newborn, you don't need a lesson in economics," William Pierce, head of the National Council for Adoption, told a reporter.[33] The article in *The New York Times* which quoted Pierce carried the banner headline: "Market Puts Price Tags on the Priceless." As Pierce suggests, where there is a shortage, the price goes up. "Many couples in search of a child are already depleted, emotionally and financially, by drawn-out fertility treatments. Still, they will pay $15,000 to $20,000 on average, even if they have to mortgage their futures, to find their babies. Some will spend much more before the day they appear in court to take legal custody of their children. And a few, people who have the money for intermediaries to do the work, pay up to $100,000 to bring home a newborn."[34]

According to its critics, independent adoption "commodifies" children and transforms the culturally "priceless" into the carefully priced. An adoption advocate criticized the potential parents who enter the market for a child: "there are people who have the basic philosophy that the more I pay for something, the better it will be."[35]

As in any other market, consumers balance their demands against the costs. And if those with material resources can find a baby who will be "just like one's own," those who cannot afford the desirable dwi reconsider the terms of adopting and, as well, the meaning of family and of kinship. If you are priced out of the white newborn market, you can choose another sort of adoption. With its sensitivity to supply and demand, and to capacity to pay, independent adoption further splits the adopting community. So there are those who search—and wait—for healthy white infants, sometimes as long as seven years.[36] Other potential parents locate brokers in their communities, or across state lines, and in the process may find themselves considering another kind of child, a non-infant or a child of another race. Finally, there is the ballooning group of parents who adopt outside the borders of the United States. Their choices of children not only provide a new chart of *desirable* traits but also add one more turn to the shift in interpretations of family endemic to modern adoption.

The Gundersons were disqualified by local agencies because, Meg told me, they were "too old." They were unwilling to spend the time and money involved in adopting internationally. In addition, they had learned of an independent broker in their area who was successfully placing children in adoptive homes. They decided to adopt through "Mrs. S.," an elderly woman who had spent nearly a quarter of a century transferring babies from unwed mothers to stable families. Angry at the agencies, and eager to have a family sooner rather than later, Meg and Todd Gunderson were overjoyed to discover how quickly Mrs. Simpson's adoptions could be expedited. Mrs. Simpson worked with a local home for unwed mothers; she spent time with the "girls" there, encouraging them to place their babies and to move on with their lives. (Those who adopted through Mrs. S. were asked to teach the girls skills, like reading and writing.) Many of the unwed mothers were African-American, and like other Mrs. S. families I met, the Gundersons adopted two mixed-race children. "Our parents were against the adoption," Meg remembered, "but as soon as they saw the children, they melted."

Those who knew Mrs. S. portrayed her as a grandmotherly type—"her stockings rolled around her knees," one mother told me. She was concerned and involved, and determined to place every child in a permanent home. Operating entirely on a face to face basis, Mrs. Simpson accomplished a goal set by the 1997 Adoption and Safe Families Act. Through her, children acquired a stable home, learned the meanings of "mother" and "father," and experienced the conditions for "thriving." Mrs. Simpson did not balk at racial differences and consequently managed the problem of children officials considered "special needs" because they were not Caucasian. From her point of view, a secure family was better than no family.

There were costs to her adoptions, too. The parents she accepted had to oppose abortion, had to prove they were regular churchgoers, and had to be married. But everyone I interviewed who had a "Simpson baby" expressed satisfaction.[37] Mrs. Simpson effectively created an adoption community, whose participants shared an understanding of adopting and of family composition.

Her methods and means came in for a great deal of criticism from outsiders to that community. Some said she "forced" vulnerable birthmothers to relinquish their babies. Others said she placed babies without providing enough information to the adopting parents. Still others expressed vague discomforts with the idiosyncratic bases ("whims," they told me) upon which she made her decisions. Nothing she did was illegal, and adoptive parents had to have a home study by a social worker before they took the case to court.

Mrs. Simpson is one of hundreds of thousands of "mediators" in non-agency adoptions. Condemnation of her methods suggests the source of a perceived danger in non-agency adoption and the appeal of an arrangement that is, after all, *independent.* The word itself is illuminating: the positive connotation of freedom of choice has a close twin in the negative connotation of lack of supervision. Independent adoption, more dramatically than agency adoption, exposes a persistent dilemma in American placement policy: having a child is supposed be "one's own" decision, while the social delegation of parenthood is supposed to be monitored by outside experts. (For her critics, Mrs. S.'s experience did not count as expertise). Independent adoptions also expose the willingness of parents to "take in" children of diverse backgrounds and to ignore the convention that matching child to parent is a guarantee of enduring solidarity. Independent adoptions ultimately demonstrate that parental choice may be the best predictor of a child's safety and security.

So do international adoptions, an increasingly large segment of North American adoption practice these days.

Going abroad

In 1993, Elizabeth Bartholet published a book called *Family Bonds: Adoption and the Politics of Parenting*. In it, she describes the process of adopting two boys from Peru. The description is an unveiled critique of North American adoption practices that, according to Bartholet, uphold a long history of racism. Her point opposes that of the NABSW and, based on her experience in Latin America, she argues for a complete acceptance of transracial adoption. *Family Bonds* avoids the issue of international politics (rich nations and poor nations)[38] and instead attacks policies whose racial ideologies leave thousands of children in the world homeless. Support for international adoption, in which parents often do not match the children they adopt, the book suggests opens the boundaries of adoption altogether. "Foreign adoption can help create a climate that is more sympathetic to wide-ranging forms of support for children everywhere."[39]

Along with its argument for a breakdown in racism at home and of barriers to adoption abroad, *Family Bonds* also reveals the persistence of conventions about making a family in the United States. Matching disappears, but as-if-begotten creeps back in. Phrases like "falling in love," the "bonds" in her title, and mention of the ease with which the boys "belonged" evoke one dimension of the as-if-begotten in American adoption policy. The boys, Bartholet writes, were "so clearly the children meant for me."[40] In her case, as in others, a humanitarian goal shapes the decision to go abroad but proof of the solidity of the relationship lies in personal feelings of attachment. Charitable motives succeed, *Family Bonds* shows, when they give way to parental love.

International adoptions have risen phenomenally in the past three decades. The number grew from 7,000 in 1990 to nearly 17,000 in 1999.[41] The countries from which these children come, as well as the ages at which they are adopted, uncover the persistence of "as if" when individuals consider the form an adoptive family will take. A categorization of nations develops based on the kind of children they have to offer. As one book notes, China offers "children 0 through 2," while Korea offers "children 0 through school age" (though "0" must be rare).[42] Very young children are "as-if-begotten" inasmuch as they can be molded in the image of the adopting parents. If not exactly a blank slate, a young child is thought to carry little of the past and few of the behavioral traits time accords an individual. The child, then, is potentially "just like" the adopting parent or parents.

International adoption upholds as-if-begotten in another way as well. Americans adopt from a short list of countries, and the choices stem from notions of parenthood as much as from diplomatic or humanitarian considerations. In 1999, the primary "sending countries" were "Russia [4,348 children], China [4,101], Korea [2,008] and Guatemala [1,002]."[43] The smallest number of children comes from African countries.[44] The rise in numbers of Russian children is astonishing: from 324 in 1992 to nearly 5000 a short eight years later.[45] Given that a majority of those who adopt abroad are white, the fact that Russia supplies an increasing number of children suggests that race (and color) plays a continuing part in individual decisions about family.

International adoption may distance altruistic or humanitarian adoption from the requirements of an act that addresses a domestic crisis. To the extent that international adoption replicates and reinforces traditional notions of the family, it veers from the adoption proposed in the Adoption and Safe Families Act. A child that can be raised in one's image and that may in appearance be similar to the adoptive parents falls into a quite different category from the children who need adoption within the borders of the United States. Unlike the independent adoption the Gundersons undertook with Mrs. Simpson, international adoptions hive away from the public problem of at-risk or special needs children.

The debate over good and bad adoptions that once focused on agency and non-agency methods now focuses on international versus domestic adoptions. The newer debate is as heated as the older, and like the older indicates how closely adoptive parenthood is tied to definitions of community and to national interests. A series of letters to *The New York Times* expose the passion and the value attached to the choice of a way of adopting. An adoptive mother wrote: "Nurturing a child is among the most selfless of activities; furthermore, adopting an infant does not increase the world's population." The humanitarian reasons cited in one letter appear on the same page as a reference to the "right" to choose one's family. "Where does Deborah R. Wells (letter, Aug. 26) get the right to tell couples who are adopting Chinese babies that they should be choosing American black or hispanic infants instead?" The letter continues: "Should they have been admonished to select their marriage partners on racial or ethnic grounds? It is time that the piety police stop telling others how to behave." [46]

International adoptions, then, cast a bright light on aspects of North American adoption that previously remained in the shadows. Articulated reasons for adopting abroad expose the uneasy link between adopting to help or rescue a child and adopting to have a child who will blend into the family as if he had always been there. The outcomes of international adoptions, too, expose the parameters around family still subscribed to in many pockets of the American population: an emphasis on inherent likeness (particularly race) or on resemblances that can easily be cultivated. In deconstructing the connection between cultural identity and a child's well-being, however, proponents of international adoption also offer a perspective on transracial adopting at home. As a woman who adopted a Romanian orphan told a *Time Magazine* reporter: "There is no culture or pride in orphanages, only a brute form of survival." [47] This says that "cultural politics" should be ignored when a child's life is at stake.

Still, race on the one hand and income on the other hand influence independent adoptions. These newcomers in the adoption field, drawing publicity, deflect attention from the role of race and income in most American adoptions. The costs of adopting are high, regardless of the route a person chooses. The scale of value, however, is more obvious in independent and international adoptions, where it intertwines directly with other measures of value, like race and national origin. In 1998, for instance, an agency outside of Philadelphia estimated a cost of approximately $18,000 for adopting a child from China, and $22,000 for a Vietnamese child. Nationwide, the average cost for a Chinese child is

$12,000 and for a Russian child slightly more, $14,000.[48] A child from Ethiopia costs on average $5,000.[49]

The open exposure of differential costs has the side benefit of allowing customers to calculate exactly what they can afford in adopting. The benefit is dual: opening the "pool" of adoptive parents and overcoming the obstacles that the strict criteria established by agencies impose on domestic adoptions. "As a single, nonrich white woman, I wanted to adopt a healthy infant of any race," wrote the "proud parent of a wonderful Asian Indian daughter" who had been rejected by an agency. She turned outside the United States: "It soon became clear that healthy infants in this country are mainly available through private adoptions, a murky legal area."[50] Like Alan, she assumed parenthood despite the checks and hoops of agencies, and despite common cultural conceptualizations of a "fit" parent. Like Alan, too, this "proud parent" occupies a place in the vanguard of adopting adults, persons who do not accept a disqualification from parenthood on the basis of their marital status, their sexual preference, or their level of income. And while the desire to have a child may be culturally constructed (and even enforced), the claim of diversity in being a parent is equally powerful. More and more participants in American adoptive kinship fall off the pages of manuals for adoptive practice, pages that are themselves undergoing rapid revision to reflect the petitioners for children, the implicit message in federal acts, and the trend in so-called natural families throughout the United States. Participants in adoptive kinship will soon again be *just like* everyone else, but that is because "everyone else" has swept well beyond the popular images of the 1950s and 1960s.

Agencies adjust the "costs" if not the criteria

The recent burgeoning of independent adoption has compelled agencies to reconsider their own strategies for creating new adoptive families. One result is that agencies increasingly refine their fees in a straightforward supply and demand calculation that would have been anathema just ten years ago. In the twenty-first century, agencies are no longer on the fringes of a competitive market but right in the fray; advertising and discriminating among products are as much a part of agency adoption as of independent arrangements. The Edna Gladney Home, one of America's most prominent and elite agencies, now "has a lower-cost program for African-American and biracial children. 'Unfortunately, we had to create a separate program because adoptive parents were simply not coming forward,' Ms. Smith said. Under that program, the agency charges $8000" for an African-American adoption, and $50,000 for the adoption of a white infant.[51]

"Gray market" adoption customarily refers to adoptions outside of agencies, in which money is spent on services (to a broker) and not on buying a baby. "Gray" refers to the middle position between the "white" of arrangements in which the fee is unmistakably for professional services and the "black" of an illicit market in baby-selling. Growing demand for adoptable babies, combined with exclusion from agencies, opens the door to those who can respond to the demand, sometimes unscrupulously and exploitatively but sometimes not. The American public hears of the scandals, the individuals who receive payments from two couples for one baby and the individuals who "extract" babies from poor women at home or abroad.

In 1999, two Long Island housewives discovered the hungry demand for babies among potential adopters. They also discovered the possibility of bringing babies from Mexico to New York, expediently and without much legal obstruction. But the transaction did not remain closeted, and a *New York Times* reporter nosed out the whole story. Relishing the "housewife" designation, the paper played on the fears, the alarms, and the needs and desires that surround the social construction of parent-child relationships in American culture. The several articles also played on the inequities of wealth in adoption, not just between Long Island adopting parents and Mexican birthparents, but also between those who would adopt legally and those who would adopt illegally. The dichotomy is not self-evident. Breaking the laws of Mexico and of the United States is one thing, but, as the Edna Gladney Home illustrates, accepting differential abilities to pay into adoption practice is another. The Long Island housewives were arrested. "Federal prosecutors today accused two Long Island women and a prominent lawyer near the Arizona-Mexico border of running a baby-smuggling ring in which at least 17 Mexican infants were illegally sold to unwitting adoptive parents in the New York area."[52]

Selling babies is not acceptable in American culture. But actions that evoke a market are: for instance, acknowledging the differential "worth" of different kinds of children, advertising services and capacities, and adjusting fees to balance the ratio of supply and demand. The issue of independent adoption focuses a debate that is neither new nor easily resolvable. Independent adoption may be outlawed inasmuch as the arrangement is perceived to allow the marketing of babies for profit; alternatively, independent adoption may be closely regulated, by state laws or by federal guidelines. At the moment, policy-makers, professionals, and participants in adoption stand in a gray area between acknowledging the benefits of market principles and recognizing the necessities of close regulation when children are the subjects. As long as placement agencies do not respond to *all* clients, independent adoptions serve the best interests of children as well as of adults. As long as choice remains central to understandings of having a child, independent adoptions satisfy a cultural premise about kinship and family. Even critics of independent adoption who argue that accredited agencies should supervise all transactions in children cannot avoid the significance of laws of supply and demand, or the need to adjust availability to desire, or the competition that makes advertising a crucial step toward increasing the number of adoptions. Ads for children and for parents are now a prominent part of agency and non-agency adoptions in every state, regardless of the specifics of the laws of adoption.

II. Modern Modes of Placing Children

"Happy and adorable": advertising in American adoption

"The first commandment for couples wanting to adopt babies is: Put yourselves across. And they do, in spunky performances on videotapes, in lush scrapbooks and in professional portraiture smiling on the Internet."[53] The same commandment applies to those who have children to place: put *them* across, make their virtues and appeal known in all possible ways. The Internet has enormously expanded the role of advertising in adoption, but the "putting across" phenomenon has been part of North American adoption for at least half a century. Available children have to appear "adoptable" to individuals considering adoptive parenthood; applicants for adoptive parenthood, in turn, have to sell themselves to birthparents, mediators, social workers, and lawyers. The line between an advertisement and a favorable presentation is as fine as the line between "secrecy" and "privacy" in adoption practice.

Self-presentations and presentations of a child by an (interested) adult display the characteristics considered ideal at any particular time. These ads are a map to the *good* qualities in a parent and a child. Pleas for parents for a child, or a child for a couple echo the standards the CWLA outlines in its manuals. In addition, ads offer subtle plays on the meaning of "matching," both the importance of the concept for representing enduring attachment and the stretch of the concept in view of changes in the adoptable and the (potential) adopting population. With the pressure of persuasion, ads for children and for parents expose the lineaments of American placement practice often hidden in official texts and rules. The ads also reveal how a diversity of children and parents may be molded into one image.

Individuals interested in adopting present themselves as "kindly neighbors," with added touches that might give them an edge on other individuals looking for a child to adopt. The backyard might be bigger, the hobbies more lavish, and the careers more conventionally successful. But it is a careful portrayal, usually within the boundaries of the storybook image. These are the ads that address birthparents and whose goal is usually the adoption of a healthy white infant. These ads, then, represent one part of the American adopting population; they do not suggest the wider array of family-making. Advertisements of available children, too, borrow the cliches of American culture, the "happy and adorable" that transform a child into a *desirable* child. Changes in American adoption come out in these ads: the composite of traits that accompanies the clichés shows the expansion of an available "supply" from the infant of earlier decades to the "special needs" children of the late decades of the century. Ads appeal to birthparents looking for a good placement, to adoptive parents eager for a child of "one's own," and to people like Emily and Tom who, as Emily put it to me, "have so much, we can do more."

Ads are not ordinarily the most honest communications in the world. What about the use of advertisements to encourage and to facilitate adoptions? Emily and Tom objected to the photo albums they saw, with pictures of children that disguised their behavioral problems and that revealed nothing about a checkered past. It is in the nature of these "announcements" to hide facts and to smooth out problems. In a context in which opening adoption and disclosing information is at the forefront of debate, the increased use of advertisements by agencies, by participants in adoption, by lawyers, and by brokers is an interesting twist. So far the debate about disclosure focuses on the stage of adoption in which an arrangement is underway, not on the *before* of that stage. The prevalence of advertising in American adoption practice deepens the complexities of an assessment of secrecy in transactions in parenthood.

The Internet has intensified the use of advertising beyond measure. From campaigns organized by an agency or by an adoption advocacy group to chat rooms, exchange of information seems to be abundant. But how "open" are either the organized campaigns or the deceptively casual chat rooms? The urgency Tom and Emily saw influences virtually everything on the Internet. Electronic conversations, like the talk I heard at CUB and at ASG meetings, reveal how tangled and ambiguous "disclosure" really is. The goal determines the definition of facts and the script borrowed from cultural ideals of parenthood and kinship determines how facts are presented. Advertisements in American adoption reveal how closed the transaction still is; a resistance to full disclosure is *more* not less apparent in these texts and photos.

The "personals" of American adoption, exchanges on the Internet, in other media, and on telephone poles and bus stop signs hone to culturally correct views of a parent-child relationship. [54] One element, however, separates these presentations from the outlines in a manual or the policies of an agency: the greater emphasis on feelings and, especially, on love.

CWLA manuals warn social workers against applicants who promise *love* as the sole source of security and permanency for a child. Intake interviews probe beyond feelings, to establish the stability of an applicant. Ads on the Internet dwell more openly on love and on the emotional dimensions of being a parent. But, sharing a culture with those who use agencies, ads placed by potential adopters claim "love *and* financial security."

Examples of ads placed by potential adoptive parents are legion. In an era of baby shortage and of technological facility, ads by individuals wanting to adopt pop up on the computer screen readily. "We are Molly and Frank, and celebrate ten years of a very loving and secure marriage," reads one such ad, chosen at random. "We are each others [sic] best friend and share a wonderful and full life together. Our mutual desire has always been to have children as part of our life and our special family traditions. However, infertility prevents us from pregnancy. Therefore, we want our children to come to us through adoption. The same care that has gone into our marriage will go into providing a warm and loving environment for our child."

The description includes socioeconomic data. "Frank is a pediatrician in a group practice. He worked very hard throughout his college years and graduated in the top ten percent of his class." And, finally, next to a photograph of a substantial suburban house: "Our back yard with a grass lawn, a swimming pool, and plenty of open space, is a wonderful area for our children to play and grow."[55] The personality traits, hobbies, and pets Frank and Molly write about in their narrative cover the right bases without, as it were, opening the whole file. Nothing in the ad is identifying; nothing, really, is personal. Rather, this is an ad that presents the fairy-tale figures of adoptive parents in American culture. These are the people described in the CWLA manuals, and well beyond the "ordinary folk" Sophie van Senden Theis found in her surveys.

Like anyone else who places a notice on the Internet, Frank and Molly have a goal in mind. Inasmuch as they need to win the approval of a person contemplating a placement for her child, why not draw on the traits that adoption literature and the culture at large uphold? Whether the ad is two printed pages long, with photographs—like Frank and Molly's—or brief and to the point, the elements are similar. "Make someone you love happy. Kind caring couple, $$ secure, will give your baby a life filled with love, security and warmth. Our entire family waits with open arms."[56]

Generalizations and storybook figures protect the confidentiality of individuals. Adoptive parents offer themselves as "types," fit parents in a standardized model. The parent contemplating relinquishment surfs the net, choosing among versions of a similar stamp. There are exceptions, too, in ads placed by individuals who, unlike Frank and Molly, would be excluded by agency criteria: gay couples, single parents, older individuals. Presenting themselves as "alternatives" to the white-bread image of family, these individuals too mold information to conventions in order to attract a favorable response.

"Seeking biracial baby! Interracial couple seeking biracial baby."[57]

Members of adoption reform groups occasionally claim that American adoption is built on *lies*. Advertisements seem a prime field for supporting that accusation. Yet, like other customs, this new one has to be regarded in the context of the principles that guide adoption in American culture. As the social worker told Tom and Emily when they complained about deception, revealing everything would have "hampered" the placement of the two girls. From this perspective, non-truth in advertising serves the best interests of the children, and may lead to an increase in adoptive placements. Advertisements reflect a second principle of American adoption, the importance of *choice* when an individual contemplates her or his destiny as a parent. With the Internet, and acceptance of billboards for babies, individuals who contemplate an adoptive arrangement face the same dilemma social workers have faced: will too many facts spoil the transaction?

It is a new market, with no rules and much desire. The possibility of cheating, of exploitation, and of buying and selling children expands exponentially with the Internet. Brokers take money from more than one potential adoptive parent, promising the same baby to all of them.[58] Birthparents, too, play the field, making promises to different interested parties. Adoptive parents offer themselves as the beautiful and happily married couple. The end of a number of sad stories is an effort at control, either in a grass-roots form—*watch out* warnings in a chat room—or through advocacy groups that publish lists of "bad" participants. In a situation in which state laws range widely, however, and freedom of expression is valued, control over the terms of an exchange remains imperfect.

The Internet provides the opportunity for protection as well as for fraud on the part of individuals. "Watch this page for a listing, by first name and state, of birthmothers with whom we have had negative experiences, or from whom we have received complaints from adoptive parents, attorneys, facilitators, agencies, and/or others."[59] Various kinds of registries appear on the Internet to supervise transactions in parenthood. "There are many different search options for finding the adoptive parents who are right for you," posts the *Adoptive Parent Registry,* addressing birthparents. "New adoptive parents are listed regularly [with the Registry], so we suggest you search often. Each of the adoptive parents has something unique to offer. We hope you will take the time to 'get to know' all of them."[60]

In speeches before he signed the Adoption and Safe Families Act, former President Clinton referred to the "open arms" of America's population. Ads on the Internet display the possessors of the "welcoming hearts" he anticipated in urging a doubling of adoption by 2002. The ads on the Internet, and elsewhere, also expose a discrepancy Clinton did not delineate. Frank and Molly are eager to adopt and apparently ready to love a child; the child they want does not resemble the children who prompt concern on a federal level. As they present themselves, Frank and Molly have the option of choosing a child they want, not a child who is in need of their stability and security. Other potential parents, not necessarily voices on the Internet or clients at an agency, regard the field of "adoptable" children differently. They may constitute the consumer group—the open arms—the 1997 act requires.

In the end, given the diversity of consumers, the marketing of children remains crucial. Antithetical to American cultural views of the person, "selling" a child in terms of his or her *needs* is not a new phenomenon in American placement history. Over the course of the 1990s and into the new century, advertising of children is taking a lead in American adoption practice, as agencies and others recognize the importance of supply and demand in serving the "best interests of the children."

New possibilities for placing children, permanently

How is it possible to talk of advertising, marketing, even "offering" children in a society in which the buying and selling of a human being has been anathema for over a hundred years? The paradox reveals a good deal about American child placement practice, especially the side that involves the group of children who are not conventionally considered adoptable. The children who *need* placement are and always have been different in kind from the children designated desirable in agencies and by clients of agencies, as well as in the independent arrangements of recent years.

Child placement policies succumb to a law of supply and demand, even when that is not articulated. The persons who implement policy must assess the willingness of individuals to take available children and the availability of children for those who want to adopt. The wheel turned at the end of the twentieth century from searching for babies for parents, to searching for parents for children, many of them no longer babies at all. Yet, turn as the wheel might, the process of creating "consumers" gets caught between cultural ideals of the family and a supply that challenges these ideals. The problems are compounded by a national welfare policy that favors family placement above all other modes of caring for at risk and vulnerable children. Tolerance for *advertising* children in a culture that outlaws the purchase of a person arises from the perceived effectiveness of such techniques for altering demand and thus affecting the distribution of supply.

The advertising of children began as if it were not that at all. Pictures displayed in the corridors of a social service agency, or photographs of children and their new families in the rooms of private agencies, did not appear to be ads. But they certainly showed both the "supply" of children and the satisfactions of adopting. Cute babies attract the potential parents an agency needs. When the supply changed, new methods were needed. As early as 1979, an analyst for the Urban Institute in Washington, D.C. confronted the problem of a growing number of "hard to place" children. She suggested direct advertising. Pictures and "TV presentations of children," the bold policy analyst argued, would facilitate the permanent placement of "difficult" children.[61]

Gradually, private and public agencies took the message to heart. A cynic might say agencies had to attract customers in order to distribute a new supply of children. A more generous interpretation is that the need to place "difficult" children requires new methods of presentation—in the best interests of those children. Both views are true.

Media presentations at first appeared in limited areas, re-creating the community of earlier (and non-western) adoption. Local newspapers carried photographs of an available child above a column describing her personality, church newsletters brought children to the attention of parishioners, and agencies distributed information to people already on their mailing lists. The emphasis on community, on those who know each other, moved the ads for available children out of the realm of commerce and into the realm of gift; the locus and the style of the presentations suggest that taking a child is an act of generosity not of consumerism. The reminder is crucial, especially as techniques for displaying children expand and diffuse, so that concepts of community no longer exclude the market element.

As the crisis of at-risk and endangered children intensified, so too did efforts to broadcast these children to wider audiences. In the late 1980s, the National Adoption Exchange, located in Philadelphia, sent Senator John Heinz an announcement of current activities. "Television, newspapers and magazine features, public service announcements, and print advertisements are used to maximize awareness and visibility of waiting children and to increase the pool of prospective parents."[62] A strong advocate of adoption, Heinz saw nothing objectionable in using television and print advertisements to get children out into the open.

By the beginning of the 1990s, strategies for presenting "waiting children" were themselves publicized. Advertising children was no longer a hidden aspect of mainstream adoption services, but had come out of the closet as an effective technique for increasing placements. A newsletter for adoptive parents reported: "The Coalition of Adoption Services in Erie County (Buffalo) sponsored an open house, ads in church bulletins, and showings of videos of waiting children. A Christmas tree was decorated with stars representing waiting kids, with a booklet of information about each one." In South Dakota, "balloons representing waiting children were launched" and a local television station kept its phone lines open all night for callers.[63]

By 1997, when in the Adoption and Safe Families Act the Clinton administration offered rewards for increased adoptions, states had the means of advertising well in place. The promise of financial benefits for each adoption spurred further creativity, while legitimating a strategy now considered in the best interests of a country's vulnerable population. On the fine line of marketing, persuading families to adopt made good fiscal sense in terms of state budgets—$4000 for each adoption, $6000 for each special needs adoption. The day the Adoption and Safe Families Act was signed, the Secretary of Health and Human Services, Donna Shalala, announced the Adoption Excellence Awards. Hillary Clinton commented on the winners: some "have promoted and supported adoption in their communities, and some are parents who have opened their homes and hearts to our nation's most vulnerable children. ... And we hope that through these awards, in conjunction with this [federal] legislation, there will be many, many more in your ranks in the years to come."[64]

Media and print advertisements are only part of the presentation of children. With echoes of Charles Loring Brace's nineteenth-century orphan trains, parties and picnics abound: children mill around, under the eye of prospective adoptive parents. These parties in themselves become front-page news. In the fall of 1998, for example, *The New York Times* featured an article on one adoption party. A picture of a little girl, bedecked in a necklace made of blooming flowers, accompanies the feature; the caption reads: "In Search of a Home. Children wait in lines for games at an event to match prospective parents with children in state care in New Jersey."[65] In the fall of 2000, the *New Yorker* published a poignant short story, in which two couples compete for the twelve-year-old boy who has captured the hearts of each at a picnic. The narrator, a male, identifies with the boy, talking of the close fit in their temperaments, looks, and demeanors. The story ends inconclusively; it is not clear who will "get" the boy.

Matching again. But matching in a new arena: at parties and picnics, prospective parents match themselves with a particular child. His or her looks and behavior catch the attention of an adult; something about the child wins the heart of an individual in search of parenthood. "Bubbly and perky," read print ads, "fun-loving and responsive." "A happy and healthy boy."[66] On paper, on line, or in person at a party, surface traits strike the chord that begins a movement toward a permanent relationship. Are these encounters better or worse (more or less revealing) than the scrapbook picture of siblings Emily told me ruefully had led her and Tom to adopt two girls who turned out to have hidden depths of difficulty? Better or worse, they bring North American adoption customs close to those that occur in small and homogeneous societies of the world and in pockets of the United States itself. Magnetism and a quick identification, empathy and pity for the sweet girl in her flowery necklace: these features bring the arrangement back, through Brace, to myriad instances in which an adult in a community *takes to* and then *takes on* a needy child.

In the contexts of parties and persuasive media stories, matching, the official principle of child placement practice, comes to depend upon a spontaneous, unpredictable, and personalized response. These responses are not, however, *free*. They are constrained by expectations about "desirable" children—cute, fun-loving, and healthy—and by cultural notions of *fit* or match. The narrator in the *New Yorker* story is totally charmed by seeing himself in the twelve-year-old stranger. Agencies and mediators play on cultural constructions in their presentations: "Jennifer is an energetic, healthy girl with a bubbly personality. When she isn't watching movies, Jennifer is usually listening to music—she even choreographs her own dance steps to her favorite songs." Conventionally appealing traits overshadow the hint of difficulty: "She has been through some traumatic experiences," the column continues.[67] "Brett is a charming, mannerly 12-year old who is noted for his sincerity," another issue of the same newsletter tells readers. "He loves music, especially rap and country, and will 'bend your ear' talking about it."[68] In both instances, much is still hidden in generalizations, clichés, and the winning phrases of an effective advertisement. Yet following federal policy and consequent state mandates, these ads are in the best interests of children who otherwise have little chance of finding permanent homes. Celebrations and columns persuade an audience that, as the *New Yorker* writer discovered, a feeling of likeness can arise unexpectedly and fatefully.

"Fortunately there are people who want to adopt many of these children," the executive director of the Child Welfare League of America wrote in a *New York Times* op-ed piece, referring to special needs children. And he went on to describe the individuals: "usually the foster parents, nurses and special education teachers who have fallen in love with the children they have been caring for."[69] Despite the familiar phrase, "fallen in love with," the people he describes differ from the primary adopting population in the United States for the last half century.

In his op-ed piece, the CWLA director describes persons who care for special needs children as a career. They are not the "average members of a community" described in adoption outcome studies; they are not the Mollys and Franks whose self-presentations appear on the Internet. And they are not necessarily the people whose petitions to adopt will be accepted.

Tax breaks and subsidies

For most of the twentieth century, private and public agencies have considered financial stability and job security reliable criteria for selecting adoptive parents. Independent adoptions, too, require income stability and often a high income. Moreover, the cost of adopting a child either way has skyrocketed over the past thirty years, adding a substantial and often unmanageable obstacle to the process of applying for a child. Discouraged, many applicants simply drop out. Others take the option of requesting compensation and financial benefits for their kind of parenthood.

When adoption became a necessary safety net for children, policy-makers could not ignore the demands for remuneration made by prospective adoptive parents. By the 1990s, discussion of tax breaks and of subsidies was part of the official discourse. A small beginning occurred in 1996 when congressional legislators agreed that adoptive parents should get the same tax breaks biological parents were already receiving. The proposal did not win easy approval, either in Congress or in the popular press.

Adoptive parents spoke out in favor of tax breaks, pointing out that adoption in the United States is expensive and also arguing that their parenthood was no different from that of a biological parent. "The cost of adoption runs from $15,000 to $30,000," an adoptive father wrote to *The New York Times*. "That is only for one child. Heaven forbid you want a second! Having spent their life savings or taken out loans for the adoption process, adoptive parents who have nothing left to raise their children and send them to college would find a tax break a welcome relief." Another letter-writer emphasized that failure to grant a tax break indicated the continuing discrimination against adoptive parents: "adopting parents [deserve] the financial breaks that biological parents receive."[70]

In January 1997, Congress passed a bill granting tax breaks to adoptive parents. *The New York Times* reported in February: "Earlier this year a law took effect allowing families with incomes below $115,000 to receive a tax credit of up to $5,000 if they adopt a child. People who adopt hard-to-place children, like those who are minorities, older, disabled or have siblings, are eligible for a $6,000 credit."[71] One year later, on March 9, 1998, *US News On-line* included the tax credit as one of its "Hot Tips." "Parents who adopted a child last year may get more than a dependent exemption," the tip began, before summarizing the exact provisions.[72] *US News* calls the credit "family friendly," burying the potential implication of "paying for adoption" under the emphasis on family-building that has marked American adoption practice for over a century and, for longer than that, adoption all over the world.

Tax breaks do two things, both in line with American placement policy: one, they underline the assumption that of families as the best place for children; two, they eliminate the distinction between biological and adoptive families in the eyes of the state and, specifically, the Internal Revenue Service. If proposed tax breaks prompted controversy, proposals for directly subsidizing the incomes of adoptive families raised profound alarm. Help on taxes is one thing, but "paying" parents to care for the children they adopt is quite another thing in American culture. Income subsidy is a prolonged battle and one that, to an extent, goes on apart from the issue of tax breaks. For critics, income subsidies do look like paying parents. For supporters, income subsidies are reasonable in a culture that appoints families to pick up the slack for an inadequate welfare system.

"Arguments against supplementation [of income], especially non-medical, are that it is expensive, at least partially negating the cost savings impact of adoption, that the child may become aware that his care is being paid for unlike other children's, that annual financial assessments of parents keep the agency involved longer than is desirable and are themselves a cost factor, that subsidy has the potential for misuse by adoptive parents who could short-change the child and divert the funds to their own purposes, and that adoption should rest on conviction, not bribery. There is a danger, too, that all adoptive parents may come to expect subsidies as their right and due."[73] The argument is fiscal: subsidies can be extremely expensive. More significantly, the argument is cultural: children should not be bought; parents should not "profit" from children; and family budgets should be private, not supervised by outsiders. Adoption should be a matter of love not money, the phrase "conviction not bribery" implies.

In the late 1980s, with a flood of poor and neglected children in an era of stringent welfare payments, Congress drafted a bill that would provide financial support for adoptive families. But the lines around the support were clearly drawn, and an emphasis on unusual expenses, especially medical expenses, forestalled accusations that the bill provided payments to parents. The 1990 Adoption Opportunities Act granted subsidies to persons who adopted *special-needs* children. Decisions about distribution were left to individual states, as was the responsibility for checking on a family's right to extra monies. As usual in American placement history, the autonomy of the states resulted in close supervision of families; once the recipient of public aid, even in the benign form of an adoption subsidy, a family lost some of the privacy American culture promises a domestic unit.

Implementation of the Adoption Opportunities Act varied enormously across the nation. To avoid complete chaos, the Department of Health and Human Services issued a "policy interpretation" paper. The language reveals how persistently American child policy is constructed case by case. The DHHS paper advises that, in calculating rates of assistance, "the state should consider what it would take to incorporate a *specific* child, with his or her *specific* needs, into a *particular* household [my italics]."[74] In fact, there were few general guidelines and few federal interventions into state practices.

The 1990 act set a precedent. Subsidies emerged as a public problem alongside the emergence of calls to adopt the thousands of children entering foster care day by day, as well as the thousands of children already living in unsafe conditions. While the shibboleth, "families are best for children," provided a unified national discourse, individual states monitored the recipients of subsidies and the designation of children as "special." The existence of a national policy concerning subsidies is an illusion as long as every state allots money according to its own means tests. In every state, too, subsidies compete with other state expenditures, and debates indicate the persistence of an idea that paid parents are bad parents.

Yet, as the director of the CWLA said not so long ago, providing "loving care" for special needs children costs a lot of money. Special needs children "are often very expensive to raise." Subsidies, he adds, are not at all adequate: "The small state and Federal adoption subsidies do little to offset the costs."[75] Moreover, a point he does not dwell on, the very people in the population willing to adopt such children are frequently those with limited incomes.

The issue of adoption subsidies appears in the media almost as often as scandals about "baby brokers" or the titillating tales of "discovered" kin. That is because the issue draws on unsettled cultural preoccupations with the form and function of adoption. Discussions of subsidies expose the residual suspicion that adults adopt for selfish reasons, even if not for profit. Such a suspicion, in turn, reveals the uncertain image of the adoptive parent in the United States: is she selfish or providing a service to the state? Is the adopting parent ultimately more like a foster than a biological parent? In an American history of child placement, focus on the parents time and again distracts from responsibilities to the children.

Subsidies are an expensive federal policy. Adoption assistance subsidies rose from $701 million in 1998 to $869 million in 1999. "According to HHS [Health and Human Services], the increase is partly due to expectations that the new adoption law will reduce barriers and stimulate an increase in adoptions."[76]

In North American society, barriers to adopting reflect cultural values as much as financial concerns. Those barriers are barely touched on in federal acts and in programs for implementing federal guidelines. *Subsidies have the potential to reduce the distinctions among "substitute parents" in the United States that have shored up adoption for over a century.* When a state provides financial support for all those who "take in" children, the result is a leveling of the differences that have guided American adoption practice. Primarily, adoption subsidies could erase the class and, to some extent, the race and gender biases in American adoption. Subsidies will blur not only those major divisions in American culture but also the refinements of such divisions in adoption practice. Foster parents, child-care workers, "nurses and special education teachers," and individuals who can easily jump the hoops in a traditional agency occupy the same category in a state budget.

American policy still rests on a designation of *kinds* of parents that isolates one "adopting" case from another. Policy holds, despite the evidence of a growing breakdown in those "kinds" by participants in constructed parent-child relationships all over the country. The incompatibility between policy and practice points to the weakness of a rhetoric that claims communal responsibility for "America's children." "Beyond the obvious question of payment rates for adoption assistance lies the deeper issue of the social contract that exists between the state and the adoptive families it recruits to provide homes for its waiting children."[77]

III. Adoption In and For the Community

Love and the social contract

The idea of adoption as a social contract between families and the state is at once radical and nothing new. It is radical in a context in which adoption is equivalent to "making a family." It is not new in many societies of the world, where adoption serves the purpose of ensuring the solidarity and continuity of a community through kin-based exchanges of children. The idea of a social contract is radical, too, in a context in which adoption has an almost entirely individual character. Adoption in the United States no longer addresses *family* as an integral and lasting unit. Adoption in the United States addresses *individual* needs: an adult's need (or desire) for a child, a child's need for a home, another individual's need for relief from the responsibility of parenthood. But, if adoption in the United States is not a family affair, it is increasingly a state affair.

American adoption, distinctively, sits on a fence between individual needs and state policies. The 1997 act performs a balancing feat on that fence, assuming desire to have a child can serve the purpose of rescuing children. The expectation is optimistic and mystifying; it depends upon a shift in cultural interpretations of parenthood, kinship, and identity. The success of Adoption 2002 means a reconsideration of the "social contract."

Adoption has always, incidentally or intentionally, served the state's purposes. Since the 1909 White House Conference on Children, adoption in the United States serves to transfer the burden from a social welfare system to families. By the middle of the twentieth century, the event was clothed not in the language of charity or civic virtue, but in the language of love, belonging, and individual fulfillment. A person adopted in order to gratify a desire and mapped the relationship onto the model of a biological bond between parent and child. Adoption manuals and scholarly literature talked of instant, absolute, and unconditional love. In the 1970s and 1980s, adoption advice included: when potential parents first see a child, "it is better if they are delighted, for their first reaction may set the tone of their love of the child forever."[78]

The children available for adoption as the year 2002 approaches pose a challenge to "delight." They pose a challenge to a notion of enduring solidarity linked to delight, and without reference to wider entities of family or of community. A national exchange called Children Awaiting Parents (CAP) publicizes waiting children on the Internet. "Many thousands of children with special needs who wait for parents live in foster homes, group homes or residential treatment centers. More than half the children are of minority descent. Sadly, many of them have experienced abuse and neglect, and all have endured the trauma of being separated from their families." A plea for action comes next: "The challenges CAP's children face differ from child to child, but they all long for unconditional love, patience and understanding. These children are waiting for the day when they will have a family who can give them the stability and loving care they so desperately need ... and deserve. Can you make the difference of a lifetime for one of these children?"[79] All "special," these are children who have been in foster care for years, have been traumatized, cannot be separated from a large sibling group, have psychological and physical problems, and do not easily fit the "happy ending" script of American adoption stories.

"Applicants should have a basic love for children," instructs the CWLA *Standards for Adoption Service*.[80] An adoptive parent group that advocates special-needs adoption offers a similar prescription. "Through the application of love, patience and skill, they [adoptive parents] are often able to mitigate the worse effects of a child's early trauma."[81] When I talked with Madge, adoptive parent of a fourteen-year old, she confessed that she did not feel love for the troubled teen-ager who had recently arrived in her home. "But you can't parent a stranger from four-teen on," she said, "that's all there is to it."[82]

In her book, *The Limits of Hope*, Ann Kimble Loux frankly questions the role of love in parenting children with special needs. A total disruption of expectations and norms puts the cultural prescription of "love" into a new perspective. Perhaps, Loux admits, she did not love the adopted girls in the same way she loved her biological children. "Watching Margey and Dawn slip and fall instilled a dark terror in each of us. Why did we always feel more fortunate than they? Were we in truth more fortunate? Was there then a difference between we and they? Was it blood? Luck? Love?"[83] Did she fail, she asks, to love the adopted girls altogether? More crucially, did her failure to love predict a failure in the girls to thrive? As Nancy Scheper-Hughes has pointed out, the burden placed on a parent—especially a mother—to love automatically, instinctively, and uncondition-ally is heavy, elitist, ethnocentric and, often, destructive.[84]

A language of love pervades American adoption policy and practice. At the first moment of applying for a child, petitioners are asked to explore (or, from their point of view, be tested on) their "feelings" for children. Subsequently, like Madge and like Anne Kimble Loux, adoptive parents ask whether they have rightly used, or kept, the resource of love. In adoption discourse, love is a personal resource, a sign of character, of capability, and of worth. The interpretation appears in negotiations among members of the triad about anonymity, contact, sealed records, and secrecy. Recent congressional hearings on confidentiality show how prevalent the rhetoric is, for participants in adoptive kinship as well as for those professionals who testify. Adoptive parents base their rights to "non-interference" on the enduring love they have developed by *working* to raise the child, through diapers, measles, and school failures. Birthparents, too, base their requests for contact with a relinquished child on love, cit-ing the *natural* bond that cannot be broken by a legal arrange-ment. Birthparents I met drew from their reunion experiences a reassurance that their love put them on the same plane as the adoptive parents: the resource of love matching (or exceeding) the resource of *things*. Adoptive parents who agree to non-confidential adoptions argue that the birthparent's love can be *added* to the child's life.

Whether described as an instinctive feeling or as work, love becomes a personal capability. Central to the transaction, this interpretation of love ultimately isolates adoption from the community, resting its worth on the love a parent expresses for a relinquished or an adopted child. Yet public statements on adoption on the federal, the state, and the local level call for an action that refers to community and not to self.

Expanding the meanings of "secrecy"

Decisions like that of Ann Kimble Loux, Madge, Emily and Tom—and thousands of other individuals—to take children who do not prompt delight changes the face of American adoption. Children who do not instantly elicit unconditional and absolute devotion—who do not blend in, settle down, or release a flood of feelings are now, by fiat, the adoptable. They are increasingly the adopted. At the beginning of the twenty-first century, *participants in adoption* are definitely speaking in a different voice from the *policy-makers of adoption*.

Participants are ahead of agencies and umbrella organizations in breaking old molds. Yet, when the time comes to legalize an adoption the old forces often step in and bring up traditional cultural interpretations of a family, of kinship, and of a good parent. In the United States, racial matching enters all deliberations over legal adoptions. Petitioners for adoptive parenthood still may find their wishes to become the legal parents of a "stranger" child blocked by traditional measures and by significant ideologies about family composition. The individuals who perhaps most frequently run into the tangle of principle and of policy are foster parents who ask to adopt the children in their care.

In the spring of 1998, a Texas couple petitioned to adopt three siblings they had been fostering in their home. Their petition was refused, despite the fact that under the 1997 Adoption and Safe Families Act Texas could expect a reward for the permanent placement of the children. The couple, married and middle-class, met the ordinary standards of agency adoption. Racial differences short-circuited the adoption: the couple was white, the children black. As in many other areas, Texas social workers, lawyers, and judges sit between the same-race positions of organizations like the National Association of Black Social Workers and the crying needs of "freed" children. The National Adoption Exchange, established to facilitate the movement of children across state lines and the permanent placement of all children, warns: "Most agencies try to place children in families with similar racial and ethnic backgrounds."[85]

Throughout American adoption history change has come in small steps, cautiously taken within the parameters of notions of kinship, family, and identity. Foster parents increasingly succeed in their petitions to adopt, though not always in their inclination to cross racial lines. The bias against foster parents slowly diminishes in face of the federal turn to adoption as the solution for needy and at risk children; the growing number of foster children will only achieve permanency if a new category of parents is recognized. Under the pressure of a permanency policy, foster parents are successful in petitions to adopt. According to one survey, of the nearly 40,000 children deemed "adoptable" in 1999, 64 percent were adopted by foster parents: a remarkably high proportion.

Changes in practice may be slow, but changes in interpretations of the family are even slower. The special needs children adopted in 1999 were adopted by married couples (66 percent) and by single women (30 percent). A tiny 2 percent were adopted by unmarried couples and by single men, suggesting an intertwining of perceptions of the good family on the part of petitioners and of those who grant petitions.[86] Moreover, the importance of "matching" for creating a sense of entitlement continues to influence adoptive parents. Parents of special needs children revise matching to suit the new family constellation, and describe the likeness between themselves and an adopted child. A woman I talked with remarked on the similarity between her own "kinky Jewish hair" and the hair of her four-year-old African-American daughter. But matching has become resemblance, no small change in American adoption. The adoptive mother's comment about kinky hair and knots differs from the "laundry list" of traits potential parents were once presented with on the way to adopting. Choosing characteristics in advance is a different experience from seeing similarities emerge in the course of family life. While "similarities" and being alike leaves adoption with one foot in the old ways, definition and perception of similarities on the part of adoptive parents pushes adoption forward into new ways of conceptualizing relationships.

Birthparent and adoptee activism focuses on opening records and unsealing adoption papers. Adoptive parent activism focuses on stretching the boundaries of family and kinship. If the story ends well, those elements of adoption reform will blend, leading to an adoption policy that responds to adoption practices. Another ending is the further division of adopting parents by class, income, race, and status. The connections between non-confidentiality (full disclosure) and changes in concepts of kinship and the family falter on the positioning of the three members of the triad.

In the 1970s, as the adoption reform movement took off, adoptee groups and birthparent groups formed an alliance, uneasy but expedient. In the process, and in some of the arguments, adoptive parents were villainized, as evil as the social worker and lawyers who deny the rights of the birthparent and the adopted person. Historically, in American culture, adoptive parents have been viewed as the "well off" in the transaction, those with the ability to decide about having children. For adoptive parents, however, the picture is distorted and misleading. Adoptive parents define themselves as vulnerable, dependent upon outsiders for having a child, and forced to undergo checks that no natural parent has to experience. Petitioners and clients, adoptive parents talk of "needing" someone else in order to make a family and of the silence that need imposes on them. While birthparents and adoptees organized into activist groups, adoptive parents followed more slowly and often under the burden of a negative image created by the vociferous birthparent and adoptee.

The attribution of power and position to the adoptive parent is not entirely false to American adoption history. As a category, the adoptive parent did make the first significant dent on state adoption law, from the movement of adoption into local courts to the legal guarantees of confidentiality. By the late twentieth century, Senator Gordon Humphrey could characterize America's infertile couples as "tragic" and raise only a few eyebrows. Even now, theirs is the role that garners media sympathy and public respect. Moreover, adoptive parents influence the *distribution* of children by obeying cultural norms or, as in the past three decades, by disobeying those cultural norms. If their voices have been quiet, the stance of the dependent, their actions have been loud.

Faced with a shortage of dwi's (domestic white infants) and with tight restrictions in many agencies, adoptive parents have altered the notions of family in their wide search for adoptable children. On the one hand, the search exacerbates existing distinctions between privileged and non-privileged adopters, especially in international and in independent adoptions. On the other hand, the search makes at least some potential parents the willing recipients of children who are currently presented as "special."

As adoptive parents adopt children who look nothing like them, who could not possibly "pass" as their biological children, and who bring detailed stories of their pasts with them, the meaning of secrecy in American adoption expands. The narrow interpretation of secrecy as sealed records and closed documents vanishes under a much larger openness. Adoptive families are out of the closet, more and more frequently without the possibility of hiding their form of kinship.

Full disclosure has an abundance of meanings. The ambiguities in arguments against closed records in the 1970s, when adoption reform groups began making a case, have become legion. Furthermore, the ambiguities are created and re-created by what participants in adoptive kinship *do*—and by a steady erosion of the purity of the term "adoptive kinship." Adoptive arrangements now cross state borders and national boundaries. Adoptive arrangements also cross the rules of agencies and of licensed brokers (in states that approve of independent adoption). Last but not least, adoptive arrangements now cross customary expectations about kinship. The content, the form, and the presentation of facts are effectively open when the concept of adoptable has such a plethora of interpretations. These changes transform the meaning of a demand for "freedom of information."

There are continuities with past history too. The phrase "freedom of information" itself connects the newest moves in American adoption with a principle that is over a quarter century old. The assumption that certain facts are crucial to a person's identity also holds strong connections with concepts that are at least half a century old. Requests for information continue to be couched in the language of psychological theory, well popularized these days, and in a medical vocabulary, equally available to an American public. A presumed "science" begs the issue of multiple forms of disclosure and leaves aside the evidence that disclosure in adoption no longer involves official records. The "papers" members of CUB and of ASG focused their arguments on, while still significant, are only a part of the transaction of "knowledge" emerging in a new era of adoptive practice.

Nowadays, a description of health and well-being does not satisfy either the birthparent or the adoptive parent who wants to know about an adopted child. The birthparent is less shy about demanding contact, the face to face information that no document provides. The adoptive parent is encouraged by cultural signals to request a genetic map to fill in the conventional medical-history data. Adopted individuals, like those who fought for the Oregon initiative granting adoptees access to their birth certificates, understand that *origins* complete the information provided on a record.

Advocates of adoption reform have long recognized that the demand for knowledge is also a claim to power. Adoptive parents for years chafed under the suspicion that social workers knew more than they did about the child they had adopted and made their own. Perceived inequities in the disclosure of information contribute to the feelings of powerlessness adoptive parents recall as being central to the process of adopting. "The social workers call all the shots," a couple said to me, explaining their reluctance to ask for more "data" on available children.

The same advice comes from an advocacy group for adoptive parents: "You can't play head games with these people," cautioned Debra Harder, a spokeswoman for Adoptive Families of America. "The social workers are the ones with all the power."[87]

An alternative to the demand for information exists for all members of the triad. Birthparents, adoptees, and adoptive parents in the United States have the option of embracing the other dominant view of adoption as an arrangement established and perpetuated by *love*. "I am happier not knowing anything," an adoptive father said to me. "Then we can love her [the child] for who she is." A version of one of the oldest perspectives on socially constructed parent-child relations, his comment speaks not only of love but also, implicitly, of nurture, environment, and trust in a child's capacities: we can love her for who she is.

The argument for information more closely mirrors the vast changes in American adoption, including a newly available adoptable population and new conceptualizations of parenthood and kinship. With changes in practice, challenges to "as if begotten" abound and the desirability of passing as a biological family vanishes. These old insurances of permanency are replaced by an emphasis on facts, or knowledge, as the seal of an enduring solidarity between parent and child. Typical of adoption history in the United States, the meaning of knowledge remains particularized, determined by the parent who adopts, the parent who signs a relinquishment paper, and the child who grows up in full awareness that he or she is adopted. There are no standards yet, no manual for the amount or the kind of knowledge participants in adoptive kinship should have. Clearly, though, a substantial—and outspoken—number of individuals involved in adoption share a conviction that knowing *something* is a source of strength in a parent-child relationship and that enduring solidarity is built on disclosure rather than on secrets.

At the same time, as long as knowledge remains particularized and individually determined, the debate over disclosure isolates adoption from the needs cited in recent federal initiatives. Demands for open records and non-confidentiality do not recognize the social contract implicated by a rhetoric of responsibility for all America's children. Demands for open records, non-confidentiality, and full disclosure are put in terms of strengthening individual identity and dyadic bonds. These demands reveal that at the start of the twenty-first century, American adoption has become *singular*, in the sense of creating one-on-one bonds. Even more than in the past, contemporaneous American adoption practice establishes a parent-child tie and not a wide kinship network. In a post-modern world of flux, mobility, and a general transitoriness of relationships, the parent-child relationship is the last bastion of permanency. "The child is the source of the last *remaining, irrevocable, unexchangeable primary relationship*. Partners come and go. The child stays."[88]

This is not necessarily a message of doom. Relinquishing old notions of adoption also banishes ideas of descent and of the chosen heir. These ideas put a heavy burden on the adopted child to represent the good name and preserve the "good" property of a family. That parent-child bonds are the last irrevocable and unexchangeable relationship suits the urgency of the Adoption and Safe Families Act. Irrevocable permanency for one child, and then another and another, ultimately can diminish the shocking number of children at risk and in danger in the United States. As always in American child placement history, individuals acting out of diverse, sometimes selfish, and often non-communal motives take care of the children who need to be cared for. These actions slowly and inevitably dent the walls of practice—and eventually invade the fortress of cultural interpretations of core concepts like identity and kinship.

In this moment of American adoption history, the accumulation of individual actions places the issue of sealed documents and stymied disclosure under the larger issue of altruism, charity, and a social contract. By their actions, and in their relationships, participants in adoption revive an idea of the social contract that renders the "as if begotten" family obsolete and grants all children a chance at permanency.

Notes

1. The only comparison may be with the late nineteenth-century approach to homeless and poor children, which defined them as "adoptable."
2. DHHS Response to Clinton's *Executive Memorandum: Adoption 2002.*
3. http://www.adoptioninstitute.org/research/ressta.html.
4. http://www.adoptioninstitute.org/research/ressta.html.
5. Pertman 2000. One must keep in mind the inadequacy of record-keeping on adoption.
6. http://www.adoptioninstitute.org/research/ressta.html.
7. Personal communication.
8. Mnookin 1985; Goldstein, Freud, Solnit 1973; Katz 1974.
9. Personal communication.
10. Debate over the science versus the art of placement are common in social work literature, with some support for depending on intuition and not searching for objective measures. See, e.g., Burgess 1981.
11. Personal communication.
12. I borrow from Putnam's recent critique of American society; Putnam 2000.
13. CWLA 1985: 60.
14. Ibid: 61.
15. Bass 1975: 506.
16. Maas and Engler 1959.
17. Feigelman and Silverman 1983: 13.
18. Also by religion, but since this is not visible, it does not work in the same way to blend adoptive families into the "normal" population.
19. Hoffamn, Jan. *The New York Times* 6/2/96: E1.
20. http://www.adoptioninstitute.org/research/ressta.html.
21. State laws regarding "independent" adoption vary enormously and some states outlaw them altogether. Other states require an agency involvement before the adoption can be legalized, while other states permit an adoption to go to court without the intervention of an agency.
22. Perhaps at the insistence of Gordon Humphrey, a member of the committee with a longstanding interest in protecting American adoption.
23. Hearings, U.S. Senate Sub-committee on Security and Terrorism, 1985.
24. Ibid.
25. Because there are no national statistics on adoption, no records exist of how many adoptions go through agencies and how many are independent in the nation as a whole. Six states outlaw independent adoption altogether; in the other 44 states, regulations are as different as everything is in the arena of domestic law.
26. Meezan, Katz, Russo 1978: 227.

27. ibid.
28. Data on independent adoptions are no more available than data on all adoptions in the United States. A 1992 estimate made by the National Adoption Information Clearinghouse claims that nearly 40 percent of adoptions are handled by private agencies or independent facilitators. Pertman offers the estimate that nearly two-thirds *of all newborns* adopted are adopted independently (italics mine); 2000: 36.
29. Meezan, Katz, Russo 1978: 78.
30. ibid: 228.
31. Mansnerus, Laura. *The New York Times* 10/26/98: 4.
32. Less than 1 percent of nonwhite women relinquish unplanned babies; Bachrach, Stolley, and London 1992.
33. Mansnerus, Laura. *The New York Times* 10/26/98: 14.
34. ibid: 1.
35. ibid: 15.
36. http://www.adoptioninstitute.org/research/ressta.html.
37. By and large, interviewees are self-selective and those who shunned Mrs. Simpson may not have come forward to talk with me—at least, if they had not yet found a route to adoption. Several of my friends, adoptive parents, refused to use Mrs. Simpson, mainly because they could not accept her insistence on an anti-abortion stance and a promise of church attendance.
38. No figures exist on how many North American children are adopted by other nations.
39. Bartholet 1993: 152.
40. ibid: xv.
41. U.S. Immigration and Naturalization Service. Just this year, the INS revised its laws so that children could become citizens immediately upon adoption.
42. Bascom and McKelvey 1997: 78.
43. U.S. Immigration and Naturalization Service.
44. Approximately 100 in 1997. Bascom and McKelvey 1997: 78
45. The figure 324 comes from an article by Rachel L. Swarns in *The New York Times*. 11/28/97: 20.
46. Letters to the Editor. *The New York Times* 9/2/97: 19.
47. *Time Magazine* 10/21/91: 88.
48. Mansnerus, Laura. *The New York Times* 10/26/98: 16.
49. http://www.adoptioninstitute.org/research/ressta.html.
50. Letters to the Editor. *The New York Times* 9/2/97: 19.
51. Mansnerus, Laura. *The New York Times* 10/26/98: 14.
52. Halbfinger, David. M. *The New York Times* 5/28/99: 1.
53. Mansnerus, Laura. *The New York Times* 10/26/98: 1.
54. For a period of time, an agency in my area hung a large poster across the entrance to a tunnel, pleading for adoption of "special" children: it was about as public an ad as I had seen.
55. http://www.adoptlink.com/profile.htm.
56. http://www.adoption.com/chat.
57. http://ep.com/ep/sub.html.

58. In a case reported in *The New York Times*, through the Internet and a broker two couples were "given" the same babies; not only are they contesting each other's rights, but the birthparent has decided she wants the babies back. Lewin, Tamar. *The New York Times* 1/19/01: 12.
59. http://www.overtherainbowad.com/possible.htm.
60. http://www.adoption.com/registry/search.cgi.
61. Joe 1979: 56.
62. H. John Heinz III Archives.
63. *Adoptalk* 1991: 7.
64. http://www.adoptioninstitute.org/policy/polupd1297.htm.
65. Bernstein, Nina. *The New York Times* 9/15/98: 1.
66. Random examples from a listing I receive on "Waiting Children."
67. *Network News* Fall 2000: 2.
68. *Network News* Summer 2000: 3.
69. Liederman, David. *The New York Times* 5/4/96: 19.
70. Letters to the Editor. *The New York Times* 5/14/96: 21.
71. *The New York Times* 2/15/97: 5.
72. http://www.usnews.com/usnews/issue/980309/9tax.htm.
73. Joe 1979: 39.
74. Quoted in *Adoptalk* 1991: 8.
75. Letters to the Editor. *The New York Times* 5/4/96: 19.
76. http://www.adoptioninstitute.org/policy/polupd.htm.
77. Adoption Advocates. File:///jm%27s%20harddisk/Desktop%20Folder/.
78. Burgess 1981: 15.
79. http://www.ggw.org/cap/aboutkids/htm.
80. CWLA 1978: 61.
81. Adoption Advocates. File://jm%27s%20harddisk/Desktop%20Folder/.
82. Personal communication.
83. Quoted by Ann Hulbert, "In the Bosom of the Family." *The New York Review of Books* 6/11/98: 56.
84. Scheper-Hughes 1992.
85. H. John Heinz III Archives, CMU Libraries.
86. Adoption and Foster Care Analysis and Reporting System (AFCARS).
87. Hoffman, Jan. *The New York Times* 6/2/96: E1.
88. Beck 1992: 118.

Chapter 5

Opening the Confines of Kinship—Twenty-first Century American Child Placement

Studying American adoption

Why is American adoption distinctive, worth a study? The answer comes in two forms: one historical and the other cultural. That is, I could explain the distinctiveness of American adoption by tracing its roots through three centuries—since the United States broke away from its own parent country, England—or I could explain the distinctiveness in terms of its character: why does American adoption look different from the family of adoption systems spread around the world? Following the bent of my cultural-anthropological training, I will take the second route, delineating the distinctiveness of American ways of moving children through a kind of ethnographic strategy, isolating the major patterns constituting this version of child placement. Furthermore, also in the tradition of my discipline, I compare American patterns with other ways of doing something that might be called the same thing.[1] As has been apparent in the preceding four chapters, an anthropological analysis is never complete without its kindred historical approach. Here, however, I want to take another tack and pull out what seems emphatically "American" to me about a form of kinship—which, in fact, is far from being only kinship.

With roots in Roman traditions, in European apprenticeship and placing-out systems, and, in one state, Napoleonic Law, American adoption developed in its own way. The institution has historically demonstrated an independence of form and function, of symbolic meanings and practical realities. During the period covered in this book, the past quarter century, American adoption has diverged even more noticeably from the practices and policies of closely related societies, with similar legal systems and shared kinship structures. No other Western nation so thoroughly prescribes secrecy and so reluctantly opens the records of adoption. No other culture works so hard to persuade an adopted person of the inevitability and the benefits of adoption.

The emphasis on secrecy in the United States bespeaks an extreme ambivalence about "transactions in parenthood." The rigor with which secrecy is maintained exceeds that of near cultural neighbors like Great Britain where access to records is easier than it is in the United States. Records "open" state by state, in always contested cases.[2] Secrecy in American adoption hides an abundant—and unresolved—tension between the value of "birth" and the belief in "becoming," between nature and nurture. Entrenched in a system of sealed records and closed documents, American adoption is, in a colloquialism, *its own thing*.

American adoption is a "thing" of contradictions and inconsistencies, of ambiguities and deceptions, of rewarding with one hand and recriminating with the other. In this concluding section, I bring out the contradictions and inconsistencies in order to indicate the peculiar quality of a familiar way of moving children around: if *they* (those other cultures) seem odd, the beam of an anthropological light shows how strange *we* are.

The outstanding contradictions can be summarized. American adoption is confidential, secret, and, at the same time, a matter of vociferous public debate. American cultural conventions assume a child's identity can be totally transformed through adoption and also that "blood" is the core of identity. American adoption policy is premised on a notion of "caring for" but also calculates strictly the fitness of care-taking adults. Finally, adoption is at once a highly individualized event and a mechanism of social and cultural control. Before I topple off into my own tangle of words, let me proceed with those four major points. In amongst them lie other significant issues, like interpretations of personhood, hierarchies of race, class, and gender, and sources of change and of lethargy in the history of American adoption.

The secrecy of American adoption

For much of the twentieth century, American adoption was personally secret and publicly fascinating; what individuals do not (and often cannot) know contrasts with what the public hears, watches, and absorbs about adopting, adoptees, and adoptive families. Hidden by individuals, the transaction receives attention at congressional hearings, on television, and recently in a spate of memoirs. "Secret" but not kept a secret: the contradictions surrounding secrecy in American adoption stem from the diverse applications of the concept in the process of creating kinship. "Secret" has almost as many meanings in the history of American adoption as there are individuals who use the word to comment on the phenomenon. "Secret" appears in arguments for and against confidentiality, as well as in arguments for and against disclosing information to all participants in an adoption.

As the twentieth century came to an end, the notion of secrecy shed a bright light of publicity into virtually every nook and cranny of American adoption. Little was left out of the glare, and terms of a debate that had once been the province of participants in adoption were available to anyone who turned on a TV or opened a newspaper. Phrases like "sealed records," "closed files," and "hidden relatives" diffused out of the adoption community into a wide public arena. They were the phrases that represented the experience of adoption to an American audience. Good or bad, the "secrets" in adoption appeared to be a simple matter. Stories of an adopted person claiming the *right* to see the documents a state had sealed, or the account of a mother and child reunited after twenty (or thirty or fifty) years of being "strangers" to one another, or the photograph of a crowd waving banners demanding "freedom of information" for all participants in adoptive kinship: these are the scenes through which an increasing number of people interpret the experience of adoption in the United States. Yet the meaning and the implication of these scenes are no more straightforward than anything else in the history of child placement. Even a term that looks transparent, like "sealed records," has multiple definitions.

The records that may be sealed range from an original birth certificate to a social worker's notes, and often include the papers in an adoptive parent's desk or a birthparent's bank vault. Lips may be sealed as well. In an American context, secrecy refers to what a parent does *not* tell a child or a child hides from her friends; secrecy reflects a general perception that an adoption should not be talked about. Keeping secrets, then, can be a decision made by the parents of an adoptive child or by a social worker eager to place a child or by the adopted person unsure of how others will respond to the status. In every case, the embrace of secrecy underlines the "strangeness" of adoption, the marginality many people involved in adoption confess to feeling, and the general awkwardness about coming out of the closet and announcing one's difference from "everyone else."

The concept of secrecy dramatizes and isolates adoptive parent-child relationships in the United States. However defined, the concept clearly distinguishes adoptive from biological parent-child relationships, to which the word is rarely applied. Secrecy underlines the perception of an essential difference between *contracted* (or "legal") and *consanguineal* (or "natural") parenthood. And the more publicity the concept of secrecy receives, the more apparent it is that adoption has long stood on the outskirts of dominant cultural constructions of kinship, family, and identity. The presumed "not real," fictive, and liminal quality of adoptive kinship impinges on practice, on participants, and on professional assessments of the outcome of transactions in parenthood.

There have been stages in the evolution of secrecy in adoption well before the high profile debates of the last twenty years. Laws of confidentiality appeared on the books of almost every

state by 1920. Twenty years later, in the 1940s, adoption literature expressed growing concern about the secrets adults kept
from adopted children. An outgrowth of the post-Progressive
Era preoccupation with the best interests of children, the professional critique of secrets in adoption focused on the potential
damage to an individual child. From this perspective, keeping
secrets within a family was fertile ground for personal insecurity, unhappiness, and inability to "adjust." The critique of keeping secrets in the family had a social dimension as well. Experts
worried that secrecy at home encouraged the public perception
of adoption as a second-best way of having children, shameful
and stigmatizing, and largely a last recourse. That perception,
documented in surveys, diminishes the social function of adoption, which is to create families and to rescue children in one
transaction. Setting the groundwork for the search movement of
the 1970s, social workers had already concluded that family
secrets gave a bad name to the placement strategies they had
carefully developed.

While social workers continue to this day to match children
with parents, permitting a family to hide its adoptive status,
they also advise adopting parents to tell a child about adoption.
The result of these potentially contradictory practices has been
a substantial literature on *telling*. An early guide for adoptive
parents appeared in 1950, in a small, easily read book that told
a story of the "chosen child."[3] In the 1990s, when I did my
research, adoptees remembered the story as part of their childhood experiences; several commented on the good effects of the
story, saying they had always felt "special." Others interpreted
the story differently, saying it made them feel as if they had been
plucked from a shelf of babies, in a supermarket aisle. Choice,
and chosen, are no more clear in their implications and coloring
than these concepts ever have been in American adoption. For
all three members of the triad, a preoccupation with *choice*
pushes adoption further into the shadows of "natural" kinship.

While individuals struggle with issues of secrecy and privacy, the subject of adoption itself commands a large and fas-
cinated audience. In one of the more striking paradoxes of
American adoption history, a treasured confidentiality among

participants accompanies the unconstrained publicity about a *permanent re-delegation* of parenthood, whether by an individual who signs her name to a relinquishment paper or by the state official who defines a parent as incompetent. The fascination goes back to tales of the prince and the pauper: the "wrong" child brought up in the "wrong" family. Tales of mis-placed placement abound in adoption circles. One adult adoptee described herself to me as the "ugly duckling" who had the misfortune of growing up in a family of "beautiful swans." News stories of hospital mix-ups and of love affairs between adults who did not know they were "blood" kin are a sure sell for the media. American culture inherits numerous myths of the danger and also the *daring* in separating a child from his or her "natural" parents, and the myths endure. Today, no less than centuries ago, such myths of western civilization embody cultural interpretations of the sources of individual identity and the link between identity and social bonds. In American culture, adoption is at once romantic and risky, private and public—a secret, a shame, and a sign of something special.

By the end of the twentieth century, adoption commanded attention as an aspect of individual identity. Prompted both by an adoption reform movement and by a general cultural obsession with adjustment, fulfillment, and the assertion of one's *self*, the language of "identity quests" spread from adoption into the wider public discourse. Adoption serves as a vivid and accessible case for a complicated discussion of the sources of individual character and capability. It could not but be so, since adoption is regarded as producing a dramatic split of the person from the natural substance of her or his being. As long as adoption is perceived as an intrusion into essential connections between parent and child, adoption throws biology, blood, and, now, DNA onto the palette of identity talk. When birthparents argue that contacting a biological child "completes an identity" or when adoptees claim the importance of knowing a "face with genes like mine," they enter and influence a debate over fundamental cultural values. When adoptive parents wonder how much they should know about a child's birth family, they too perpetuate the terms of an ongoing debate. Simultaneously, to the extent that adoption is always a *contracted* relationship, the transaction insists on the other strand of cultural conceptualizations of identity: the achievement of identity and, in the triad, the transcendent importance of decision over destiny. If adoption is a *made* (the root meaning of "fictive") relationship, then the participants in adoption present an unmistakable vision of the possibility of *making oneself.*

None of this has been comfortable in American culture. This is evident in state laws of adoption and their emendations, in state policies for placement, and in the close supervision of any adoptive transaction in the United States.[4] The central assumption of American adoption law and policy, "as if begotten," is an oxymoron. Behind (and obscured) by the legal dictum is a contradiction between core cultural values: respecting the "nature" of a person and granting a person the freedom to construct an identity. The response has been the oversight I describe in the previous three chapters.

Although generalizations have drawbacks, a contrast between Oceanic and Western cultures is useful for thickening description and, in this instance, illuminating the "exotic" side of familiar interpretations of adoption. In contrast to North American customs, adoption in Oceanic cultures is open, the participants and the precipitating causes known to all and sundry—at least, to all who are interested. Furthermore, until recently, adoption in Oceanic cultures did not require the scrupulous supervision and formal legitimization characteristic of North American (and Western) procedures for reallocating parental rights. Accompanying this cultural and structural openness, throughout Oceania rates of adoption are high: children are generously given and easily transferred from household to household. In some societies, the rates of adoption involve over half of all children.[5] Adopting is a perfectly ordinary procedure, whether taken to a court or not, and without fanfare the adopted person is just like anyone else. Just because adoption is ordinary, however, does not erase its significance, socially, culturally, and personally.

Adoption in Oceanic societies presents several outstanding features. These features tell what is not—or is no longer—true of American adoption. First, adoption in Oceanic societies binds one adult to another: giver to receiver of a child. It is a genuinely social and sociable endeavor. Second, adoption in Oceanic societies does not cut the child off completely and forever from a family of birth. His or her connections remain strong and solid, as long as everyone gets along. That is, personal contact not state contract determines the rules of the game and the terms of the relationship. Third, adoption in Oceanic societies begins with individual needs, desires, and decisions and not with an outsider's assessment of parental fitness or lack of fitness.

The three features contrast with contemporary American adoption customs which by-and-large proscribe contact between giver and receiver of a child. Customs still cut the child off from a birth family and placement decisions still depend upon differential judgments of parental capability. The three features also indicate the modernization of North American, and Western, adoption customs, a process that involves shedding the very features I cited for Oceanic adoption.[6] In modern adoption, choice and contract are key concepts, and both are restricted by the state. Accepted customs and statutory provisions limit choice in adoption and place the contracts of fictive kinship under careful supervision.

One might argue that casual adoptive arrangements inspired by the feelings of participants are fine in small, tightly integrated societies, but would not work in a large, heterogeneous society like the United States. The argument begs the cultural question. In all societies, adoption is as much a matter of values as of procedures, of conviction as of regulation. The contrast between North American and Oceanic forms of adoption reflects beliefs about the family, parenthood, personhood, and identity as much as it reflects demographic and structural differences. A comparison serves to disclose the *cultural assumptions* that give American adoption the particular cast I have described in the previous four chapters.

One must then explore the cultural background of an enduring lack of casualness in American adoption. Far from being informal, the arrangement has been tightly tied by legal standards and by moral strictures for most of its history. The strength, the persistence, and the seeming inevitability of this way of arranging the exchange of a child reiterate how much the exchange absorbs. Unlike in Oceanic societies, where adoption means a child is raised by "new" adults, in the United States adoption involves a thorough alteration of the individual's kinship status, a complete change in her position in a social network, and a total transformation of identity. The immensity of what adoption is supposed to accomplish in the United States elicits the defensive reaction manifested in strict state control and in powerful cultural ideologies of the family: represented by the middle class couple behind a white picket fence. Legal regulations, formal review processes, and insistent images reinforce the effort to make "water" as thick as "blood"—and reveal the impossibility.

Transforming identity

A transformation of identity in adoption is not unique to the United States. What distinguishes American adoption is the coupling of such a transformation with a belief in the significance of blood that is as fierce as it is ambivalent. American adoption policies assume the adopted child can be "born anew" and a certificate of birth is newly written. At the same time, adoption practices show how hard it is to relinquish the idea that "birth" bequeaths traits to a child; currently, this idea is phrased in terms of *genetic substance*.[7] Official dogma about environment and opportunity drive the belief in blood underground, as it were, into the sinews and cells of individual identity. A rewritten birth certificate recognizes the importance of "genealogy" in the very effort to disguise, hide, and rewrite that connection.

A rewritten birth certificate points out how "un-normal" adoption is perceived to be in the United States, as in European nations generally. The importance of such a document is evident in the ferocity with which it is defended, a battle that currently rages more bitterly in the United States than in other western societies. Despite intermittent recognition of the justice in an adoptee's demands for access to documents, the principle of sealing the original birth certificate and filing it in state archives remains in force in most states. The new birth certificate *certifies* the permanent re-creation of kinship ties and the enduring transformation of identity. And the certificate, with an adoptive parent's name inserted as if she were the biological parent, "normalizes" the adoptee's membership in a family. "As if" loses its connotation of a simile—he is as strong as a lion—and becomes metaphorical: he is a lion. It is as if American culture cannot tolerate a *made* or a constructed bond—at least not in the domain of parent-child relationships. An adopted child is, as adoption manuals instruct, "your very own."

Adoption in the United States preserves the importance of nature in a social and legal transformation of identity. The importance of nature is marked by the replication of as-if-begotten and by the enforced disappearance of the "natural" parent. In an American culture of adoption, the birthparent *vanishes*, as CUB members put it. She vanishes precisely because she represents the genealogical connection perceived to be at the core not only of kinship but also of identity. According to the genetic lore of the past two decades, the birthparent is present through the genes she has bequeathed to the child; within this framework, her actual presence constitutes an overload on the adoptive family.

Oceanic societies harbor no similar ideas about the "thickness" of blood or its contribution to individual identity. The cultural milieu is one in which the parent by birth brings nothing more and nothing less to the child than any other adult. The parent who gave birth and then gave her child to someone else chooses the extent of her involvement and may, or may not, be chosen by the dhild to be kin. Relationships are premised on conduct and are consequently contingent. The familiar western cultural expectation that an enduring commitment constitutes a "good" relationship does not find a place in interpretations of the parent and child relationship in an Oceanic society, regardless of how the relationship originates.

Laws of confidentiality, statutes mandating closed records, and psychological theory about the dangers of "too many parents" protect more than the individuals involved in adoptive kinship. In the United States, the panoply of strictures protects cultural views of the person that are tied to increasingly articulated assumptions of *natural* endowment. The intensity of the controversy over unsealing records reveals both the significance and the peril of recognizing the tug of blood in adoption. Stringent efforts to dismiss biological origins point to the cultural importance of those origins. The continued convention of banishing the *birthparent* points to the importance of birth. All in all, an insistence that nature can be overridden in adoptive kinship has made nature ever more present in participants' views of adoption—and has inspired a reform movement in which the major plank rests on the significance of birth.

Shrouded in secrecy, blood ties have assumed special importance, manifested in quests for information, searches for kin, and demands for full disclosure. In the open, in an Oceanic society, ties of birth fit into a complex network of relationships the child has, acquires, and establishes (or discards) over time. "Blood" is not who the child *is* any more than the flower in her hair or the smoothness of his skin.

Historically, American adoption has operated under the principle that nurture conquers nature and that a child can thrive when transplanted into a new environment. How does that familiar notion fit with the outburst of searching, the spreading petitions for access to unrevised birth certificates, and the calls for open adoption of the past twenty-five years? Assessments of adoption and its outcomes—its benefits for the individual and for the community—have always referred to the consequences of being brought up without biological connections. Today's arguments for unsealing records and disclosing information, however, rearrange the old dichotomy by urging that proper nurture requires nature. An emphasis on the frailty of nurture without nature, while resonating to cultural viewpoints in general, has particular implications for adoptive kinship. So, while adoption works on an individual level because adults believe they can raise a "stranger" child, it is also true that many of those adults request information on the child's "natural endowment" in order to raise her well. And while adoption works on a societal level because of a cultural conviction that transplantation into a fresh environment will benefit a child, in practice the child's traits (however designated) determine where he or she is "best" placed. The "bad seed" story of earlier decades is silent, but American adoption practices follow a narrative in which any seed flourishes best in nearly indigenous soil. Metaphors and images play the contrapuntal theme to official policy: roots, for instance, and family trees, words like flourishing and thriving, all keep "nature" heavily in the discourse of a legally constituted kinship.

References to nature and to biological ancestry may steer clear of bad-seed analogies, but they maintain the notion of a seed in interpretations of the child's being. Looking at Oceanic adoption again exposes the inconsistencies in American adoption. In the United States, practices focus on fitting the child into the right niche, ensuring that there are no insurmountable differences between the child and his adoptive parents, and generally treating placement as a round-peg-for-round-hole task. Such a task is not an element in adoption decisions in Oceanic cultures, where the child's identity is not thought to depend so completely on a perceptible (measurable) "fit" with an adult. Rather, the child grows up under the (loving) tutelage of an adult, expected to acquire his or her own traits and tendencies along the way. The idea that identity develops, following an individual course, is characteristic of Oceanic notions of the person, but not—despite cultural emphasis on individuality—American notions. In an American context, parents work hard to make something familiar of the child and work harder when the child is a "stranger."

Assumptions about identity affect adoption wherever it occurs. In the United States, to the extent that identity is thought to depend on blood ties and to be grounded in genetics, adopting must be regarded by many as a risk. In Oceanic societies, where identity is thought to evolve in a supportive environment, adoption is considered no more risky than any other way of bringing up a child. In American culture, a risk creates a vacuum which experts step in to fill. The state intrudes in the process to make sure the environment of the adoptive family is right for the nature of the adopted child. The state intrudes in order to facilitate the permanent transfer of a child from a "poor" to a "rich" environment.

Desiring and deserving a child

American adoption policy presumes that love propels an adoption. Simultaneously, adoption policy has established elaborate criteria for designating a qualified adoptive parent. Rhetorical emphases on love, feelings, and caring go hand in hand with the refinement of measures for distinguishing one kind of parent from another, producing a contradiction that plagues members of the triad. And yet the gesture of applying objective criteria to parenthood perfectly suits an American culture in which calculation is thought to minimize risk. By mid-twentieth century, it was clear that adoption *was* considered risky, for the child and for the adults. Described as it might be in a language of love, adoption struck many observers, and some participants, as the solution to a crisis. According to one expert: "The adoption of a child is, in human terms, always a painful and potentially traumatic event. In our culture, adoption occurs only when something has gone quite seriously wrong."[8]

As a "painful and potentially traumatic event," adoption drew the attention of professionals. A century ago, charity workers determined the decisions that were made about a child. Half a century later, a profession of social workers took over the task of establishing criteria for parenthood; conveyed to a public, these criteria shaped ideas about the best interests of a child in private arenas as well. The criteria were refined, systematized, tested and evaluated, inevitably becoming part of the discourse on adoption for birthparents, adoptees, and potential adoptive parents. If the elaboration of standards indicates the degree of outside interference in an adoptive arrangement, such elaboration also influences self-perceptions, and in this most self-conscious of kinship arrangements transforms a relationship between parent and child into an event based on forms and findings.

Premised on love, an adoption plan is institutionalized through the calculation of benefits, interests, and capacities. In the CWLA *Standards for Adoption Service*, phrases like stability and emotional maturity distract from the "gush" of emotion ordinarily associated with wanting a child or being a parent. Ultimately, love seems to fade from the process, only to return after the participants have moved back into their domestic privacy. Love, in other words, does not explicitly enter the proceedings in an agency, a lawyer's office, or a courtroom. In the paradox that outspoken birthparents voice, under some circumstances love may be regarded as *antagonistic to* the best interests of a child.

The entry of trained professionals into adoption proceedings accompanied the passing of adoption laws state by state. Justified as a protection of the child's interests, the presence of experts also defends adoption against accusations that the exchange represents the selfish interests of adults. Over the course of the twentieth century, American adoption policy increasingly constructed the interests of adults as antithetical to those of children; between the lines, texts assumed that adult interests were self-serving, not charitable or altruistic or, even, good-hearted. Systematizing the criteria for a good parent constituted a rearguard action against the assumption, enforcing a separation between the *placement* and the *exchange* of a child. The horror of "marketing babies" as much as anything else upholds the role of professionals in adoption. The presence of experts removes market principles from adoptive transactions by obscuring the presence of such principles.

At the same time, few participants in adoption deny the importance of choice. The element of choice, and the capacity to fulfill one's desires, brings a supply and demand ratio in the front door and market principles slide in the back door of adoption. The ratio suffers ups and downs, the roller coaster ride of any relationship between "availability" and "demand." Despite the rhetoric of care, concern, and commitment, appropriate to the exchange of a child, market principles influence the distribution of children in the United States. Rules set by agencies and by state officials gloss over the consumerism while in effect determining the terms of a trade. As popular and some professional literature indicates, the line between choice and consumerism, desire for a child and willingness to pay, is reed-thin. Both media accounts and manuals for participants in adoption emphasize the importance of choosing—other parents, a child, a form of adopting. The same accounts and manuals reveal how close to the commercial domain adoption is. Moreover, the recent expansion of international and independent adoptions inserts market principles quite blatantly into the transaction, with deep cuts into cultural interpretations of parenthood and family. There are advantages to a "market". That those who can pay can have a child means that the non-conventional, the single, the gay, the lesbian, and even the old find an opportunity for being a parent once not theirs.

At the same time, the part supply and demand play in adoption practice prevents "gift" from being the model for American customs. While forms of exchange have changed, issuing in new conceptualizations of the parents who are bound together in the transaction, resistance to "gift" suggests how important market principles remain. In many ways, of course, gift is the culturally appropriate model, with its connotations of generosity and of intimacy, of trust and ongoing reciprocity. Yet "gift" seems threatening, underlining the chaos and lack of regulation some commentators already condemn in independent adoptions. Perhaps gift is more threatening inasmuch as the concept is used by those who object vociferously to the hoops and checks plaguing American adoption. In this rhetoric, "gift" constitutes a resistance to the importance of material resources in the placement of a child and to the intrusive supervision the state imposes on this particular form of family. The concept of gift prevails especially in the rhetoric used by advocates of open adoption, which does not help. But the model suits the diffuse arrangements of open adoption; despite their differences, open adoptions all assume a connection between the adults who share an interest in the child and some assume a personal contact between those adults. Open adoption links adults in their involvement with the child rather than separating them as unequal "bargainers" for the child's future.[9] From this perspective, the direct, reciprocal, and personal exchange of a gift is the proper model for the transfer of a child.

Resistance to open adoption is strenuous throughout all fifty states. Besides the articulated objections, that the arrangement is unreliable and confusing to a child, the unarticulated heart of the matter lies in exactly what gift implies: the creation of bonds between adults, the spontaneous expression of concern, and the focus on connections that extend beyond those between a parent and a child. While opposition to open adoption is phrased in terms of the interests of children, the source of the intensity lies in its perceived attack on the integrity of the family. In the United States, adoption is regulated precisely because it serves the function of upholding an ideology of the family. Gift undermines the ideology by (apparently) introducing whim and wish into a social institution, dissolving the normative unit with a bevy of individual interactions. The courts that formalize an adoption present a model of the family not an imprimatur on the exchange of a child.

A grandmother in Hawaii looks askance at the rules and regulations characteristic of American adoption, with their apparent elimination of generosity and love from the transaction in parenthood. She has raised her daughter's child since that child's birth, without questioning her motives, desire, or capacity to parent. She wants to help her daughter, she loves her grandchild, and she respects the centuries long Hawaiian custom of giving the first girl grandchild to the mother's mother. Whether or not she matches the child or is deemed competent on someone else's scale of parental behavior does not enter her narrative. She talks instead of her feelings for the child, of pride in her own generosity, and of the "natural" gesture of taking in a child who needs security and permanency. Her story, however, is not well-received in the American courtroom where she has taken a petition to become the legal parent of her granddaughter. Over the bench, the judge looks down, wondering whether the grandmother is the "best" parent for the child. Depending on his background, training, and personality, he may apply criteria strictly or loosely; he may simply leave the child where she is loved or he may request a report from a child welfare agency on the condition of the home and its residents. Two cultures come together in that courtroom, with contrasting ideas about the best interests of a child.

The principle of "best interests" does not provide a certain guideline in the Solomonic judgments of a child's future. In the end, the principle primarily has symbolic significance. "Best interests" reminds participants, professionals, and the public that children are not being moved arbitrarily, to satisfy the (selfish) desires of an adult. Reference to best interests, too, legitimizes an external assessment of parental capability, by the moral legislators of a community, by the judge in a divorce case, or by social workers in the case of neglected, abandoned, relinquished, or at-risk children. Moreover, "best interests" glosses over the fact that these assessments are (often) determined by categories that have little or nothing to do with the *person* of the child. Rather, they are based on contemporaneous interpretations of race, gender, and class. Best interests naturalizes these interpretations by linking them to a child's well-being.

With the child as the center of concern, the state delegates parenthood by applying familiar social and cultural classifications. Agents and officials who carry out the state's authority draw on such categorical discriminations in order to systematize decisions about parenthood. Dependence on categories exists wherever the state plays the main part in transactions in parenthood, but the categories themselves vary from time to time and place to place. North American adoption history can be written around the virtually unchanging categories of race, class, and gender; evaluations of a child's welfare are premised on distinctions that can be traced to interpretations of these categories. Applied by officials and internalized by participants, such categories come to seem a "natural" way of determining the best placement for a child. Moreover, as I have shown in the previous four chapters, the categorical distinctions among kinds of parent stand fast through shifts in policy and in the adopting population. As long as categories are applied case by case, the fortress is strong. Another condition of state discipline, however, is resistance to the particular forms of discipline a state imposes.

Under conditions of "modernity," legal historian Lawrence Friedman writes, state discipline penetrates the most intimate domains of life.[10] American adoption is a prime example of such penetration. American adoption is also a prime example of resistance to intervention in intimate domains. The resulting struggle dominates the narrative I present in this book: the multiple ways in which individuals who take on or who relinquish parenthood challenge state discipline and, with it, the categories a culture enforces. The previous chapters delineate another condition of modernity, the diversity of interpretations on subjects as close to home, and to the social order, as parent-child relationships and individual identity.

Adoption as a social problem

Given short shrift in scholarly literature, adoption for a long while was treated as simply a personal event. Even Jack Goody's seminal comparative analysis of forms of adoption throughout the world (and over time) treats the phenomenon in terms of *individual* management—of resources, of infertility, of marriage strategies, of upward mobility, and so forth.[11] The two volumes on adoption in Oceanic societies I have cited expanded anthropological perspectives by delineating the social causes and consequences of distinctive patterns of adopting.[12] Little scholarship exists, so far, on the fourth of the contradictions I listed. In the last decades of the twentieth century, a famously *secret* phenomenon, adoption became one of the most *exposed* issues in industrialized societies. Sealed records and closed files are open to a wide public as a matter of divisive debate.

By the end of the century, too, personal experiences of adoption were well out of the closet. Memoirs and autobiographies, marches on the Washington, D.C. Mall, and pleas for access to information brought individuals forward, and multiple voices now shape the meaning and the significance of adoption. The resulting negotiations over the policies and the practices of child placement demonstrate that while members of the triad may look like the average neighbors on any street, they are often the harbingers of new modes of forming relationships. Frequently, they do not look like the "average neighbors:" two men pushing a baby carriage, a middle-aged woman with tiny Korean children in tow, a white family with brown children—these are the new adoptive parents of a new century, once dismissed by agencies and by independent mediators in child exchange. Such new parents are incompletely acknowledged elements in a new problem, that of thousands of bereft, abandoned, and at-risk children.

The 1997 Adoption and Safe Families Act treats the neglect and the desperate plight of children as a social problem. "A 'social problem' is a category of thought, a way of seeing certain conditions that provide the source for a claim to change through public actions. The concept is a part of modern language; the idea is a part of modern culture."[13] In this instance, the "public actions" the act calls for are subsumed under a concept of adoption, which is to say under the triad of parenthood, family, and kinship. The way the word adoption appears in the act reflects the perceived urgency of the problem. Throughout the text, the word has a conventional meaning that is designed to recruit adoptive applicants. But this gesture ignores the very individuals who in their practices boldly and persistently revise American adoption.

The Clinton Administration is not the first nor will it be the last to consider adoption a key approach to the plight of children living in unsafe situations. The 1997 act puts a big burden on adoption, not only to shore up the failings in (some) parents but also to compensate for a terribly weakened welfare system. As presented, adoption solves several social problems. This, too, has precedent in the history of North American adoption, which early on served the wider purposes of social control through public (legislative, judicial, or professional) decisions about parent-child relationships. Adoption proceedings sanction one behavior through the condemnation of another; the "taker" of a child contrasts with the giver, who is pictured as an "immoral mother," an "irresponsible girl," or a "promiscuous teen." However pictured, the individual *loses* when her parenthood comes under scrutiny. Surrender reinforces moral values as thoroughly as do the state appointed agents who re-place a child. TPR (termination of parental rights) dramatizes an existing pattern of judgment that is as caught by convention as by concern for a child's best interests. On the level of symbolic politics, Clinton's adoption initiative preserves the moral and the normative functions American adoption has historically had.

On the level of real politics, Clinton's adoption initiative proposes an apparently unproblematic solution to the astonishing fact of over half a million at-risk children in the most advanced nation in the world. Sweeping advocacy of adoption complements the federal government's reluctance to intervene in the child welfare and foster care systems that are managed by states. The act does not challenge the rights of states to disburse child welfare funds according to their own fiscal and legal strictures. Instead, the act promises monetary awards for each new adoption a state deems legal. Successful programs for placing children permanently receive not only money but also kudos from the federal government. Clinton's Adoption 2002 initiative will undoubtedly continue under a new administration which, like the old, supports "family" as the best guarantee of security for a child.

Regardless of administration, the solution to the crisis of neglected, abandoned, and abused children is a case by case one: child by child, family by family, and state by state. Focus on the particulars is a persistent feature of American adoption history, and a turn from communal to familial responsibility has a long past. Without doubt, the permanent redelegation of parenthood is a *personal* event; if not a response to trauma, certainly in the United States an event with enormous impact on an individual's circumstances and sense of self. The extremely personal emphasis in American cultural views of adoption appears in programs for implementing the 1997 act. Many of these programs depend on persuading potential parents of the appeal of a particular child: a young girl who is sweet and good-natured despite a history of abuse; a young black boy who loves sports and would respond to a caring family; siblings who must be placed together, and so on. While these ads effectively win the hearts of potential parents, they demonstrate how fully American adoption policy avoids the structural and economic conditions that create an ever-expanding supply of available children.

Personalizing also works to bring the best interests principle down to earth. The principle is most persuasive as an interpretation of a particular child's needs and an assessment of the environment that will meet those needs—that is, the family that can provide permanent safety and security. This view of the best interests principle justifies the intense scrutiny of applicants for permanent parenthood and the measures that, as I have described, narrow the criteria by which applicants are judged. Moreover, a case-by-case interpretation of best interests legitimizes the intrusion of experts into the transfer of children.

The "unfit" and the "fit" parent come to be judged by criteria that often have little to do with a person's motives for giving or receiving a child. The criteria instead serve to delineate good and bad *kinds* of parent, an outcome that is accentuated by the increased use of TPR proceedings which are more punitive than the "surrender" about which members of CUB complain. The Adoption and Safe Families Act presents the paradox of at once putting adoption to vast new uses and leaving intact the restrictions on participants in adoptive relationships. Like the federal guidelines for child placement policy promulgated in earlier decades, the adoption initiatives of the mid-1990s obscure the ultimate *impersonality* of standards of parenthood by assuming shared cultural understandings of parenthood and family.

In fact adoption practices expose the delusion in assuming shared understandings of parenthood and family. Deliberated and contracted, adoption exposes an array of understandings that run parallel to the rules and regulations prevailing in the public domains of the transaction. Independent and international adoptions constitute one version of guerilla actions against official doctrine, and these are complemented by the numerous agencies that for one reason or another radically alter their practices of placing children. Adoption turns the private and intimate matter of family composition into a public and legislated affair of the state; in the face of this, adoption relentlessly inspires subversive actions to protect the "private." The confrontation is especially sharp in periods of imbalance between the supply of and the demand for adoptable children. In recent American history, the imbalance has occurred in times of a radical reconstruction of the family that has nothing to do with adoption. The combination dismantles the old shibboleths guiding best-interests decisions.

Federal and state policies dealing with the placement of children uphold the ideal of a nuclear family, a married couple, and a stable income for ensuring the safety and security of a child. Furthermore, official dictates continue to maintain the importance of *matching,* albeit transformed into a claim that a stranger child should be as familiar to the adoptive parents as possible. In recent decades, matching practices too demonstrate widely diverse interpretations—for instance, an adopted child with a laugh like his adoptive father's—with one primary exception. Even with a majority of those half a million at-risk children belonging to minority groups, matching by race regulates placement practice.

Maybe necessarily. Adoption *is* a personal event, and in a culture in which personal identity continues to be linked to a notion of "roots," matching serves a personal purpose. More than that, matching reflects the persistent cultural purpose adoption serves, extending beyond the care of children at risk and beyond the satisfaction of an adult's desire for a child. Adoption maintains certain *kind*s of kinship. And to the extent that it does, that function stands in the way of reaching the goal Clinton's 1997 act set: providing safe, secure, and permanent placement for every American child. Maintaining a certain kind of kinship does not serve the sweeping social-political goals of the act. The act addresses the sudden plight of a generation of children who are at risk of *not* thriving, but it follows old precedents of disciplining parents and regulating families. The Adoption and Safe Families Act sidesteps the conditions that put thousands of children in a highly industrialized nation at risk of their lives. It minimizes the accumulation of policy decisions that have deprived individuals of the resources for constructing (or rehabilitating) their own parent-child relationships.

There are chinks in the wall and breaks in the mold. The "precedents" in American adoption history are not only court cases, judicial opinions, and legislative acts. They are also individuals who give and take children, who assume permanent responsibility, and who relinquish the as-if-begotten ideal for having a child. *Contracted* kinship sounds constrained; in fact, contracted kinship is as close to "chosen" kinship as anything we have. In practice, the meanings of adoption are undergoing steady modification and revision. Without the indigenous practices and interpretations—the distinct and individualized, daunting and innovative actions taken by participants in adoption—, the solution in the 1997 act would be a fantasy. Instead, the goal of increasing adoptions in the twenty-first century has a chance of working—and of unmistakably altering adoption.

Reconfiguring kinship and family

Every bit of encouragement for adoption in the act and in the DHHS reports on its implementation changes the meaning of adoption. An emphasis on racial matching and on placing a child in an environment that looks like her or his "natural" environment persists. At the same time, interpretations of the meaning of the principle—of what, simply, "likeness" signifies—do not persist. The "open arms" Clinton relished in his rhetoric exist, largely because they encompass far more than he dared to announce in speeches and in texts. The open arms are far more important to American adoption in the twenty-first century than are open records, for they tell of all the possible arrangements any number of individuals can make concerning the (permanent) transfer of a child. The argument for open records, and for contact with biological kin, is conservative inasmuch as it takes up the discussion of genetic engineering, biological endowment, and DNA that fills much of public discourse these days. Truly open arms, by contrast, banish the interpretations of kinship that are grounded in (presumed) facts of genetic heritage and persistent traits. This is not to say that genes are irrelevant to a person. It is to say that in adoptions as they develop despite policy, genes are irrelevant to the parent-child relationship.

Changes in American adoption have always come about from the bottom up. Centralized child placement policy, in the form of ideologies of the family, is continually threatened by centrifugal forces. While the 1990s initiative depends on a familiar (and familial) connotation of adoption, it is rescued by the existence of multiple perspectives on the transaction in parenthood. Those perspectives constitute the bedrock for the success of a policy that advocates permanency for all children.

The lessons an anthropologist can draw from adoption in small-scale, homogeneous societies are especially pertinent to the circumstances of adopting in the heterogeneous and complex society Clinton's initiative addresses. No longer the baby of a stranger, the child of adoption is now an older child, a child who will know and visit his biological parents, and a child who comes from a culture that is vastly different from that of the adopting parents. The extent to which records are open and documents accessible to every participant becomes an aspect of the reformulation of kinship these arrangements require and not any longer the central issue in adoption. Like adoptions in traditional cultures, adoptions in twenty-first century American society lean on the openness of individuals to various modes of relating to the knowledge inscribed on papers and to the actions and expressions of unfamiliar kin. There is little opportunity for closed files and hidden information in these situations. There is also little opportunity for imposing distance and with it discriminatory judgments, on the participants in such intimate and chosen adoptions.

Perhaps, adoption will now serve the best interests of the children. Perhaps, too, in serving the best interests of the children, adoption can now serve the function of expanding rather than narrowing the meaning of a parent-child relationship. As the DHHS report insisted in 1997: the time is now, the chance is ours.

These developments make it clear that in the United States, at the beginning of the twenty-first century, an individual child is not the sole subject of an adoption. The pretense that fictive kinship exists solely for the child's sake vanishes. The reality of bonds between adults enters adoptive arrangements. Should these signs of social and communal solidarity persist, the result would be placement policy that is—at last—in the best interests of children.

Notes

1. In an early essay comparing American with Oceanic forms of adoption, Vern Carroll rightly points to the difficulties of using one word to cover the diversity of ways in which children are permanently "reallocated" to new parents. Carroll 1970.
2. Oregon joins Kansas, Alaska, Delaware, Tennessee, and Alaska in granting adoptees access to unamended birth documents; that is, six of the fifty states grant access.
3. Rondell and Michaels 1951.
4. Independent adoptions are threatening to the extent they escape this supervision—or seem to.
5. Carroll 1970: 11.

6. The process of modernization throughout the Pacific produces a tension between customary modes of adopting (exchanging) children and those represented by modern, capitalist (imperialist) societies.

7. My book has discussed only "stranger" adoptions, inasmuch as these reflect and reveal core assumptions about kinship and identity in the United States. It would be interesting to explore the interpretations of kinship and of identity for children adopted by relatives, by a parent's new spouse, and so forth.

8. Brinich 1980: 107.

9. Modell 1999.

10. Friedman 1990.

11. Goody 1969.

12. Carroll (ed.) 1970; Brady (ed.) 1976.

13. Gusfield 1996: 18.

Bibliography

Adoptalk. Newsletter for Adoptive Parents. Minneapolis, Minn.
Adoption Advocates:
   file:///jm%27s%20harddisk/Desktop%20Folder/
Adoption and Safe Families Act:
   file://C/ProgramFiles?Netscape/Navigator/Program/
   useftp.cgi
Allegheny County, Department of Human Services. 1998.
   *Redesigning Human Services Delivery in Allegheny
   County*. Ms. in author's possession.
ASG Newsletter. 1985-1998. Gibsonia, Penna.: ASG
   Headquarters.
Bachrach, Christine. 1986. "Adoption Plans, Adopted Children,
   and Adoptive Mothers." *Journal of Marriage and the
   Family* 48: 243-253.
Bachrach, C., P. F. Adams, S. Sambrano and K.A. London. 1990.
   Adoption in the 1980's. Hyattsville, Md.: U.S. Department
   of Health and Human Services.
Bartholet, Elizabeth. 1993. *Family Bonds: Adoption and the
   Politics of Parenting*. Boston: Houghton Mifflin.
Bartholet, Elizabeth. 1999. *Nobody's Children: Abuse and
   Neglect, Foster Drift, and the Adoption Alternative*. Boston:
   Beacon Press.
Bascom, B. B., and C. A. McKelvey. 1997. *The Complete Guide
   to Foreign Adoption*. New York: Pocket Books.
Bass, Celia. 1975. "Matchmaker-Matchmaker: Older-Child
   Adoption Failures." *Child Welfare* 54: 505-512.

Beck, Ulrich. 1992. *Risk Society: Towards a New Modernity.*
Thousand Oaks, Calif.: Sage Publications.

Becker, Gary S. 1991. *A Treatise on the Family.* Cambridge,
Mass.: Harvard University Press.

Bellingham, Bruce. 1986. "Institution and Family: An
Alternative View of Nineteenth-Century Child Saving."
Social Problems 33 (6): 33-57.

Benet, Mary Kathleen. 1976. *The Politics of Adoption.* New
York: Free Press.

Best, Joel. 1990. *Threatened Children: Rhetoric of Concern
about Child Victims.* Chicago: University of Chicago.

Blustein, Jeffrey. 1982. *Parents and Children: Ethics of the
Family.* New York: Oxford University Press.

Brady, Ivan (ed.). 1976. *Transactions in Kinship.* Honolulu:
University Press of Hawaii.

Brinich, P. M. 1980. "Some Potential Effects of Adoption on
Self and Object Relations." *Psychoanalytic Study of the
Child* 32: 107-133.

Brodzinsky, D. and M. Schechter (eds.). 1990. *The Psychology
of Adoption.* New York: Oxford University Press.

Brodzinsky, D., M. Schechter, and R. M. Henig. 1992. *Being
Adopted: The Lifelong Search for Self.* New York:
Doubleday Anchor Books.

Burgess, Linda C. 1981. *The Art of Adoption.* New York: W.W.
Norton.

Burke, Kenneth. 1971. *A Rhetoric of Motives.* Berkeley:
University of California Press.

Campbell, Lee. 1979. "The Birthparent's Right to Know."
Public Welfare 37: 22-27.

Caplan, Lincoln. 1990. "An Open Adoption," Parts I and II. *The
New Yorker.* May 21: 40-65, and May 28: 73-95.

Carp, E. Wayne. 1998. *Family Matters.* Cambridge, Mass.:
Harvard University Press.

Carrieri, Joseph R. 1991. *Child Custody, Foster Care, and
Adoptions.* New York: Lexington Books.

Carroll, Vern. 1970. "Introduction: What does 'Adoption'
Mean?" *Adoption in Eastern Oceania.* pp. 3-17. Honolulu:
University Press of Hawaii.

Carroll, Vern (ed.). 1970. *Adoption in Eastern Oceania*.
Honolulu: University Press of Hawaii.

Child Welfare League of America (CWLA). 1978. *Standards for Adoption Service*. New York: CWLA.

Children's Home of Los Angeles. n.d. Ms. in author's possession.

Cole, E. and K.S. Donley. 1990. "History, Values, and Placement Policy Issues in Adoption." Brodzinsky and Schechter, *The Psychology of Adoption*. pp. 273-294. New York: Oxford University Press.

CUB Communicator. 1970-1990. Dover, N.H. (1979-1986): CUB Headquarters; and Des Moines, Iowa (1986-1990): CUB Headquarters.

CUB New Member Information. Dover, N.H.: n.d.

Derdeyn, A. 1990. "Foster Parent Adoption: The Legal Framework." Brodzinsky and Schechter. *The Psychology of Adoption*. pp. 332-347. New York: Oxford University Press.

Developments. Penna.: University of Pittsburgh Office of Child Development. 1994-2000. Pittsburgh.

Evan B. Donaldson Adoption Institute.
http://www.adoptioninstitute.org

Executive Order, Adoption 2002. 1996: file://C/ProgramFiles/ NetscapeNavigator/Program/2002body.htm.

Feigelman, W. and A.R. Silverman. 1983. *Chosen Children: New Patterns of Adoptive Relationships*. New York: Praeger.

Fisher, Florence. 1973. *The Search for Anna Fisher*. New York: Arthur Fields.

Friedman, Lawrence M. 1990. *The Republic of Choice: Law, Authority, and Culture*. Cambridge, Mass.: Harvard University Press.

Gediman, Judith S. and L.P. Brown. 1989. *Birth Bond: Reunions Between Birthparents and Adoptees*. Far Hills, N.J.: New Horizon.

Gillis, John. 1996. *A World of Their Own Making*. Cambridge, Mass.: Harvard University Press.

Goldstein, J., A. Freud and A.J. Solnit. [1973] 1979. *Beyond the Best Interests of the Child*. New York: Free Press.

Goldstein, J., A. Freud and A.J. Solnit. 1979. *Before the Best Interests of the Child*. New York: Free Press.

Goldstein, J., A. Freud, A.J. Solnit and S. Goldstein. 1986. *In the Best Interests of the Child*. New York: Free Press.

Goody, Esther N. 1982. *Parenthood and Social Reproduction: Fostering and Occupational Roles in West Africa*. New York: Cambridge University Press.

Goody, Jack. 1969. "Adoption in Cross-Cultural Perspective." *Comparative Studies in Society and History* II: 55-78.

Gordon, Linda. 1988. *Heroes of Their Own Lives: The Politics and History of Family Violence*. New York: Viking Penguin.

Gritter, James. 2000. *Lifegivers: Framing the Birthparent Experience in Open Adoption*. Washington, D.C.: CWLA Press.

Grossberg, Michael. 1985. *Governing the Hearth: Law and the Family in Nineteenth-Century America*. Chapel Hill: The University of North Carolina Press.

Grossberg, Michael. 1996. *A Judgment for Solomon: The D'Hauteville Case and Legal Experience in Antebellum America*. New York: Cambridge University Press.

Gusfield, Joseph R. 1996. *Contested Meanings: The Construction of Alcohol Problems*. Madison: The University of Wisconsin Press.

Heinz, H. John III. Archives. Carnegie Mellon Libraries.

Herring, David. 1998. "The Role of the Child Welfare Agency Caseworker in the Involuntary Termination of Parental Rights." *Developments* 12 (1): 5-7. Pittsburgh, Penna.: University of Pittsburgh Office of Child Development.

Hocking, Ian. 2000. *The Social Construction of What*. Cambridge, Mass.: Harvard University Press.

Hollinger, Joan H. 1998 [1988]. *Adoption Law and Practice: 1998 Supplement*. New York: Matthew Bender.

Hulbert, Anne. 1998. "In the Bosom of the Family." *The New York Review of Books*. June 11: 54-56.

Inglis, Kate. 1984. *Living Mistakes: Mothers Who Consented to Adoption*. Boston: Allen and Unwin.

Joe, Barbara. 1979. *Public Policies Toward Adoption*. Washington, D.C.: The Urban Institute.

Katz, Sanford. 1971. *When Parents Fail*. New York: Beacon Press.

Kirk, H. David. 1984. *Shared Fate: A Theory and Method of Adoptive Relationships* (2nd ed.) Port Angeles, Wash.: Ben Simon Publications.

LaShawn et. al. v. Sharon Pratt Dixon (Washington, D.C.). 1991. Ms. in author's possession.

Levy, Robert. 1973. *The Tahitians: Mind and Experience in the Society Islands*. Chicago: University of Chicago Press.

Lifton, Betty Jean. 1977 [1975]. *Twice-Born: Memoirs of an Adopted Daughter*. New York: Penguin Books.

Lifton, Betty Jean. 1979. *Lost and Found: The Adoption Experience*. New York: Harper and Row.

Lifton, Betty Jean. 1994. *Journey of the Adopted Self*. New York: Basic Books.

Lindsay, Jeanne Warren. 1987. *Open Adoption: A Caring Option*. Buena Park, Calif.: Morning Glory Press.

Loux, Ann Kimble. 1997. "The Catch That Came With Our Adoption." *The Washington Post*, November 23, 1997: C1-C2.

Maas, H.S. and R.E. Engler. 1959. *Children in Need of Parents*. New York: Columbia University Press.

Mason, Mary Ann. 1994. *From Father's Property to Children's Rights: The History of Child Custody in the United States*. New York: Columbia University Press.

McKelvey, C.A. and J. Stevens. 1994. *Adoption Crisis: The Truth Behind Adoption and Foster Care*. Golden, Colo.: Fulcrum Publishing.

McRoy, R.G., H.D. Grotevant and K.C. White. 1988. *Openness in Adoption*. New York: Praeger.

McRoy, R.G. and H.D. Grotevant. 1991. "The American experience and research on openness in adoption." *British Journal of Adoption and Fostering* 15 (4): 99-111.

Meezan, W., S. Katz and E.M. Russo. 1978. *Adoption Without Agencies: A Study of Independent Adoption*. New York: Child Welfare League of America.

Meezan, W. and J. Shireman. 1985. *Care and Commitment: Foster Parent Adoption Decisions*. Albany, N.Y.: State University of New York.

Mnookin, Robert. 1985. *In the Interest of Children*. New York: W.H. Freeman and Company.

Modell, Judith S. 1986. "In Search: The Purported Biological Basis of Parenthood." *American Ethnologist* 13 (4): 646-661.

Modell, Judith S. 1988. "Meanings of Love: Adoption Literature and Dr. Spock, 1946-1985." Stearns, C.Z., and P. Stearns. *Emotion and Social Change*. pp. 151-192. New York: Holmes and Meier.

Modell, Judith S. 1992. "How do you introduce yourself as a childless mother?" Rosenweig, G. and R. Ochberg. *Storied Lives: The Cultural Politics of Self Understanding*. pp. 76-94. New Haven: Yale University Press.

Modell, Judith S. 1994. *Kinship with Strangers: Adoption and Interpretations of Kinship in American Culture*. Berkeley: University of California Press.

Modell, Judith S. 1999. "Freely Given: Open Adoptions and the Rhetoric of Gift." Layne, Linda. *The Rhetoric of the Gift: Transformative Motherhood in a Consumer Culture*. New York: New York University Press.

Network News: Statewide Adoption Network. 1990-2000. Pennsylvania Department of Public Welfare, Office of Childcare, Youth and Families. Harrisburg, Penna.

Paton, Jean [Ruthena Hill Kittson]. 1968. *Orphan Voyage*. New York: Vantage Press.

Pertman, Adam. 2000. *Adoption Nation: How the Adoption Revolution is Transforming America*. New York: Basic Books.

Prager, B. and S. A. Rothstein. 1973. "The Adoptee's Right to Know his Natural Heritage." *New York Law Forum* 19: 137-156.

Putnam, Robert D. 2000. *Bowling Alone: The Collapse and Revival of American Community*. New York: Simon & Schuster.

Rillera, Mary Jo. 1991. *The Reunion Book* Vol 1. Westminster, Calif.: Triadoption Publications.

Rondell, F. and R. Michaels. 1951. *The Adopted Family*. New York: Crown Publishers.

Ratterman, Debra. 1986. "Judicial Determination of Reasonable Efforts to Preserve Families" *Children Today*. Nov-Dec: 29-32.

Sanger, Carol. 1996. "Separating From Children." *Columbia Law Review*. 96 (2): 375-517.

Schechter, M. and D. Bertocci. 1990. "The Meaning of the Search." Brodzinsky and Schechter. *The Psychology of Adoption*. pp. 62-90. New York: Oxford University Press.

Scheper-Hughes, Nancy. 1992. *Death Without Weeping: The Violence of Everyday Life In Brazil*. Berkeley: University of California Press.

Scheper-Hughes, Nancy and C. Sargent (eds.). 1998. *Small Wars: The Cultural Politics of Childhood*. Berkeley: University of California Press.

Schneider, David M. 1984. *A Critique of the Study of Kinship*. Ann Arbor: The University of Michigan Press.

Silber, K. and P.M. Dorner. 1990. *Children of Open Adoptions*. San Antonio, Tex.: Corona Publishing Co.

Smith, J. and F.I. Miroff. 1987. *"You're Our Child": The Adoption Experience*. New York: Madison Books.

Solinger, Rickie. 1992. *Wake Up Little Susie: Single Pregnancy and Race Before Roe v Wade*. New York: Routledge.

Solinger, Rickie. 1994. "'Race and Value': Black and White Illegitimate Babies, 1945-1965." Glenn, E.N., G. Chang and L.R. Forcey. *Mothering: Ideology, Experience, and Agency*. pp. 287-310. New York: Routledge.

Sorosky, A.D., A. Baran and R. Pannor. 1979. *The Adoption Triangle*. New York: Anchor Books.

Talbot, Margaret. 1998. "Attachment Theory: The Ultimate Experiment." *The New York Times Magazine*. May 24: 24-38 and 50-54.

The New York Times. 1986-2001. Miscellaneous articles.

Tiffin, Susan. 1982. *In Whose Best Interest? Child Welfare Reform in the Progressive Era.* Westport, Conn.: Greenwood Press.

Time Magazine. 1991. October 21: 88.

U.S. Government. *Adoption Assistance and Child Welfare Act.* 1980. PL 96-272.

U.S. Government. *Adoption and Safe Families Act.* 1997. PL 105-89.

U.S. Government. *The Multiethnic Placement Act.* 1994.

U.S. Government. *Congressional Hearings before the Subcommittee on Children and Human Development of the Committee on Labor and Human Resources.* April 1980.

U.S. Government. *Congressional Hearings before the Senate Sub-committee on Security and Terrorism.* 1985.

U.S. Government. *Congressional Hearings, Oversight on Adoption Reform Act.* 1980.

U.S. Government. *Oversight on Adoption Reform Act. PL 95-266.*

U.S. Government. *Congressional Record.* 1989. 135 (106), August 11.

U.S. Government. Immigration and Naturalization Service. Reports

U.S. Government. *Department of Health and Human Services Response to Clinton Initiative.* 1998.

Waltner, Ann. 1990. *Getting an Heir: Adoption and the Construction of Kinship in Late Imperial China.* Honolulu: University of Hawaii Press.

Washington Post National Weekly Edition. 1998. Miscellaneous articles.

Waterville (Maine) Sentinel. 1981-1983. Miscellaneous articles.

Webber, Marlene. 1998. *As If Kids Mattered.* Toronto, Canada: Key Porter Books.

Wolf, A. and C. Huang. 1980. *Marriage and Adoption in China, 1845-1945.* Stanford: Stanford University Press.

Wegar, Katarina. 1997. *Adoption, Identity, and Kinship.* New Haven: Yale University Press.

Websites:

http://www.adoptioninstitute.org/research/ressta.html.

http://www.adoptlink.com/profile.htm.

http://www.adoption.com/chat.

http://www.overtherainbowad.com/possible.htm.

http://www.adoption.com/registry/search.cgi.

http://www.adoptioninstitute.org/policy/polupd1297.htm.

http://www.usnews.com/usnews/issue/980309/9tax.htm.

http://www.ggw.org/cap/aboutkids/htm.

http://www.cubirthparents.org/presidents.htm.

http://ep.com/ep/sub.htm.

Index

A

Abortion, adoption argument against, 62-63, 100
The Adopted Break Silence (Kittson), 28
Adopted child syndrome, 39
Adoptees
    access to closed/sealed records, 36-38, 55-56, 177, 198
    "biography" of, 54-55
    characteristics of, 198
    as child in a transaction, 28
    disruption of identity formation, 34-35, 55
    experiences of searching, 54-59
    "good cause" plea for information, 57-58
    "remarkable intimacy" with a stranger, 57
    reunions by adoptees, 56-60
Adoptees Liberty Movement Association (ALMA), 29
Adoptee Support Group (ASG)
    adoptees experiences of searching, 54-59
    adoption practice reforms, 76
    ASG Newsletter, 33, 57
    Disclosure (internet), 150

    freedom of information, 170
    membership of, 33
Adoption
    As academic subject, 3, 4
    adoption triad, 11-12
    And American foster care, 79-95
    charitable adoptions, 113-15
    common law adoption, 108-9
    crossing state boundaries, 115-21
    family-building to child-rescuing, 76
    focus on secrecy, 26-27, 166-72, 178-84, 199n.3, 200n.6
    fully-disclosed, 64-65
    "hard to place" and "waiting" children, 154-58
    history of American adoption and secrecy, 179-82
    in federal policy, 18, 107-15
    income-based tax subsidy, 20, 110, 158-63
    international, 11, 143-46, 189-90
    on the Internet, 11, 149, 150, 151-52, 164

matching practices, 7-8,
117-18, 157, 196-97
minority children, 112-13,
115, 164
Multiethnic Placement
Act, 117
new forms of adoption,
64-68
policies and practices,
75-123
professionalization of
state agencies, 133,
189
Public Law 105-89, 75, 76,
78, 106, 107, 108
racial policies in
American adoption,
118-21
rehabilitation of birth
families, 96
sanctions and stigmas,
194
semi-open, 64-65
serving the state's
purpose, 163-66
of sibling groups, 12
significance of
faith/religion in open
adoptions, 67
as a social transaction, 26
of "special needs"
children, 12, 111-15
traditional closed
adoption, 64-65
See also American
adoption
Adoption 2002, 107-8, 110, 120,
195
Adoption and Safe Families Act
of 1997, 75, 76, 78, 83
adoption as a social
problem, 193-94, 196,
197
criteria for adopting, 125,
127, 131
charitable and social
emergency motives,
127

expanded definition of
adoptable children, 125
financial benefits for
adoption, 156
foster care and adoption,
79-80, 109
impact of international
adoptions, 144
kin care, 127
professionalization of
state agencies, 133,
189
reunification with
biological parent,
95-107
role and place for foster
parents, 127-28
shift in child-welfare
philosophy, 107
on special needs and
minority children, 113,
115
Adoption Excellence Awards,
110, 156
Adoption Opportunities Act, 99,
161
Adoption practices
African-Americans, 2,
119, 123n.75
Hawaii, 16, 88, 108-9,
122n.55, 191
Native-Americans, 2
non-Western societies, 4
Polynesian fosterage and
adoption, 90, 122n.29
The Adoption Triangle
(Sorosky, Baran, and
Pannor), 35
Adoptive Families of America,
171
Adoptive kinship, 169-70
Adoptive Parent Registry, 153
Adoptive parents of the 21st
century
Adoption and Safe
Families Act, 125-28,
131
adoption in and for the
community, 163-72

adoptive kinship, 169-70
criteria for adoptive
  parenthood, 127, 129-
  32, 146-48
advertising in American
  adoption, 148-54
agencies, 146-48
assuming adoptive
  parenthood, 129-48
baby brokers, 139, 141-42
bias against foster
  parents, 167
breaking old molds of
  adoptive parents,
  166-70
charitable and social
  emergency motives,
  127
CWLA criteria for
  adoptive parents, 134,
  149
demographic factors, 129,
  168
disclosing information
  about a child, 150,
  170-71
"gray market" adoptions,
  147-48
"hard to place" and
  "waiting" children,
  154-58
history of adoption
  agencies, 132-36
independent
  adoptions/private
  channels, 136-42
international adoptions,
  143-46
irrevocable permanency,
  172
love and the social
  contract, 163-66
markets and consumer
  choices, 129,137-38
modern modes of placing
  children, 148-63
new possibilities for
  permanent placement,
  154-58

"ordinary" parents, 135-
  36, 151
parents matching with a
  child, 157
presentation of self as
  parent, 148-49, 157-58
pool of adoptive
  applicants, 125
role of "papers," 132
secrecy, expanding
  meanings of, 150,
  166-72
single-parent families,
  127
social work and criteria
  for parenthood, 188-89
stable marriage as
  criterion, 124-29
status of special needs
  caretakers, 162
tax breaks and subsidies,
  158-63
traditional cultural
  interpretations of a
  parent, 166
uniform standards for
  adoptive placement,
  132-36
vulnerability of adoptive
  parents, 168-69
Advertising in American
  adoption, 148-54
African-Americans
  adoption practices, 2
  cost for adopting an
    African-American
    child, 147
  racial policies in
    American adoption,
    118-21
  relinquishment, 119,
    123n.75
Alabama, access to closed/sealed
  adoption records, 55
American adoption
  access to closed/sealed
    adoption records, 177,
    199n.2

adoption as a social
  problem, 193-97
as-if-begotten, 182
"best interests of the
  child," 63, 191-92
contracted and
  consanguineal
  parenthood, 179, 182
contracted kinship, 197
contrasting with
  adoptions in Oceanic
  societies, 182-83, 184,
  185, 187, 200n.6
desiring and deserving a
  child, 187-92
genetic substance, 184
"gift" model, 190, 191
history of American
  adoption and secrecy,
  179-82
identity quests, 181-82
marketing principles in,
  189
matching practices, 7-8,
  117-18, 157, 196-97
myths of mis-placement,
  181
open adoption and
  resistance to, 190-91
reconfiguring kinship and
  family, 197-98
sanctions and stigmas,
  194
searches for blood
  ties/biological ancestry,
  186-87
secrecy of, 178-84, 199n.3,
  200n.6
social work and criteria
  for parenthood, 188-89
standards of parenthood,
  195-97
state discipline and
  parenthood, 192
study of, 176-78
"telling," 180, 199n.3
ties to legal and moral
  doctrines, 183-84

"transactions in
  parenthood," 177
transformation of
  identity, 184-87, 200n.7
American kinship,
  understanding of "family," 2
An Open Adoption (Caplan), 66
ASG Newsletter, 33, 57
As-if-begotten, 5-8,
  22nn.7,8,10,11, 171
Autonomy, 2

B

Baby brokers, 139, 141-42
Banishing secrecy,
  confidentiality, and opening
  adoption, 24-74
    activating bonds of "flesh
      and blood," 56-57
    activism and adoption
      groups, 25
    adopted child syndrome,
      39
    adoptee as child in
      transaction, 28
    adoptee experiences of
      searching, 54-60
    Adoptees Liberty
      Movement Association
      (ALMA), 29
    adoptee support groups,
      rhetoric, 32-40
    The Adoption Triangle
      (Sorosky, Baran, and
      Pannor), 35
    "best interests of the
      child," 63
    "biography" of an
      adoptee, 54-55
    birthparent experiences of
      relinquishment, 40-54,
      72n.22
    birthparents in support
      groups, 30, 31-32
    Concerned United
      Birthparents (CUB),
      24-27, 31, 40, 69

contact between adoptive
and birthparents,
61-62
diversity in adoption
arrangements, 64-68
ending a sealed and secret
kinship, 24-27, 72n.2
"fictive" to "functional"
kinship, 68-71
focus on personal identity,
26-27, 34-35
"good cause" plea for
information, 57-58
identity politics and CUB,
44-48
impact of DNA and
genetic engineering, 35
information activities to
reunion, 48-54
information request from
sealed records, 36-38
Missing in Adoption
(MIA), 42-43
moral differences of
adoptive and
birthparents, 70
National Council for
Adoption (NCFA), 27
new allies in adoption
reform, 60-71
opening records, 24-26,
27-32, 72n.2
"psychological need" for
sealed record
information, 37
reunions, 49-51, 56-60,
73n.37
right to privacy by
birthparents, 55-56
search and reunions,
60-71
secrecy and American
adoption, 26-27, 72n.4
"sharing" a child, 70
shift to non-agency
adoptions, 61
statistics on adoption, 25,
72n.2

"sunshine" laws, 27,
72n.4
Bartholet, Elizabeth, 143
Berry, Marion, 86
Betrayal, 2
*Beyond the Best Interests of the
Child* (Goldstein, Freud, and
Solnit), 89-90, 108
Birthparents
advertising in American
adoption, 148-54
banishing of, 185, 186
contact between adoptive
and birthparents,
61-62
experiences of
relinquishment, 40-54,
72n.22
impact of Adoption and
Safe Families Act,
95-107
reform groups, 19
rehabilitation of birth
families, 96
reunions, 49-51, 73n.37
rights to privacy, 2, 55-56
role in adoptive family,
165-66
shame and stigma, 52-53
shift to non-agency
adoptions, 61
in support groups and
reform, 30, 31-32
"surrender" and
"papers," 40-44,
72n.22
termination of parental
rights, 96-107
woman's issue, 46-47
Blood and biological ties,
primacy of, 6, 22n.10
Brace, Charles Loring, 77, 156,
157
Brokers, 11, 139, 141-42

C

California
    Los Angeles Department
        of Adoptions, 135
    placement rate of foster
        children, 116
    redesign of adoption
        arrangements, 64
Campbell, Lee, 24, 56
    birthparent experiences,
        40-41, 42, 44
    CUB Communicator,
        44-48
Caplan, Lincoln, 66
"Child exchange," 3
Children Awaiting Parents
    (CAP), 164
Children's Home Society of
    California, 64
Child Welfare League of
    America (CWLA)
    criteria for adoptive
        parents, 134, 149, 151
    special needs children,
        158, 161
    *Standards for Adoption
        Service*, 134, 164, 188
    systematizing child
        placement in state
        agencies, 133-35
Child Welfare Reform and
    Adoption Assistance Act of
    1980 (Public Law 96-272), 97
China, international adoptions
    from, 143, 145-46
Clinton, Hillary, 110, 136, 156
Clinton, William J., 21, 75-79,
    104, 136
    Adoption 2002, 107-8,
        110, 195
    Adoption and Safe
        Families Act, 110, 111
    adoption to save children
        at risk, 126, 194
    Executive Memorandum
        1996, 21
    "open arms" of America,
        153, 198

welfare system, 194
Concerned United Birthparents
    (CUB)
    adoption practice reforms,
        76
    birthparent rhetoric and
        experiences, 41-54
    coercion, 100-101
    disclosure (internet), 150
    freedom of information,
        170
    identity politics and,
        44-48
    membership of, 43
    role of birthparent, 185,
        186
    support group formation
        and reform, 24-27, 31,
        40, 69
    on termination of
        parental rights and
        Adoption and Safe
        Families Act, 96-97,
        196
Confidentiality,165, 178-84
Congressional Coalition on
    Adoption, 100
CUB Communicator, 41, 42,
    44-45
Cultural anthropology, study of
    adoption, 4

D

Department of Health and
    Human Services (DHHS),
    78, 81
    adoptive parenthood
        category, 127
    implementing Adoption
        and Safe Families Act
        of 1997, 107, 108,
        122n.53, 197-98, 199
    interpretation of
        Adoption
        Opportunities Act, 161,
        162

jurisdictional barriers and
state child welfare
systems, 115, 116-17
state control over
adoption process,
126-27
Disclosure, debate over, 64, 150,
170-71
District of Columbia,
Department of Human
Services (DHS), 86
"Domestic white infants"
(dwi's), 136, 140, 169
Drug abuse/chemical abuse
"crack-baby epidemic,"
102
family rehabilitation and
reunification, 98
termination of parental
rights, 103-6

E

Edna Gladney Home, 147
Ethiopia, international
adoptions from, 146

F

*Family Bonds: Adoption and
the Politics of Parenting*
(Bartholet), 143
Feigelman, William, 39
Fictive kinship, 2, 8
to functional kinship,
68-71
new "kinds" of adoptive
parents, 126
Fisher, Florence, 29
Forbes, Lorna, 135
Foreign adoption, 143-46
Fostadopt programs, 93
Foster children/foster care
Adoption and Safe
Families Act, 75, 76,
78, 127-28
*Beyond the Best Interests
of the Child* (Goldstein,

Freud, and Solnit),
89-90
bias against foster
parents, 167
children at risk, 78-79
children in limbo, 86-91,
121n.25, 122n.29
Department of Health
and Human Services
(DHHS), 78, 81
economics of, 83-84
fostadopt programs, 93
foster care as a system,
81-83
from foster care to
adoptive families,
91-95
foster parents as servants
of the state, 84-85, 91-
95, 121n.15
history of American foster
care, 79-95
kin-care, 81-82
leverage of foster parents,
85, 91-95
love and foster care, 92-
95, 122n.34
negative views of, 81, 82,
86, 87-91
Public Law 105-89, 75, 76
role in welfare system,
82-83
Smith v. *Offer*, 91
traits of foster parents,
91-95
Friedman, Lawrence, 192

G

Genetics, 12
access to closed/sealed
adoption records, 36-
38, 198
genetic substance, 184
impact on adoptee reform
groups, 35
Goody, Jack, 3, 193

Government. *See* Adoption and Safe Families Act of 1997
"Gray market" adoptions, 147-48
Guatemala, international adoptions from, 144

H

Haley, Alex, 35
Harder, Debra, 171
Hawaii
common law adoption, 108-9, 122n.55
hanai (customary) adoption, 88, 191
practice of "exchanging" children, 16
Heinz III, H. John, 85-86, 97-98, 155-56
Herbert, Bob, 104, 122n.49
Humphrey, Gordon, 62-63
adoption argument against abortion, 99-100, 101, 102, 103
infertile couples, 169

I

Independent adoptions/private channels, 136-42
Inheritance and property rights, 3, 6
International adoptions, 143-46, 189-90
Internet
Children Awaiting Parents (CAP), 164
role in advertising adoption, 149, 150, 151-52
Irrevocable permanency, 172

K

Kefauver, Estes, 99
Kin-care, 81-82

Kinship
activating bonds of "flesh and blood," 56-57
adoptive kinship, 169-70
alternative kinship, 13
and American adoption, 176-200
birth as core to kinship, 15
changes in adoption and interpretations of kinship, 14, 197
contracted kinship, 197
cultural interpretations of parenthood, 166
from "fictive" to "functional" kinship, 68-71
reconfiguring kinship and family, 197-98
searches for blood ties/biological ancestry, 186-87
symbols of, 10, 15
Kinship with Strangers (Modell), 17
Kittson, Ruthena Hill, 28
Korea, international adoptions from, 143-44

L

Levy, Robert, 17
Lifton, Betty Jean, 28-29, 32, 33, 34-35, 38, 39
The Limits of Hope (Loux), 165
Lost and Found: The Adoption Experience (Lifton), 32, 39
Loux, Ann Kimble, 114-15, 165, 166

M

Maryland, access to closed/sealed adoption records, 56
Matching practices, 7-8, 117-18, 157, 196-97
Meezan, William, 84, 95

Mexico and baby smuggling
operations, 147-48
Minority children, 112-13, 115,
164
Missing in Adoption (MIA),
42-43
Missouri, family preservation
programs, 98
Mnookin, Robert, 85
Mothers/motherhood
concepts of motherhood,
46-47, 63
opening the subject of
adoption, 9-10
Multiethnic Placement Act, 117

N

National Adoption Exchange,
155, 167
National Adoption Month, 77,
128
National Association of Black
Social Workers (NABSW),
118-19, 167
cultural assumptions and
placement practices,
119-20
National Council for Adoption
(NCFA), 27, 37, 56, 140
Native-Americans, adoption
practices, 2
New Jersey, adoption parties,
157
North American Council on
Adoptable Children, 83
North Dakota, placement rate
of foster children, 116

O

Oceanic cultures and adoption,
182-83, 184, 185, 187, 200n.6
"Open adoption," 64-68
Oregon, access to closed/sealed
adoption records, 1-2, 10, 53,
55, 69, 170
Orphan Voyage (Paton), 28

P

Parents/parenthood. *See*
Adoptive parents of the 21st
century
Paton, Jean, 28
Pennsylvania
Adoption Legal Services
Project, 111
family preservation
programs, 97-98
placement rate of foster
children, 116
Pierce, William, 27, 37, 38, 140
birthparents right to
privacy, 56
Polynesian fosterage and
adoption, 90, 122n.29
Public Law 105-89, 75, 76, 78,
106, 107, 108
adoption of "special
needs" children, 112

R

Racial policies in American
adoption, 118-21
Reconceptualizing American
adoption
access to sealed birth
certificates, 1-2
adoptee and birthparent
reform groups, 19
adoption as academic
subject, 3, 4
adoption as a public
problem, 13-17, 18
adoption and foster care,
19
adoption in the media, 1-4
adoption triad, 11-12
adoptive parents as
clients and consumers,
11
alternative kinship, 13
alternative to abortion, 19
as-if-begotten, 5-8, 11, 12,
22nn.7,8,10,11
autonomy, 2, 4

betrayal, 2
birth story and family
tree, 9, 22n.13, 33
breaking silence/sounds of
change, 8-13, 22n.13,
22nn.15,16,17
changes in interpretations
of kinship, 14
"child exchange," 3, 4
collapsing biological
bonds, 13-14
criteria for a fit parent, 14
debate on definition of
family in United
States, 18
diversity and division of
adoptive parents, 21
federal guidelines for
adoption, 20
fictive kinship, 2, 8
genealogical models in
American adoption, 5,
22n.8
Hawaiian practice of
"exchanging" children,
16
inheritance and property
rights, 3, 6
issues of genetics, 12
market principles and
adoption, 4
matching practices, 7-8
mothers/motherhood,
9-10
open/openness, 2
Oregon and access to
sealed birth
certificates, 10
parenthood and federal
tax laws, 20
primacy of blood and
biological ties, 6,
22n.10
protected rights and
entitlements of
adoptive parents, 10-
11, 23n.17
"rescue" of endangered
children, 18

resemblance adding to the
bond, 6-7, 22n.11
search and access, 2
secrecy and sealed
records, 3-4, 17-22
statistics on adoptees and
birthparents, 10,
23n.15
"stranger" adoptions, 4
symbols of kinship, 10, 15
"transferring" children,
1, 4
Resemblance adding to the
bond, 6-7, 22n.11
Ridge, Tom, 111
Roe v. *Wade,* 100
*Roots: The Saga of an American
Family* (Haley), 35
Russia, international adoptions
from, 144, 146

S

Scheper-Hughes, Nancy, 165
Schneider, David, 3, 15, 17
Scoppetta, Nicholas, 84, 87, 91,
111
Search and access, 2
The Search for Anna Fisher
(Fisher), 29
Secrecy
expanding the meanings
of, 166-72
focus on, 26-27, 178-84,
199n.3, 200n.6
in history of American
adoption, 3-4, 26-27,
72n.4, 179-82
See also Banishing
secrecy, confidentiality,
and opening adoption
Senden Theis, Sophie van, 80,
135, 151
Shalala, Donna, 156
Shireman, Joan, 84, 95
Smith v. *Offer,* 91
South Dakota, advertising
"waiting" children, 156

"Special needs" children,
111-15
Standards for Adoption Service
(CWLA), 134, 164, 188
"Stranger" adoptions, 4
Surrender by birthparents, 40-
44, 72n.22
Surrender versus termination
of parental rights (TPR),
105-6, 194

T

Tahitians (Levy), 17
Tax breaks and subsidies, 20,
110, 158-63
Tennessee, access to
closed/sealed adoption
records, 55, 199n.2
Termination of parental rights
(TPR) versus surrender, 105-
6, 194
Texas, disclosure and contact
between adoptive and
birthparents, 64
Thompson, Tommy G., 103-4,
122n.49
"Transferring" children, 1
*Twice Born: Memoirs of an
Adopted Daughter* (Lifton),
28, 29, 33, 35, 39

U

Urban Institute, on "hard to
place" children, 155

V

Vietnam, international
adoptions from, 145

W

Wells, Deborah R., 145
Wilson, Pete, 103, 104
Wisconsin, custody of drug-
addicted pregnant women,
103-4